G000241329

White

Sou

55 classic runs for kayakers and rafters in France and North West Italy.

Peter Knowles

L.M.

Rivers Publishing U.K.

Photographs are as credited. **Front cover:** Roman bridge on the Ubaye race course, photo Harry Wood. **Back cover:** Kayaking the Séveraisse, photo Charlie Wood. Alan Ellard & Mike Abbott surfing at the Argentière slalom site, photo Heather Gunn. Hinckley Canoe Club rafting the Guil, photo Caragh Mathew.

Cover Design by Leon Reichel. **Maps** were drawn by Fiona Firth & Peter Knowles.

Drawings and cartoons are by Jeannie Tracey, Louise Mathews, Colin Hill (Chill), Alan Fox (Foxy), and Jo Sayers. Historic etchings are reproduced by kind permission from the collection of the Museum Dauphinois in Grenoble.

IISBN: 0-9519413-7-2.

A CIP catalogue record for this book is available from the British Library.

Printed by Biddles Ltd in England.

Trade enquiries:

- **U.K. and Europe**: to Cordee Outdoor Books & Maps,
  3a De Montford St, Leicester LE1 7HD, UK, Fax: 0116 247 1176.

- **Other countries**: to Rivers Publishing U.K.
  125 Hook Rise South, Surbiton, Surrey KT6 7NA, UK, Fax: +44 208 391 5114.

Disclaimer

The information and advice given in this book were written in good faith, but the reader is warned that nothing in this book should be regarded as 100% accurate: this book was written by humans so there are bound to be errors, rivers and rapids change, and some information is out of date before it is printed. All advice and information should be treated with caution and checked locally. The publishers, authors and contributors can accept no responsibility for any loss, injury, or inconvenience sustained by any person as a result of information or advice contained in this guide.

A typographic error in the guidebook had forced Henry into a difficult situation ...

WARNING Printed using Laser-phobic ink
This may degrade if scanned by photocopiers or similar devices.

The Author

Peter Knowles has led expeditions and first descents in many different countries all over the world. He simply enjoys paddling rivers but amongst other accomplishments he introduced rescue throw bags to the UK (the famous 'Green Slime Throwbags'), helped organise white water cardboard canoe races, served for ten years as chairman of the BCU Expeditions Committee, hand paddled some 120km down the Kali Gandaki, won a couple of freestyle rodeos, and co-founded London River Rats. He is a member of the Alpine Kayak Club, and a fellow of the Royal Geographical Society.

He has spent a lot of time exploring the rivers of the Himalayas and this inspired his first guide book 'White Water Nepal'. He returns each year to the Himalayas, helps run the Nepal Rodeo, and in the last few years has also made several exploratory kayaking trips to Bhutan, including filming for American television.

Despite paddling in all these wild and exotic countries Pete returns every year to paddle in the Alps - he says simply to run the rivers, but friends speculate that this might also be something to do with French and Italian food and wine?

Pete is now a professional guide book publisher and in the winter months he tries to stay warm and dry sitting in front of a computer, writing about rivers - but friends keep dragging him out to get nasty cold and wet yet again!

"Who put that ferret in my boat?"

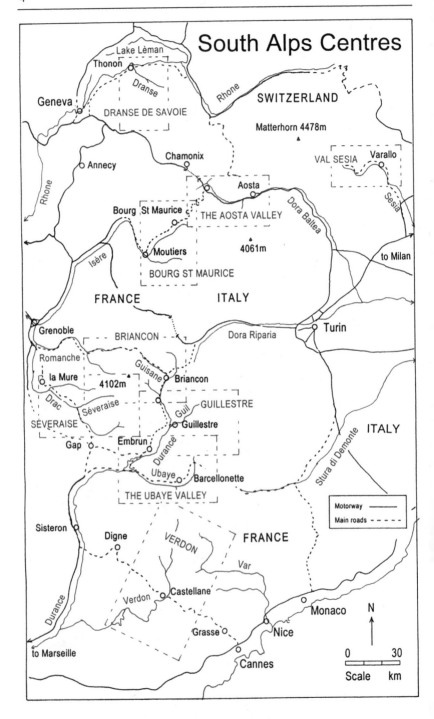

South Alps Centres

Centre: Dranse de Savoie

Name of run	Class	Stars	Scen	Km	cms	Notes
Middle Dranse	3 (3+)	★★	❀❀	6	20	popular run
Upper Dranse	4 (5+)	★★	❀❀	3	20	1 portage

Centre: Bourg St Maurice

Isère from Bourg	3+	★★	❀	8	20	a fine training run
Isère from Gothard	4	★★★	❀❀	11	20	a classic
Doron	4	★★	❀❀	4	10	

Centre: the Aosta Valley

Dora Baltea Gorge	3+ (4)	★★★	❀❀	6	30	Lots of interest
Dora from Pre-St Didier	4+	★	❀	2	20	Powerful
Dora from Montbardon	3+	★	❀❀	5	20	Continuous
Dora from La Salle	5	★★	❀	2	25	Technical
Dora from Lenteney	3	★	❀	3	25	Cold but fun
Canyon de l'inferno	4+	★★★	❀❀	2	30	Impressive
Grand Eyvia	4	★★	❀❀	4	15	Varied

Centre: Val Sesia

Middle Sesia	4 (5)	★★★	❀❀	9	15	2 portages
Lower Sesia	3+(4+)	★★	❀❀	9	20	a fine run
Sermenza	5- (6)	★★★	❀❀	6	10	several portages
Upper Sesia - from Balma	4-	★★	❀❀	4	10	fast and shallow
- from Curgo	4+ (5-)	★★★	❀❀	3	10	fast and steep
- from Scopello	3	★★	❀	5	15	fast and shallow
Sesia Gorge	4 (6)	★★	❀❀❀	2	10	Best in low water

Centre: Briançon

Upper Guisane	3 (4-)	★★	❀❀	11	10	fast and scenic
Lower Guisane	4	★★★	❀❀	6	15	1 portage, great!
Romanche	4+	★★	❀❀	5	25	full-on late season
Durance Gorge	4 (5)	★★★	❀❀❀	8	15	a mini-expedition
Briançon Gorge	3	★★★	❀❀	2	10	fine little paddle
Upper Durance	2	★	❀	7	30	confidence builder
Middle Clarée	4	★★	❀❀	4	5	fast and furious
Lower Claree	3	★★	❀❀	12	10	beautiful valley
Gyr	4+(5)	★★★	❀	3	15	"flat out"
Onde	3+	★★	❀❀	3	5	best early season
Gyronde	3+	★	❀❀	6	20	good training
Vénéon	4+(5)	★★★	❀❀	4	20	A hard alpine gem

Centre: Guillestre

Name of run	Class	Stars	Scen	Km	cms	Notes
Lower Durance	3- (3+)	★★	⊕⊕	16	60	Big and bouncy
Middle Guil	4 (5)	★★★	⊕⊕	9	25	True classic
Middle Durance	2 (3)	★★	⊕⊕	19	40	Good intro.
Upper Guil - from Abries	3	★	⊕⊕	4	4	High Alpine valley
- from Aiguilles	3+ (4)	★★	⊕⊕	17	5	Fine little gorge
Château Queyras	4+	★★★	⊕⊕	1	7	Committing
Guardian Angel	4+ (5)	★★	⊕⊕	3	7	Much scouting
Guil Gorge	4+ (5)	★	⊕⊕	4	15	Russian Roulette?
Lower Guil	3-	★★	⊕⊕	7	25	Pretty and fun
Biaisse	5 (6)	★★★	⊕⊕	8	7	A gem

Centre: Séveraisse

Name of run	Class	Stars	Scen	Km	cms	Notes
Séveraisse	3+ (4)	★★	⊕⊕⊕	8	15	Scenic
Bonne	4 (6)	★★	⊕⊕	6	10	tight gorge
Drac Blanc	3+	★★	⊕⊕	4	10	fast and furious
Drac Noir	5	★	⊕⊕	5	10	tight and rocky
Drac	3+	★★	⊕	20	30	high water run

Centre: the Ubaye Valley

Name of run	Class	Stars	Scen	Km	cms	Notes
Ubaye Race Course	4	★★★	⊕⊕	8	30	Justly popular
Upper Ubaye	3	★★	⊕⊕	13	10	recommended
Ubaye from Jausiers	2 (3)	★	⊕	13	20	high water run ?
- from Les Thuiles	3 (4)	★★	⊕	5	25	large, open valley
- from La Fresquière	5	★★	⊕⊕	2.5	25	challenging run
Ubaye Gorge	5- (6)	★★★	⊕⊕⊕	4	20	low water run
Le Bachelard	4	★★	⊕⊕	8	10	May-June

Centre: Verdon

Name of run	Class	Stars	Scen	Km	cms	Notes
Grand Canyon	4 (5)	★★★	⊕⊕⊕	30	18	An expedition!
Pre-Canyon	3 (4)	★★★	⊕⊕	13	18	recommended
Verdon from Castellane	2 (3)	★	⊕⊕	6	18	Friendly
- from Allos	4	★	⊕⊕	7	7	Early season run
- from Colmars	3-	★	⊕⊕	15	10	Early season run
- from Pont Clos	3+	★★	⊕⊕	18	10	Early season run
Var - Gorges de Daluis	3	★	⊕⊕	7	10	Committing

Notes

★ **Stars** for paddling are 1-3, a subjective measure of satisfaction at that grade.

⊕ **Scenery** - our subjective measure from 1-3.

Acknowledgements

A lot of water has been down those rivers since the first edition, but with perhaps surprisingly few major changes - so the updates to this edition are many but minor, including more maps, photographs, and websites.

Over the last two years friends and myself have had the onerous job of paddling all the rivers to check out the runs, (well not quite every one) and of course the research did require us to check out a few restaurants and bars!

All at your insistence - because one of the requests from users was a few more tips on places to eat and drink. One of the nicest things about this job is talking to, and getting feedback from readers, and much of the updates and I hope improvements in this book are from you the readers - so please keep them coming.

This book is the product of many people's input, ideas and help and I should like to say a big thank you to all the many paddlers who have shared their time and experience. Throughout this book you will see that I have used the 'Royal we' as an acknowledgement that this is the work of many. Whilst it's not practical to name everyone, I would like to say a special thank you to Stuart Woodward, Roberto Chilosi, and Robin Knapp who helped a lot with this edition. We have told a few pernicious lies about some of the main contributors in Appendix G (if we've missed you out, you should probably be grateful!). This gives some idea of the wide cross-section of people that are attracted to this deviant sport of Alpine paddling!

I hope you enjoy this book and have some great trips in the Alps.

Good Paddling!

Peter Knowles,
England,
March 2003.

p.s. Note our website for updates and feedback -

www.riverspublishing.co.uk.

Dedication

This book is dedicated to Gianni Bestopho who died on the Guil in May 2002 - he was kayaking his favourite river when he had a heart attack. Gianni spent all and every summer paddling in the South Alps travelling around with his girlfriend Paola in their camper van. Many readers of this book will have padded with Gianni or will have shared a drink with him on the Rabioux campsite, whilst talking rivers - his knowledge of the rivers of the Southern Alps was immense and he was always happy to share this.

Gianni was a small guy with a big heart - a naturally quiet, gentleman, he was always a pillar of help and friendly advice and he gathered a wide circle of friends from all the many nationalities of boaters that paddled the French & Italian Alps.

His ability as a river runner was top draw - watching him eddy down an alpine rapid was like watching movements from a ballet. His leading technique was very simple - as he put it "eddy-eddy, lookie-lookie". Paddling was a sport he excelled at, and when asked once why he did not climb or parrapont, his reply was "if I come out of my boat I can swim, but if I fall - I cannot fly"!

He will be missed and remembered with great affection.

Gianni Bestopho

Using this guidebook

Why the Alps?

Great white water and sunshine in beautiful mountain scenery!

However, the Alps also offer so much more: for centuries they have been both a barrier and the cross roads of Europe, they are steeped in history and rich in local culture. Every valley has its own picturesque traditions and customs and even the language may change from one valley to the next. Exploring the rivers in this guide book will take you away from some of the main tourist valleys and into some fascinating places known only to the locals. Let us also remind you that mountain people have a tradition of good food and drink - something dear to most river runners.

Tourism is well developed in the French Alps: rafting and kayaking are recognised as an important, and ecologically friendly, source of tourist revenue (probably worth at least 90 million pounds per year in indirect revenue for Europe as a whole). There is now an increasing awareness throughout Europe that free-flowing rivers are a natural asset that should be protected from dams and pollution - the economic benefits of white water tourism has greatly strengthened this argument (in contrast, the current situation in most areas of England and Wales involves bigoted angling clubs refusing to share the rivers so that local communities lose out).

Our message is to come to the Alps, run these wonderful rivers and spend your money in local communities: you will be made welcome, and you will be helping to protect the rivers that you enjoy. Note that throughout the Alps (as in most of Europe) you are welcome as a tourist to run the rivers without permit, payment or licence - you are merely asked to follow any local regulations and to behave considerately.

We are often asked for advice on whether to take a holiday in the south Alps or the northern ones: both areas, as can be seen from our guidebooks, offer a wide variety of rivers and runs. Generally speaking though, the rivers of the south Alps are slightly friendlier, warmer, and offer a wider choice of easier runs. Travelling time, and costs will be roughly similar and for many people the choice will be based more on general ambience and subjective things like whether they prefer Austrian or French food - or Italian ice cream.

Classic runs

This book and its companion volume which covers the North Alps concentrates on the 'classic' runs in the Western Alps that are class 3 and 4 and which are probably of most interest to the recreational kayaker and rafter. To qualify as a main **classic run** we feel that it should have good scenery and white water (normally a combination of 4 stars on our rating system), be of reasonable length (normally over 6 km) and have good chance of water through the peak summer months of June and July.

Where a river is quite exceptional then we relax some of these criteria. We have included a few easier classics and also one or two harder ones. If a river doesn't satisfy all these criteria, but is still worth including then we call it a **'Lesser Classic'** and give it a shorter write up - many of these runs are excellent, but only have sufficient water in the spring months. Lastly, just to whet your appetite, we have a third category where we just give the river a mention in **'Other Rivers'** at the end of the centre notes - we also try and give an idea where to find out more information.

Centres
We have grouped runs by centres as this seemed to us more natural than long alphabetical lists that you have to search for on the map. It also has the advantage that we could write a little about the area and as someone put it 'occasionally lift paddlers' bleary red eyes away from the river'.

River Descriptions
We have tried in this book to give a 'feel' for each run and the important things that most paddlers would probably want to know if they were thinking of running it. What these river descriptions are not is a blow by blow account of how to run each rapid - this would take the fun out of paddling! We have normally noted major rapids or other hazards, but be warned - these often get washed away and new ones appear.

1. Suggested **start** and **finish** points are those that are we feel give the best run at that class of difficulty - often a difficult decision; where there are alternatives, we have tried to make this clear in the text.
2. **Gradient** is for the total length of the run and is expressed in metres per kilometre - 10 m/km is roughly equivalent to 50 ft per mile.
3. **Stars** is our subjective rating of the run for total interest and enjoyment on a scale of one to three stars. We have tried to do the same thing for scenery.
4. **Time** is how long most kayakers would take to do the run including a little play and rest. Rafting times for most runs will be roughly similar.

How Difficult?
Note that the **class of difficulty is for the stated flow** - with a higher volume the difficulty will normally increase and the river becomes very dangerous.

We have used the standard International Classification of Difficulty (see Appendix A) when grading these runs, and like many other modern guide books we have used + and - grades and ( )s. We think that these two ideas make the classification scheme a lot, lot, more meaningful.

In the course of researching this book we have been surprised how much consensus there was between experienced paddlers about the grading of a particular run or rapid. Ten years ago there were much greater inconsistencies between different countries and paddlers - as international paddling has spread and grown so the grading has become more uniform.

One of the problems of the International Classification is that the majority of white water is class 3 and 4 and in fact there is a vast difference between an easy grade 4 and a hard one. Hence the use of + and - grades to be more definitive:

1	2	3	3+	4-	4	4+	5-	5	5+	6

Where we call a run **class 4-** we mean that in our opinion this is the overall standard - there may be long sections of lower difficulty, but to do the run safely you need to be 100% capable of paddling at this level.

Class 3 (4+) means that in our opinion the overall standard of the run is Class 3, but there are a few (normally one or two) class 4+ rapids that can usually be easily portaged if required.

This international classification is very subjective: it tends to rely on consensus and peoples' experience to interpret the rather woolly definitions.   **Class 5** can be objectively differentiated because the definition requires 'inspection' - by implication from the bank and not by eddy scouting. This means that if someone says that they did a run without bank scouting - safely and under control - then that run cannot be class 5, and this leads us to a definition for the next grade down.

'Class 4+ often requires bank inspection but may include very continuous and difficult white water that can be run by experts without scouting from the bank - note that a powerful, committing. and continuous class 4+ run like this can be more difficult and potentially dangerous than a pool-drop class 5 run'.

"...It looked a grade III from the bridge..."

The differences between say class 4- and class 4 are more subjective - paddlers love to argue about what to grade a certain run, and much depends on the water level at the time. Rivers **do** change and what may be a class 4- one year may be a class 4+ the following season - thankfully this is relatively rare, but don't rely on this or any other book to be more than a guide!

We have based our opinion on the class of difficulty of the river as it was when we, or our informants, ran it. Earthquakes, landslides, roadwork's, floods, etc. may completely change a river and make it easier or harder - it's always sensible to seek up-to-date advice from other paddlers or rafting companies.

Water flows and gauges

Quoted figures are normally rough estimates only for the optimum flow for that run and as such they are a useful indication of the size of the river. Flow is expressed in cubic metres per second - cumecs in paddlers jargon (scientifically these should be expressed as m^3/s), 100 cumecs is roughly equivalent to 3500 cubic feet per second. Unfortunately detailed hydrographic information is surprisingly difficult to come by for most Alpine rivers. Gauges are also sadly unreliable - a winter flood can scour out the river bed and make a gauge reading dangerously misleading. The golden rule is to use your experience and common sense and if gauge readings and flow rates don't seem right, then seek local advice.

Sketch maps

The sketch maps that accompany the river descriptions are just that: they do not pretend to be 100% accurate: they are merely a guide, from different sources and our own research on the ground, as to the nature of things at the time of writing. We have tried to indicate most of the information that would be of interest to paddlers, as clearly and as simply as possible, so have been selective in the detail we have included.

Planning your trip

When to go
This book is written mainly for those taking a summer holiday - which for most people means end of May through to September. If you do have a choice of when to go in the year, then **late June is probably the best time**, with wild flowers, hot sun, and good water levels.

Many groups go to the Alps in the half-term week at the end of May, however going at this time of year, you need to be prepared for high water levels and possible cold weather (think twice about camping!). If you plan to come in the main summer months then note that the French summer vacation is two months long - almost the whole of July and August.

However, most families go away only from mid-July to mid August so this is high season and the prime time to avoid if you possibly can. Campsites, and tourist facilities are all quiet after the 14th August so this is a good time to be a tourist, but water levels on most of the rivers will be disappointingly low (note that in France the 15th August is like an unofficial New Year's Day with many facilities closed).

Climate
June, July and August are normally hot and sunny, with temperatures often in the 20's and sometimes the 30's. The higher up the valleys you are, then the cooler you will be - for both river and air temperature). Summer storms are fortunately rare, but can come at any time, bringing torrential rain and cold winds. They also bring the very rare (but real) risk of flooding.

Before you go
A little bit of time beforehand on reading and research can make your holiday a much better quality trip and save you time and money.

We suggest that you spend some time on the internet, and write off, or fax for information from tourist offices in the main centres that you are planning to visit. Note that almost all tourist offices speak English and are only too delighted to answer a phone call from overseas. It's also a good idea to obtain up-to-date travel information from your motoring organisation or other source. If you are driving from Britain, then you should check with your car insurance company and extend the cover to other European countries if necessary.

Car breakdown insurance gives peace of mind but can be expensive. It's worth looking hard at the policies and doing a 'what if' scenario. If you do two or more trips a year then it's worth thinking about annual cover for the whole of Europe.

Medical cover

We recommend that you take out specialist medical and travel insurance for your trip to the Alps. If you are involved in an accident and are injured it is likely that you will incur not only hospital charges, but also ambulance transfer fees and even helicopter call out fees in some cases. Serious accidents may also need subsequent air ambulance and repatriation to your home country.

Some general insurance policies will include canoeing cover but most exclude white water kayaking as they view this as high risk. So if you plan to paddle on class 2 or above then in our experience you are better talking to a specialist company (see the 'Suppliers Directory'). Policies bought direct from companies like these are normally much better value than those bought through second parties - in some parts of the travel industry the mark up on insurance can be as high as 100%.

If you travel regularly then an annual multi-trip policy is well worth considering, but again, do make sure that any high risk activities are specifically covered - it should also cover you if you break your leg one weekend hill walking!

Most European countries (**but not Switzerland)** have reciprocal health agreements with the U.K. A form DSS E111 (available from post offices) helps in administering medical expenses claimed back from the NHS in the U.K. and is a useful thing to have. This is particularly recommended if you choose not to take out travel insurance as it will help you claim back some of your medical expenses. But note that it is not an alternative to insurance, many hospitals and rescue services will still insist on you paying the bill or producing evidence of insurance.

Planning your programme

Alpine rivers may well be more powerful and challenging than those you are used to, so we urge you to be conservative in your plans:

- **Give yourself time** - don't aim to do too much paddling - remember that there are many other enjoyable things to do in the Alps.

- **Build confidence and experience on easier rivers** - plan your itinerary so that you start easy then progress to more challenging rivers - you will see that our example itineraries do this.

- **Be flexible** in your plans and adjust them if for example you're feeling tired or if local river conditions and/or weather are bad.

Paddlers do die on Alpine rivers and usually it's because events, time or people have pressurised them to do a run, which, if they were alive to reflect on it, they should not have attempted that day.

Try to plan your outline programme so that you minimise driving and shuttles. The experience of most people is that it is better to stay in one centre for a few nights: moving on every night can be very tiring; but, to stay in one centre for two weeks can be almost as tiring, as it will involve you in some long daily drives to reach the more distant rivers.

What to take

Although the weather in the Alps is often hot and sunny you should remember that some rivers are fed by glacial melt water and you will need suitable equipment for paddling very cold rivers, and to survive the odd swim. We recommend a long john wet suit, thermal tops, pogies and dry-top paddling jacket, besides your normal paddling equipment.

Paddling in the Alps is a bit of an expedition, so your equipment should reflect the fact that you may be at the bottom of a gorge and remote from outside help - you group should be self sufficient and suitably equipped for most emergencies with first aid, safety, and rescue gear.   This is a 'where to go' rather than a 'how to do it' book - if you feel you need further guidance then we recommend a practical course at a good kayak or rafting school.   It's also worth packing some some spare paddling gear and a repair kit.

It's perhaps obvious, but a French or Italian phrase book will repay its price many times over. The south of France can be very hot - up to 40 degrees - so it's worth planning for this. An ice box is essential if you are camping (some people swear by a small portable fridge) - most campsites will pop your freezer pack in their freezer for a small charge, so take several and mark them with your name.

The author setting off the Alps.   *Dave Manby*

One of the most useful items to take is a tarp or flysheet so that you can rig this as a sun awning or rain fly. We take a table and folding stools that take up almost no room in the bottom of the boot, but there are some very comfortable folding armchairs available if you have the room. A hammock is another accessory that takes up little room but sets the right holiday tone!

French stores and supermarkets often have a wider range of camping accessories, like chairs and ice boxes, than your home camping store, and often substantially cheaper!

Most foods that you can buy in your home country are available in the Alps and at roughly comparable prices so it usually makes little financial sense to load your car down with food from home - you will eat much better if you buy fresh local produce, and this is surely one of the pleasures of a foreign holiday? You might want to consider though a stock of your favourite breakfast cereal and any other favourite speciality food: Brits will probably want to take fresh tea bags; Australians, vegemite; and Americans, peanut butter.

Money

The introduction of the Euro has made travel in Europe so much easier. But, in truth you don't really need much cash - the French in particular, just love their Visa Cards 'la Carte Bleu' and it has become a nation that is almost more credit card friendly than North America. (forget about bringing travellers cheques). You will need cash for the occasional drink or campsite fee but this is easily obtained from a cash dispenser using either your credit or bank card, as long as you know your PIN number, or over the counter at larger banks (you will need your passport).

Note that UK credit cards will not work in most automatic 24 hour petrol stations, so don't run short of fuel when driving at night, or on Sundays.

A cry for help

It was late in the afternoon as the three kayakers drove up the valley in the Maritime Alps with the idea of one last short paddle before the drive back to England. The weather was warm, and it was supposed to be an easy run so they just changed into shorts and paddling jackets. John volunteered to shuttle the car and cycle back whilst the other two sunbathed.

They set off and enjoyed a fine paddle, too short, but just as well, because the sun had gone in and they were all starting to feel cold as they arrived at the take-out. They got out of their boats, pulled them up the bank, and headed for the car with thoughts of warm dry clothes, food and a brew.

But, getting back to the car - they looked around with horror as they saw it wasn't where John had left it. Slowly they realised, but didn't want to accept, that it must have been stolen - it had contained all their possessions. They stood there shivering in their swim shorts by the roadside as the sun went down, and so did their spirits as they realised the horrible truth - they had taken nothing with them in their boats, so they had no clothes, no money, no friends and no papers.

The despairing cry "Mother" echoed up the lonely valley .....

Security

Local people in the Alps are honest and hard-working and in our experience you are less likely to have anything stolen than in your own home city, however you are on holiday so it does pay to take basic precautions:

- Leave valuables in the safe keeping of your hotel or campsite guardian.

- Photocopy important documents (e.g. passport) and keep these separate.

- Take important phone numbers and money with you on the river in a waterproof pouch on your person.

- Take two cable locks so that you can lock boats both to your roof rack and if you leave any at your campsite.

Flying to Europe from North America

Flying with rafts and inflatable kayaks from North America is relatively straight - forward, many airlines, however, don't like plastic kayaks and will try to charge you air cargo rates if you contact them beforehand. Best thing is to phone and ask them in advance if they take surf boards, and provided they do, turn up on the day to check in with your 'surf kayak'. Some airlines will waive excess charges if you only check in one bag - a long thin plastic one!

Airlines change their policies from year to year. KLM are notorious in not carrying any kind of adult sporting toy, so don't even think about flying with them, whereas most paddlers experience with BA has been pretty positive. Air India actually promotes itself as 'the kayak friendly airline'. In our experience it's normally easier flying boats back from Europe to the States than vice versa, so you may want to consider the idea of buying a kayak to take back with you.

"I think we can get your kayak on board now, Sir -
if you would like to just let me have your paddle ...."

It is perfectly feasible to fly in, hire a car and go from there. The biggest problem you are likely to encounter is that very few hire companies have roof racks (note some cars have built in side rails. If you only have one of two boats then the simple solution (in our limited experience and without prejudice) is to just tie them flat on the roof of the car with some padding as protection. You can hire boats from one of the kayak schools or shops that advertise in this book - most speak good English.

Flying from the U.K.
Budget airlines like Easy Jet, Ryan Air, and Buzz, have now made it a really economic and easy option to fly over to France or Italy for a long weekend kayaking in the Alps. Popular airports are Grenoble, Geneva, Turin, and Nice. Contact the airlines direct for their latest policy on kayaks. At the time of writing most would fly short kayaks either free, or for a small extra charge.

Driving from the U.K.
Driving to the Alps from a channel port normally takes about 12 hours on the motorways. If you have 2 or more drivers then it's worth considering cruising the motorways through the night: we recommend that you leave room in the car so that you can stretch out when not driving; we normally switch drivers every two hours so that the driver is always fresh, and stop for a coffee, loo and petrol every four hours.

If you only have one driver, or a fractious family, then you might want to make an overnight break and the cheap hotel chains like Formule1 (20 euros for a room) are well worth considering (www.hotelformule1.com). Note though that French friends advise us that the car parks of these cheap hotel chains have a reputation for being insecure, partly because these chain hotels are often located in poor areas on the fringes of large cities - so a small family hotel in the country is usually better security and may be better value.

If you have a choice of vehicle, remember that in most of Europe, diesel fuel is a lot cheaper than petrol.

French motorways normally charge tolls (Belgium and German ones don't): in 2002 the toll charges for a car from Calais to Grenoble was approx. 50 euros. If you drive on a Swiss motorway you must have a special tax disc that costs about 50 euros. French motorway rest stops and picnic sites are relatively quiet and un-crowded and it appears to be common practice for people to sleep in them overnight.

The different channel crossings all have their pros and cons. The ferry companies naturally want you to book long in advance, and usually offer discounts for so doing. In our experience **substantially cheaper fares** can be obtained through companies like Ferrysavers (www.ferrysavers.com). It is also worth noting that (whatever time or date you may have booked for), our experience is that if you turn up at the check in, at a different time or date, and there is room on the next departure, then they will normally wave you through with no penalty or problem - so don't bust a gut just to get to your ferry on time (as many people turn up early as turn up late). (I suppose one can be too blasé - I turned up once at Dover, presented my ticket and was told "but your ticket is for tomorrow Sir - from Ramsgate....." My girlfriend was not amused !)

Routes

Recommended route to the southern French Alps is to avoid Paris by taking the French motorway system from Calais through eastern France via Reims and Dijon to Lyon. If you want to save money then use main roads (RN) for the quieter, long stretches cross-country and motorways to take you around the larger cities - these sections are usually free.

For **Dranse de Savoie:** head East at Macon and south of Geneva to Thonon.

For **Aosta Valley** and **Val Sesia** as above, and then through the Mont Blanc tunnel.

For **Bourg St Maurice:** after Lyon head for Chambery and then the N90 to Albertville.

For **Briancon**: head for Grenoble and then take the N91 - dramatic and scenic!

For **Séveraise** and the **Ubaye Valley:** head south from Grenoble on the N85.

For **Guillestre:** follow one of the two routes above.

For **Verdon:** the fastest route (all-be-it boring and expensive) is to take the motorway south from Lyon to Orange and Aix-en-Provence.

Whichever route you choose, try to avoid the weekend rush - city people drive to the mountains on a Friday evening and then back on Sunday afternoon. Also try to avoid the weekends at the start and end of the French summer vacation.

Ubaye, approaching Fresquière bridge.   *Robin Knapp*

Itineraries
for
kayakers

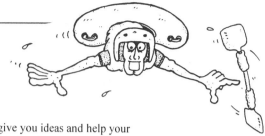

Here's some suggestions to give you ideas and help your outline planning. Please remember that extremes of weather often make rivers more difficult (or easier) and we recommend that you **try to keep your plans flexible** so that it's not a problem to move on if the weather or river conditions are unsuitable.

Warm up rivers

A popular idea for less experienced groups is to spend a few days on the more friendly and warmer rivers of the Massif Central before hitting the faster and more powerful rivers of the Alps. If you look at a map of France, the Alps is to the east of the Rhone valley, the Massif Central is the area opposite to the west of the Rhone - so only a few hours drive away. The most popular and obvious river is the **Ardèche Gorge** - 30 km of class 2 (3) through a very scenic limestone gorge and National Park. This is an excellent choice earlier in the summer, but it gets very busy and crowded in high season and should especially be avoided at weekends. Probably a better choice for most paddlers is the upper **Allier** - which has a guaranteed dam controlled flow all summer from a huge reservoir near its source - several varied sections of paddling from class 2 to class 3 (4). See Appendix E - which gives a summary of rivers in our guidebook **'White Water Massif Central'**.

En route to the Alps, just off the autoroute, 50 km south of Lyons, is the artificial white water course at **St Pierre-de-Boeuf**. Many groups have recommended this as an ideal place to stop off for a warm up, the course is easy and more like a natural river, there is a friendly welcome and camping is allowed either on the course or at the adjoining campsite. Contact: 'Espace Eau Vive Fédéral, 42520 St Pierre-de-Boeuf, Tel: 04 74 87 16 09, email: stpierre@ffcanoe.asso.fr.

Itinerary No. 1. A small group of class 4 kayakers, 1 week, early June.

River levels will be high and many runs will be more difficult

Day 1   Drive to the **Séveraisse** valley and camp at la Chapelle.

Day 2   Paddle the **Séveraisse**, 3+(4), relax.

Day 3   Drive round to the Durance valley, run the **Drac**, 3+, on route, then set up camp at **Guillestre**.

Day 4   Paddle the **lower Guil**, 3-, and the **lower Durance** 3-. Evening walk around Mont Dauphin and restaurant meal.

Day 5   Paddle the **Upper Guil** 3+(4) and check out the Middle Guil.

Day 6   Run the **Middle Guil**, 4(5).

Day 7   Run the **Lower Guisane**, 4, in the morning. Explore Briancon in the afternoon.

Day 8   Repeat your favourite run, then drive home.

No. 2. A small group of mellow class 3 kayakers, 2 weeks, mid June.

River levels in the main Alps will still probably be high so we suggest a warm up on in the Massif Central & then some sunny runs in the Verdon.

Day 1   Arrive at the **Ardèche Gorge** * and set up camp near Pont d'Arc.

Day 2   Paddle down to Pont d'Arc and play.

Day 3   Paddle the **Ardèche Gorge**, 2(3).

Day 4   Move camp to the **Upper Verdon** near St Andre.

Day 5   Paddle the **upper Verdon** from Colmars, 3-.

Day 6   Paddle the **upper Verdon** from Pont Clos, 3+.

Day 7   Hike in the Grand Canyon du Verdon.

Day 8   Paddle the **Verdon Pre-Canyon**, 3(4).

Day 9   Move camp to **Guillestre**.

Day 10   Paddle the **lower Guil**, 3-, and the **lower Durance** 3-. Evening walk around Mont Dauphin and restaurant meal.

Day 12   Drive over the Col de Vars and run the **Upper Ubaye**, 3.

Day 13   Run the **lower Claree** 3 or Upper Guisane 3(4-).

Day 14   Drive home.

* N.B.   *the Allier would make a fine, less crowded, alternative to the Ardèche.*

The Ardèche Gorge   *Peter Knowles*

No. 3.   A small group of class 4/5 kayakers, 2 weeks start of July.
this itinerary is planned to include the Grand Canyon du Verdon
- check water releases with the local tourist office beforehand.

Day 1   Arrive at the **Séveraisse** valley & paddle the **Séveraisse**, 3+(4).

Day 2   Paddle the **Bonne, 4(6).**

Day 3   Move camp to the Durance valley - Argentiere? - and run the **lower Durance,** play the Rabbious wave.

Day 4   Run the **Durance Gorge** 4+(5) if water levels right and the **Gyr,** 4+(5)?

Day 5   Run the upper and **Lower Guisane**, 4, and Middle **Claree**, 4?

Day 6   Mountain Biking the ski slopes at Puy St Vincent.

Day 7   Run the **Middle Guil** 4(5).

Day 8   Run the **Chateau Queyras** and **Gaurdian Angel Gorges** 4+(5). Move camp to the Ubaye

Day 9   Paddle the **Ubaye Race Course** 4, also the Ubaye from les Thuiles 3(4)?

Day 10   Scenic drive over the pass and camp at the Grand Canyon du **Verdon** - run the opper Verdon enroute?

Day 12   Paddle the **Verdon Pre Canyon**, 3(4).

Day 13   Paddle the **Grand Canyon du Verdon** 4(5).

Day 14   Rest and relaxation.

Day 15   Drive home.

High Water and Bad Weather?

What do you do if you arrive at your centre only to find that all the rivers are big, brown and horrible? You could stay put and try to just paddle one or two easy runs, whilst you hope that river levels fall, but if a period of bad weather has set in, as sometimes happens, then in most cases the better option is to cut your losses and move elsewhere.

If for example the Durance valley is huge and honking, then recommended alternatives to consider are -

- Drive west for a few hours to the small & friendlier rivers of the **Massif Central**,

- Especially if its cold, wet, and raining - drive south to the **Verdon Centre** where it is more likely to be hot and sunny,

- If it is late May or June then think about driving over into Italy and heading for the beautiful **Sesia** valley which has its own micro-climate.

No.4. An intermediate level school group, two weeks, end of July.

The group can all roll, but only the leaders have been to the Alps before. (Check that you won't be driving out on the weekend at the start of the Paris holidays)

Day 1   Arrive at **St Pierre-de-Boeuf** and camp.

Day 2   Paddle and train on the **white water course**.

Day 3   Drive to the Durance valley and set up camp at the Argentiere Slalom Course. More experienced paddlers have a play?

Day 4   Run the **Lower Guil**, 3- and **lower Durance**, 3- with lunch at the Rabious.

Day 5   Repeat the **Lower Durance**, 3-, again in the morning (a confidence boost). Run the **Gyronde** 3+, back to the campsite in the afternoon?.

Day 6   Visit the old town of Briancon in the morning then run the **Upper Guisane**, 3(4-) in the afternoon. On return, a well earned Pizza in Chateauroux.

Day 7   Mountain excursion, or climb a Via Ferata, or hire mountain bikes?

Day 8   Drive over the Col de Vars and run the **Upper Ubaye**, 3, then visit the Fort de Tournoux.

Day 9   Paddle the **Middle Guil**, a class 4 run, but levels will be low and there is good support from the road alongside. Afterwards, drive up and scout the Chateau Queyras Gorge? or visit Guillestre?

Day 10 Any survivors do a morning run on the **Lower Guisane, 4**.

Day 11 Pack up camp and drive to **Bourg St Maurice**, and camp.

Day 12 Run the **Isère** from Bourg, 3+ then play on the Slalom course.

Day 13 Run the **Isère** from Gothard, 4, farewell meal..

Day 14 Drive home

No. 5. A small group of mellow class 4 paddlers, 2 weeks, end of July.

Day 1   Drive to the **Séveraisse** valley and camp at la Chapelle.

Day 2   Paddle the **Séveraisse**, 3+(4), relax!

Day 3   Check water levels and if o.k. run the **Bonne**, 4(6), or the Drac.

Day 4   Drive round to the Durance valley and set up camp at **Guillestre**. Call in and play on the **Rabious** on route.

Day 5   Paddle the **lower Guil**, 3-, and the **lower Durance** 3-. Evening walk around Mont Dauphin and restaurant meal.

Day 6   Drive over the Col de Vars and run the **Upper Ubaye**, 3.

Day 7   Drive up to the Pain de Sucre 2744m and a mountain walk. Scout the Guil on route. Run **Chateau Queyras** Gorge, 4+?

Day 8   Run the **Middle Guil**, 4(5).

Day 9   Move camp to le Lauzet in the **Ubaye valley**.

Day 9   Paddle the **Ubaye from les Thuiles**, 3(4), then the **Ubaye Race Course**, 4+ back to the campsite.

Day 10 Move camp to the **upper Guisane** valley, picnic lunch and play at the Rabious on route.

Day 12 Paddle the **Upper Guisane,** 3(4-). Evening barbecue with magnificent glacier views

Day 13 A horribly early start to drive over the pass to la Grave and a morning's **skiing on the Glaciers** at 3000m altitude.

Day 14 Run the **Lower Guisane**, 4. Explore Briancon. Farewell dinner in the restaurant at les Boussardes

Day 15 Drive home

No. 6.   A group of keen class 4/5 kayakers, one week, mid-August.

Day 1   Arrive at the **Rabious**. Run the lower Durance down to the Rabious and play on the rapid as a warm up.

Day 2   Run the **Lower Durance** 3-(3+) from the campsite in the morning and then the **Lower Guisane,** 4, in the afternoon.

Day 3   Run the **Middle Guil** 4 (5) in the morning and then the Chateau Queyras and Gaurdian Angel Gorges 4+(5).

Day 4   Run the **Durance Gorge,** 4+(5) **or** the **Biaisse**, 5(6), depending on water levels.

Day 5   Shift camp to le Lauzet in the Ubaye valley. Paddle the **Ubaye from les Thuiles**, 3(4), from **la Fresquiere**, 5 & then the **Ubaye Race Course, 4+**.

Day 6   Paddle the **Ubaye Gorge** 5-(6) and then the **Gyr, 4+(5)** on the way to camp to the top end of the Guisane Valley.

Day 7   Run the **Romanche**, 4+ & the **Veneon**, 4+(5). Camp in the Veneon valley.

Day 8   Drive home.

No. 7. **A group of keen, class 4 kayakers, 3 days end of August.**

Day 1 Arrive at **Bourg St Maurice** around Midday. Run the **Isère** from Bourg to Centron, 4, then play on the Slalom course.

Day 2 Drive over to the **Aosta valley** - magnificent scenery! Run the **Dora Gorge**, 3+(4) and perhaps the Canyon de l'inferno, 4+.

Day 3 Run the **Grand Eyvia**, 4, then drive home via the Mont Blanc Tunnel.

No. 8. **A small group of keen class 4 kayakers, weekend in Jul/Aug.**
*this itinerary is planned to include the Grand Canyon du Verdon
- check water releases with the local tourist office beforehand.*

Day 1 Fly with kayaks to Nice or Marseilles, hire a car and drive to the Verdon. Paddle the **Verdon Pre Canyon**, 3(4).

Day 2 Paddle the **Grand Canyon du Verdon** 4(5). Drive and fly home.

N.B. *A support driver is strongly recommended.*

Durance, Argentière Slalom Course, Alan Ellard.   *Heather Gunn*

Notes on France

Introduction - the Centres and runs

The French Alps offer some of the best white water paddling in Europe with a huge variety of rivers and runs so it is difficult to try to summarise what each area offers -

The **Verdon**, with its unique Grand Canyon is the most southerly centre and paddling here is good from Easter through until July. Note that there are now dam releases twice a week in the summer. **Bourg St Maurice** is a famous kayaking centre, but a little limited in its runs - we feel that like its neighbouring centre in Italy, the **Aosta valley**; this is a better destination for middle and late summer.

The other centres: **Briancon, Guillestre**, the **Ubaye valley** and **Séveraisse** all offer a wide variety of runs throughout the summer (the best time for paddling is usually mid-June to mid-July): the first three centres are well known and justly popular; the Séveraisse is more limited in its runs but is well worth a visit. The **Dranse** is a good river on which to warm up on the way to other centres.

Rivers elsewhere

France is a large country and has a huge number of rivers suitable for canoeing, kayaking, and rafting - some 700 according to one guidebook. Whilst the French Alps is the premier region for white water sports, the rivers of the Pyrenees (see our guidebook **'White Water Pyrenees'**) are an alternative for early summer and the rivers of the Massif Central are also a popular destination for white water and touring paddlers looking for easier rivers - famous names are the Tarn, Ardèche, and the Allier - for more information see our guidebook **'White Water Massif Central'**.

Language

The French are proud of their language and culture so naturally they appreciate you attempting to use it, but these days most young people speak English. We visited many tourist information centres and all had staff who spoke good English. Most rafting centres and kayak centres also had one member of staff who spoke some English - generally someone who had paddled in New Zealand, Nepal, or North America - it's nice to see that white water paddling has become quite international!

Food and Drink

France has its pizza, 'pomme frites' and MacDonald's. This is a country, however, which is still proud of its heritage of good food. Lorry drivers will sit down to a four course lunch at a 'Routiers' restaurant and French housewives still walk to the local market to buy their fresh produce. When in France, we recommend that you do as the French: have lots of barbecues and picnic style meals with salads and locally grown, fresh produce.

We suggest that you try to do most of your **shopping** in local markets and small shops as it's lots more fun, the food is much better, with superb flavoured fresh local produce, and remember, you will be both interacting with, and supporting local people. A Boulangerie is a bread shop, and a Patisserie is a fancy cake shop that often makes its own chocolates and ice cream - don't let anyone loose in here with the team kitty! A Charcuterie is a pork butcher, but often more of a delicatessen, with freshly roasted chickens, pies, hams and sausages, freshly made salads, and mouth-watering quiches - great for picnic lunches or suppers - well, after a few bottles of wine, who feels like cooking?

Sassenage   *Victor Cassieu*

Driving

French roads are generally good and it's almost a pleasure to drive on their motorways. Short sections of motorway around the larger cities are usually free, but other motorways have toll charges that can be quite expensive. Main trunk roads, called 'Route National' (RN) have improved considerably in the last few years and are worth considering if you are on a budget and have more time as they take you through all those interesting old towns and villages. Minor roads are often bumpy and poorly marked so night driving on these can be as exciting as class 4!

Where to stay

Camping

Most canoeists enjoy the outdoor life and camping is an obvious choice. One of the attractions of camping is the flexibility it gives you to move on when you feel like it - if rivers conditions are not up to expectations, or if the weather turns bad.

French campsites are numerous, and good value. Almost all have hot showers and a wide variety of facilities and are graded from one to five stars. Typically in 2002 we were paying about 3 euros per head per night on a three star site. Some of the smaller, more attractive sites do get fully booked in the main summer holiday period but there are usually plenty of other local sites. If you plan to stay for a while then you may prefer to book ahead for peace of mind, and it is usually possible to select and reserve an individual pitch - they can usually fax you a site plan.

We have listed selected sites in this book, however tourist information offices and webbsites have full listings of all sites and their facilities.

Several families we know with small children have booked holidays with companies such as Eurocamp, who provide not only all the camping tents and gear but also a full social programme to keep the kids amused. This saves you carting loads of camping gear with you half way across Europe - leaving room in the car for those important things like aquatic toys, and wine on the return! These are especially good value outside the main school holiday period.

Gites and Apartments

Gites are self-catered French holiday cottages or houses. Local tourist offices can supply you with a list, or you can rent these through various commercial agencies in France and the UK. A specially good bargain are **apartments in ski resorts**, which are heavily discounted out of season in May and June - besides being warmer and drier, they may then actually be **cheaper than camping.** (so if the weather turns cold and wet on you - pop up to the Tourist Office and see if you can do a deal.)

Gites d'Etape

These are another alternative to camping, especially worth considering earlier in the season. These are small independent hostels that have to satisfy national standards. Typical price for a bed for the night is around 11 euros and many have twin bed rooms. These are great places for meeting and socialising with outdoor-orientated French people, food is usually substantial and often excellent.

Hotels

French country hotels are incredibly good value typically being about half the price of what you would expect to pay in the U.K, so again well worth considering.

Notes on Italy

Introduction - the Centres and Runs

In researching these books, we spent two months searching and researching for white water in the Italian Alps and were deeply depressed at how little remains - and it seems incredible that even these few rivers are under threat of damming - there seems to be little national regard for the environmental destruction or the loss of white water tourist revenue. But that being said, the white water that is left, is beautiful!

The classic white water runs that remain are grouped in three beautiful and diverse centres, the Val di Sole, the Sesia valley (in the Piedmont), and the Aosta valley. The Val di Sole is in the North East of Italy near Bolzano and so is covered in our North Alps guidebook. The **Aosta valley** is a major tourist valley and its river, the Dora Baltea, drains many major glaciers near Mont Blanc so is large and powerful and at its best for paddling late in the summer. The **Sesia** valley in comparison is a quiet, cul-de-sac, awkward to get to, immensely beautiful, and an absolute delight to paddle in early summer.

Rivers elsewhere

As noted above, there is little other white water of interest in Italy for the average recreational paddler in the main summer season. The expert class 5 paddler however, should consider the area to the north of the Sesia Valley that has some very difficult but beautiful runs, at their best in early summer.

Language

The Italian language sounds wonderful but have no worries if you don't speak it - young people usually speak some English so you can get by with little other than a phrase book. In the valleys near the borders people usually understand and speak either German or French, sometimes as their first language.

Food and Drink

Forget the paddling - this is really what you come to Italy for! Ask people about their visit to Italy and one of their main memories will be some delicious restaurant meals - excellent value, great cooking, and cheap wine. Pizzas are always a good standby, but do try some of the local dishes, which are often much more tasty and better value if you order the fixed price meal. Let us just remind you that Italian ice cream is the best in the world and we'll leave your imagination and tummy to write the rest of this paragraph!

Driving

Italian drivers are famous for their driving - and yes, they do have a certain flair, but really they're not that much different to other European drivers. Italian roads though, are often worse than their counterparts in other Alpine countries - you will notice the difference as you drive over the border. They are often poorly maintained and badly marked so it's better to try to limit your night driving to the motorways.

Motorways normally have a toll to pay, but at the time of writing this was reasonable and well worth it for most journeys. The price of fuel was broadly comparable with Britain.

Italy is a very bureaucratic country with, it would seem, lots of minor regulations that no one takes too much notice of. One of these is a rule that overhanging loads on a vehicle, e.g. kayaks, must have a special board and lights - this might be worth checking with your motoring organisation if you have a long overhang.

Where to stay

Camping

Italy is a relatively cheap country for the tourist paddler, so it's a bit of a surprise to find that most campsites are expensive and crowded. If you want to camp then we recommend that you try to inspect several sites. In the peak months you may find that both hotels and campsites are full, so you may have no alternative other than to find somewhere unofficial to camp.

Wild camping may break some local ordinance, but in practice you will probably have no problem as long as you arrive late and pack up your tent early the next morning - especially if you've been drinking in the village bar with local officials the night before! Note that many villages have a municipal barbecue site in some quiet, scenic setting, unsigned and far from the main road. These usually have toilets, fire pits and running water, and are ideal for a long evening barbecue ....

One of the attractions of camping is the flexibility it gives you to move on when you feel like it - important if rivers conditions are not up to expectations, or if the weather turns bad. Tourist information offices and webbsites have full listings of all campsites and their facilities.

Apartments

Local tourist offices and webbsites can supply you with a full list of holiday apartments and chalets, or you can rent these through various commercial agencies in Italy or your home country. A specially good bargain are **apartments in ski resorts,** which are heavily discounted out of season in May and June - besides being warmer and drier, they may then actually be **cheaper than camping.** (so if the weather turns cold and wet on you - pop up to the Tourist Office and see if you can do a deal.)

Hotels

Italian country hotels are incredibly good value, (typically being about half the price of what you would expect to pay in the U.K) and of course have lots of ambience and style, so again are well worth considering and especially out of season.

White water slalom course, Bourg St Maurice. *Tony Tickle*

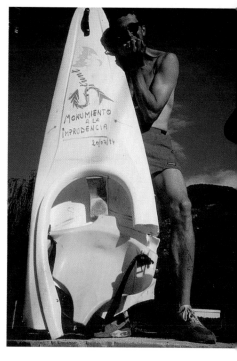

re fun off the river? *Peter Knowles*

One stunt too many. *Gianluca Ricci*

Sesia Gorge.

Peter Knowles

pper Sermenza.

Gianluca Ricci

Guardian Angel Gorge.

Peter Knowles

Middle Sesia.

Alan Fox

Rafting

Introduction

Twenty years ago and white water rafting was almost unknown in the Alps -
now it's a multi-million pound tourist industry with a million client trips a year.
There is a wide selection of rafting runs in the South Alps as can be seen from the
table below, from the scenic float trip to an aquatic bob sleigh ride - but all relatively
short and there are no long multi-day trips that you get in countries like Nepal.

Most people book for just one or two short raft trips as part of a more general
holiday, but there is great scope here for an enjoyable specialist rafting holiday - an
excellent week could be based around the Briancon, Guillestre, and Ubaye centres.
Some of the larger companies do offer a programme combining rafting trips on
several rivers, but it's probably better to get your own group of enthusiasts together
and then organise your own programme.

France now regulates commercial rafting and all companies and guides must be
licensed. This in theory does not apply to private rafts - as tourists you are welcome
to use the rivers, without payment, permit or licence - all that the French ask is that
you respect any local regulations and are considerate to other river users. There
have been the odd occasions, however, usually after accidents, when the French
police have had doubts about the non-commercial nature of overseas groups and
ordered them off the river.

How Difficult

Rivers are graded for difficulty on an international scale of 1 to 6 and if you prefer
an easier trip then you should chose a river that is mainly class 3: the most popular
easy run in the south Alps is the Lower Durance which is big, bouncy, and relatively
warm and friendly.

Many people are naturally a little bit apprehensive if they haven't been on white
water before, but after the first rapid are 'hooked'. In our experience most active
people would be happy booking on a river of moderate difficulty (class 3 to 4).
Remember that we grade a run on the hardest sections and most trips have sections
of easier water in between the rapids in which to relax.

More difficult, class 4+ or class 5, white water runs are exciting and add a spice
of danger: to book a trip on one of these rivers you should be active and comfortable
around water and have some previous rafting experience.

Paddle rafting

Paddle rafting is all about group participation and teamwork. All (or most) of the
rafters have paddles, propel the raft down the river and manoeuvre it through the
rapids with the Guide wielding a steering paddle at the back of the raft and 'calling
the shots'. Paddling your own raft is a lot of fun, challenging, satisfying, and builds
a great team spirit. Because paddle rafting is such fun, it is standard in the Alps and
you rarely come across the oar rigs that are used on other continents.

Note that on most rivers, it is not all intense activity - you will spend some time
drifting along quietly, letting the current do the work and enjoying the scenery.

Who enjoys Rafting?

Most people enjoy rafting, but **women in particular** in our experience: for many different reasons, so don't ask us - ask them!

A rafting trip can be an excellent holiday experience for older children - but this obviously depends on your family and how confident they are about water. Many rafting companies have an easy run for family groups including children 6 or older. Children of 12 years and older may be considered for runs such as the Lower Durance, whilst for more difficult class 4 rivers the age limit is often 18. Older children like to be active and involved so where possible it's better to chose a paddle rafting trip on an easier river. They also get cold quickly so we advise against a long trip on a cold day.

There is no upper age limit for rafting: the nice thing is that it can be as leisurely or as active as you wish. In our experience most older people enjoy the river experience (Cam MacLeay tells of two 70-year old widows who booked on a raft trip down the Zambesi Gorges (BIG water class 4+) in the mistaken idea that it was "a Gin and Tonic sunset cruise' and he says "they just loved it'!)

If you or friends have disabilities, then a river trip can offer real freedom and the opportunity for adventure in the natural world - one possible option is to paddle your own inflatable 'hot dog'.

Safety

Most people's image of white water rafting is one portrayed by films and the media and almost everyone who hasn't done it imagines it as a horrendously dangerous sport. The truth is the reverse: accidents, even minor ones, are rare and rafting in the Alps has a much safer accident record than say skiing, or mountain biking.

This is because when you are on the river you are in a relatively protected vehicle - inside a nice big bouncy rubber raft controlled by an experienced professional guide. This isn't to say that rafting doesn't have risks; if you run class 4 white water then there is always the possibility of a capsize, moving water isn't a rigidly structured, precise environment, it wouldn't be much fun if it was! However, if the worst does happen, and you do take an accidental swim - then because water is a nice soft landing, it's not likely to be anything worse than an involuntary ducking.

However we have to stress that white water rafting IS an assumed risk sport. It relies on good practice to keep it relatively safe and you should always book with a reputable company and with a licensed professional guide.

Note that one of the most basic safety rules is that there should always be **two rafts**, or more on a trip (or safety kayakers). A recent trend is for companies to have 'safety boaters' in kayaks to accompany trips on the more difficult rivers, particularly in high water conditions. Rafting trips at this time are more dangerous and exciting! Do **ask about river levels** and if in doubt chose an easier trip.

Summary of the main rafting runs

Name of run	Class	WW	Scen.	Km	cumecs	Notes
Middle Dranse	3 (3+)	★★	❀❀	6	20	popular easy run
Isère	4	★★★	❀❀	19	30	true classic
Doron	4	★★	❀❀	4	10	tight & fast
Dora Gorge	3+ (4)	★★	❀❀	6	30 = lw	recommended
Lower Sesia	3+(4+)	★★★	❀❀	9	20	a fine run
Upper Guisane	3 (4-)	★★	❀❀	11	10	fast & scenic
Lower Guisane	4	★★★	❀❀	6	15	fast & exciting
Romanche	4+	★★	❀❀	5	25	full on - late season
Lower Durance	3-(3+)	★★	❀❀	16	60	popular, big & bouncy
Middle Guil	4 (5)	★★★	❀❀	9	25	fast and fun
Guil Gorges	4+(5)	★★★	❀❀❀	4	7	Pin ball machine!
Séveraise	3+ (4)	★★	❀❀❀	8	15	highly scenic
Ubaye Race Cours	4+	★★★	❀❀	8	30	a must do
Upper Ubaye	3	★★	❀❀	13	10	friendly introduction.
Ubaye Gorge	5-(6)	★★	❀❀❀	4	20 = lw	challenging

Besides these 15 main runs, there is least the same number of less popular runs that are rafted when water levels are right - please see centre and run descriptions for more information.

'Paddle rafting is all about group participation'

Equipment

Rafts come in various sizes: the most popular is 5 metres long, and normally takes a crew of 8 plus guide. They are very tough and rugged so it's rare for them to be damaged or punctured - even if the latter happens, this is usually not serious as they have several compartments to keep them afloat.   Self-draining models with an inflatable floor are now standard.   Smaller rafts are more manoeuvrable and used for smaller, more technical rivers, but theses are more likely to be 'flipped' on a wave.

Good **life jackets** (Buoyancy Aids or Personal Flotation Devices) are obligatory. Modern ones are comfortable and well-fitting and have adjustable straps and buckles to ensure a snug and secure fit.   Do make sure to keep yours done up tight.

Helmets are strongly recommended on any white water trip.   On a paddle raft the helmet is more to protect your head from the paddle strokes of your over enthusiastic team mates!   Try to select and adjust your helmet so that it fits well and provides good protection for your forehead.

For white water trips, the raft should be rigged with "flip lines' so that it can be righted in the event of a capsize and it should also carry a first aid kit and **throw bags** for rescuing swimmers (ask your guide to give you a demonstration).

Personal Equipment

Your rafting company should provide all specialist equipment that you will need - this will normally include life jacket, helmet and waterproof nylon paddling jacket; and if the river is a cold: then a **wet suit** and perhaps wet suit boots.

Note that cotton **clothing** is really cold when wet and wicks the heat away from your body so we advise against wearing the ubiquitous cotton tee shirt. Much better to wear a **thermal top** or fleece next to your skin. - ones made by companies like Helly Hansen, Patagonia or Sub Zero are quick

Most rafters wear wet suit boots or an old pair of training shoes on their feet, sometimes with woollen socks for extra warmth.   If you wear **spectacles** make sure that these are fastened with a retaining strap or tied on with a thin length of string.

'Hot Dogs', Inflatable canoes, and 'Hydro-speeds'

Rafts are the usual craft for commercial river trips, but it's worth mentioning that many companies in France now have one or two person inflatable canoes that are called les **'Hot dogs'** (Americans call these 'duckies') that are used on the easier runs.   These are great fun - a typical comment is: "I got a great buzz out of paddling my own boat!"   Some companies also run smaller 'mini-rafts' which you captain yourself after suitable training.   On one or two smaller and easier rivers it is even possible to go 'tubing' sitting in a tractor inner tube.

'Hydro-speeding', or 'nage in eau vive' is a French invention and consists of swimming rivers with a special toboggan-like float to protect and support the upper body (see page.....).   Your group of hydro-speeders are guided down the river like a, sinuous line of fish, with a swimming leader at the front and usually accompanied by a safety kayaker. You wear swimming flippers and a thick wet suit with heavy padding to protect the lower body.   If you're a reasonable swimmer with flippers then do have a go at this - you're even more intimately involved with the water than a kayaker, feel every nuance of the current, and yet (unlike kayaking) this is something you can do with almost no experience!

Extreme Rafting

The Chateau Queyras and Guardian Angel Gorges on the Guil are notorious: steep, tight, technical, and difficult kayaking. I would never have believed that it was possible to raft them. I was up at Chateau Queyras researching this book and bumped into Vincent Lhote who I had met in Nepal. He was the head guide on the Guil and when I asked him about the gorges, he said that they rafted them three times a day. I expressed disbelief so he invited me to "come rafting" and try it for myself.

The trip turned out to be like no other rafting other trip I've ever done anywhere else in the world. It was more like an aquatic pin ball machine!

Because the river is so tight, the company, AN, use special mini-rafts, super tough, self-bailing, with inflatable floors and big tubes. The raft guides are experts on this river and know every rock and every nuance of the current. They will deliberately ram a rock to slow the raft down and then perhaps rotate the raft around the rock to line it up for the next drop.

A good third of the drops we did backwards, deliberately, so that we would be better lined up for the next move. I don't know which felt worse going forwards down some three metre shoot looking at some awful headwall just below, or just drifting down backwards and a horrible feeling of not knowing what was to come! Another technique was to deliberately bounce the raft into a rock so that it rebounded into an eddy - one that would be impossible for a raft to catch in any other way.

The rafts were kept slightly under-inflated so that they could squeeze through narrow gaps - a bit like toothpaste out of a tube. Meanwhile, the rafters all 'high-sided' up on one tube or we executed what the guide called 'le sandwich', where we piled into the bottom of the raft and the raft folded like a crepe around us! The paddling was intense, non-stop action - it was 'forward', 'stop', 'hold tight', 'forward left', 'back right', 'forward all', 'hold', 'back all', 'hold tight', 'highside left', and occasionally - 'relax' ....

There were a few shallow stretches and again, the guides had a special technique for these: 'le shuffle' where all seven of us would bounce the raft, up and down in unison so it shuffled and hopped over the shallows like a giant children's space hopper.

Thankfully there were a few pools and eddies so the guide would give us a rest, to let our heartbeats get back to something like normal, our fingers unclench from the paddle, and also to look around with wonderment, because of course, there is no other way into this these magnificent gorges except by river.

This was the most fun, and different white water experience I've had for a long time. If you're fit, active, and adventurous, I highly recommend it!

Peter Knowles

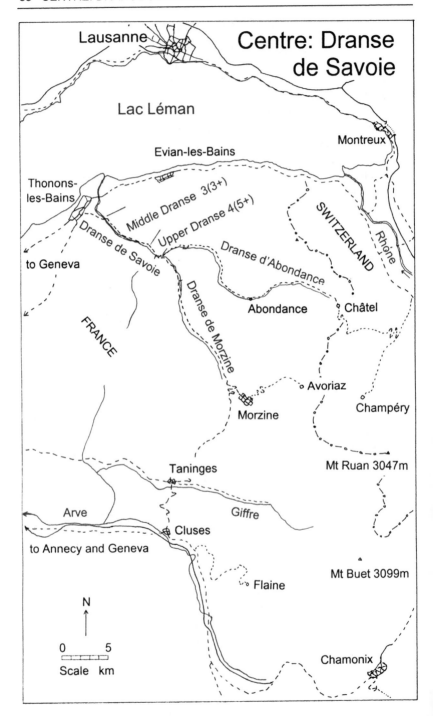

Centre: Dranse de Savoie

Lausanne

Lac Léman

Montreux

Evian-les-Bains

Thonons-les-Bains

Middle Dranse 3(3+)

Upper Dranse 4(5+)

Dranse de Savoie

Dranse d'Abondance

to Geneva

SWITZERLAND

Rhône

Abondance

Châtel

FRANCE

Dranse de Morzine

Avoriaz

Champéry

Morzine

Mt Ruan 3047m

Taninges

Giffre

Arve

Cluses

to Annecy and Geneva

Mt Buet 3099m

Flaine

N

0   5
Scale km

Chamonix

Centre: Dranse de Savoie

The Runs

Name of run	Class	Stars	Scen.	Km	cumecs	Notes
Middle Dranse	3 (3+)	★★	❀❀	6	20	popular run
Upper Dranse	4 (5+)	★★	❀❀	3	20	syphons, 1 portage

The Centre

Mention the Dranse to the average British paddler who has been to France and the chances are that they have never heard of it - they probably think you are talking about the Durance! So, a little known river - but one that offers reliable white water in pleasant surroundings and close to Geneva (30 km). The area only offers this one classic run, but it's conveniently en route to other paddling centres and we think it makes a good stop-over.

On the River

The Dranse de Savoie rises near the ski resort of Morzine to the south of Lake Geneva (Lac Léman) and flows in a steep wooded valley carved through verdant rolling hills, and then on into the lake at Thonon-les-Bains. The waters of the three branches of the river are captured for H.E.P. but fortunately returned into the river at the start of the scenic 'Gorges de Dranse'. Flows are regulated to provide good levels for rafting and kayaking throughout the summer.

Navigation is allowed from 9 a.m. to 6 p.m. from mid-March to October, subject to a minimum flow of 6 cumecs for canoes and kayaks (12 cumecs for rafts).

In the summer, there are no other rivers in the immediate area with sufficient water to be of much interest to white water paddlers.

Commercial Rafting

The proximity to Geneva makes this a popular river, with some 60,000 trips a year - something of a miniature version of the American Ocoe river!

The most popular run is what we call the middle Dranse starting from 'la Cassine': this can be rafted, and is also a great section for 'les hot-dogs' (duckies), and 'nage en eau vive' ('hydro-speeding'). The upper section is commercially rafted, but in our opinion, this short run is not worth the dangers involved.

Off the River

These south shores of Lac Léman comprise a very pleasant, affluent, tourist area with green rolling hills, the blue waters of the lake and the snow covered Alps in the distance. Thonon-les-Bains is a large, well-heeled, spa town but doesn't have that stifling 'awfully nice' atmosphere of many such places. It has a good choice of reasonably priced bars and restaurants, a lively waterfront, and a thriving market on Thursday evenings - we recommend a night out here.

There are good facilities for swimming and boating and a pleasant public park and beach (suitable for kayaks) at St Disdille on the lakeside 4 km north east of Thonon. There's also a nudist beach 2 km south of here.

Campsites

'la Prairie' at Champanges is a village site 3 km east of the river, in a pastoral setting on hills overlooking the lake.

Hospital

Thonon-les-Bains, near the station.
Telephone 18 in case of accident (fire/ambulance/rescue).

"English Persons!"

In the days before polyethylene the continental paddlers all used heavy glass fibre tanks that were strong enough to stand on. We, however, just took out our normal lightweight craft, straight from the last division two slalom. Their boats were strong enough; ours weren't. This, however, is only apparent with hindsight; at the time we had all sorts of theories about light boats being essential to give the acceleration and high performance needed to escape from trouble!

Our alpine paddling in those days resembled stock-car racing. Often, at least one boat-rebuilding day was needed for each day on the water and sometimes paddling the harder rivers became simply a matter of seeing who could get the furthest.

On those rare occasions when we all actually arrived intact at the end of a run, our German friends, who were highly amused by our antics, used to cheer with delight and we would arrive to loud shouts of "ENGLISH-PERSONS - sehr gut!"

Jerry Tracey

Maps

IGN TOP100 sheet 45, covers this centre and the surrounding area so is our recommended 'best buy'. IGN TOP25 sheet no. 3428ET, covers the river in more detail if you need it.

Tourist Office   www.thononlesbains.com
Thonon-les-Bains, Tel: 04 50 71 55 55.

Rafting Operators
AN Rafting Dranse, Tel: 04 50 71 89 15   www.anrafting.com
A7 Aventures, Tel: 04 50 26 28 96   www.A7aventures.com
Aqua Alpovine Rafting, Tel: 04 50 70 06 98

Kayak schools / clubs / shops
Thonon Canoe-Kayak Club,
Chemin des Clerges, 74200 Thonon,
Tel: 04 50 26 41 40
River Equipment Service (a good shop),   www.river-equipment-service.fr.
16 avenue de la Dranse, 74200 Thonon,
Tel: 04 50 71 26 97.

Middle Dranse, 'la Cassine'.   *Canoe-Kayak Magazine France*

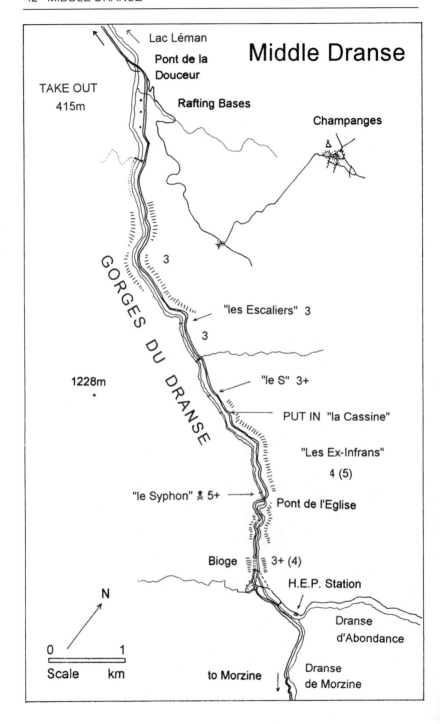

Middle Dranse de Savoie

From:	la Cassine	Difficulty:	3 (3+)
To:	Pont de la Douceur	Gradient:	10 m/km
Distance:	6 km	WW Stars:	★★
Time:	1½ hours	Scenery:	✿✿
Best months:	May to Sept	Flow:	20 cumecs = MW
Bank support:	good	Gauge:	bridge above the put in
Water temp:	warm / cool	Ass. runs:	Upper Dranse and
Water quality:	average		tributaries.

Summary
Good white water, a guaranteed flow throughout the summer, convenient access, and pleasant scenery make this a very popular river.

Special points
Please don't park on the rafters' lay-bys at the put-in. Watch out for the traffic!

The River
The Dranse de Savoie cuts a 200m deep wooded gorge through rolling hills. The left side of the valley is quite wild, almost pathless, with dense green woodlands roamed by wild boar. The river is normally a clear green, flowing over stony rapids with the occasional small orange cliff face and sombre grotto. It reminded us of rivers in Wales or the Appalachians.

Rafting
This is a fun raft trip with plenty of rapids and nothing serious to worry about. It can be done as a morning or afternoon run and there is a good choice of companies. For the more adventurous, we recommend this run for le 'hot-dog' (inflatable self-bailing kayaks) or 'Hydro-speeds' (white water swimming).

Access and Logistics
The main road between Thonon les Bains and the ski resort of Morzine follows the river closely and gives good access - too closely perhaps: local rafters reckon that more motor cyclists have died in the river than on the road and more river runners have died on the road than in the river!

The put-in at la Cassine is fairly obvious as you drive up the road - the last big lay-by before the big rapids and cliffs - but be careful not to put in too high, particularly in high water. Parking can get very congested, and it is important that the larger lay-bys are kept free for the buses and trailers of the raft companies (if there were no rafting there would be no water releases). Please park so that you are out of the way whilst you unload, and then shuttle your vehicle and park at the bottom of the river (the shuttle driver can usually get a lift back up with a raft company).

The best place to take out and park is near one of the raft company take outs (The Pont de la Douceur used to the favourite take out but several cars have been broken into here in recent years - of course, its just coincidence that there is a travellers camp over the road....). Note that the larger raft companies normally schedule their departures from la Cassine at 10 a.m. 12 a.m. and 2 p.m. so it's well worth planning to avoid these times on busy days, if you don't want to be part of a convoy of rubber buses down the river.

The Run

This is an ideal run for intermediate paddlers, with many rapids, almost all with pools below in which to recover. There's plenty of variety and character and for the expert there is the occasional surfing wave and play spot. It's easy to see why the Dranse is so popular with local paddlers from the Geneva area.

Check water levels with the local rafting companies or at the River Equipment shop on the outskirts of Thonon. Water levels between April and the end of June are normally between 20 and 50 cumecs, but may occasionally rise to 100 cumecs! In July the release is normally held at between 18 and 21 cumecs. In August and September the hours of release are normally 9 a.m. to 2 p.m. and the level is held at around 15 cumecs. If there is a drought then the hours will be progressively reduced to 9 - 12 a.m. It takes some two hours for the water to flow down the river.

Description

'La Cassine' is the classic start for slalom, down river races, rafting and other assorted river rats. Straight after the put-in is **'la Grille'**, class 3+, a series of shoots and eddies between big rocks with one notorious stopper that has been known to back loop down river racing K1s! This is followed by **'le S'**, two curving drops with undercuts and dangerous underwater currents - class 3+. Less experienced paddlers are advised to put on just below here.

The next kilometre forms the slalom course and makes an ideal play-ground for would-be competitors and those less seriously inclined. Class 3 water continues down under a footbridge and some 500m further is **'les Escaliers'** (the staircase) on the approach to a left bend: this is a long rapid, class 3, with a series of great little play waves leading into a rock garden, then look out for a rock on the right that the current piles up against.

Three more class 3 rapids follow in the next 2 km with lots of play spots, the last is **'la Grotte'** with a small drop on the left - it's possible to stop in the grotto and surf a nice little wave (Note that in high water, 50 cumecs+, this becomes a heavy class 4 and the biggest rapid on the river). A metal bridge marks the final class 3 rapid, where the main tongue heads straight onto a big boulder in the middle of the river.

The next kilometre is class 2 and runs past the rafting bases down to 'le Pont de la Douceur'. Take out here on the left just below the bridge and carry up to the old road. Time for another run - or perhaps an ice cream and sunbathe down at the lake?

Lesser Classics

Upper Dranse de Savoie

From:	Bioge	Difficulty:	**4** (5+) syphons
To:	la Cassine	Gradient:	20 m/km
Distance:	3 km	WW Stars:	★★
Time:	1½ hours	Scenery:	❀❀
Best months:	July - Aug	Flow:	20 cumecs = MW
Bank support:	good	Gauge:	no

Summary

The kilometre of river down from le Pont de l'Eglise is known as 'les Ex-infrans' (translates as the 'old unrunnable') and is a dangerous section with **many siphons and undercuts.** The rock is a coarse conglomerate that traps trees and debris (more so than limestone rivers like the Verdon); it also has a strange attraction for plastic to which it clings tenaciously, and on average someone drowns here every two years. However, having given due warning, this is a great run for the experienced paddler: we recommend that you talk to local paddlers for advice on hidden hazards and scout well from the road beforehand. It is best run at low to medium water levels.

The section before this, the first 2 km down to le Pont de l'Eglise, is less serious - several class 3+ rapids and one that might be a 4. Put on 200m downstream of the HEP station on river left below a small footbridge. Make sure you scout the take-out, before the rapid above the bridge, beforehand otherwise you will be committed to 'le syphon'.

N.B   A new bridge is being built at the time of writing so paddling is 'interdit' for 200m up and down stream - due to be completed in 2003?

Other runs

The **lower Dranse** de Savoie below the Pont de la Douceur is class 1 & 2 for two kilometres, then there is a nasty weir under the railway bridge, after this are sewage outfalls, industry, some gravel workings called a 'nature reserve' and 'navigation interdit'.

The 3 branches of the river, the Dranse d'Abondance, Dranse de Morzine, and the Brevon, all have fine stretches of white water but only in periods of good water, normally from mid-March to the end of June.

In 2003, Canotier is planning to publish a new detailed French language guidebook to the Alpine rivers to the South and East of Lac Leman - this will cover both Haute Savoie and Suisse Romande, so will give more information on rivers near to the Dranse.

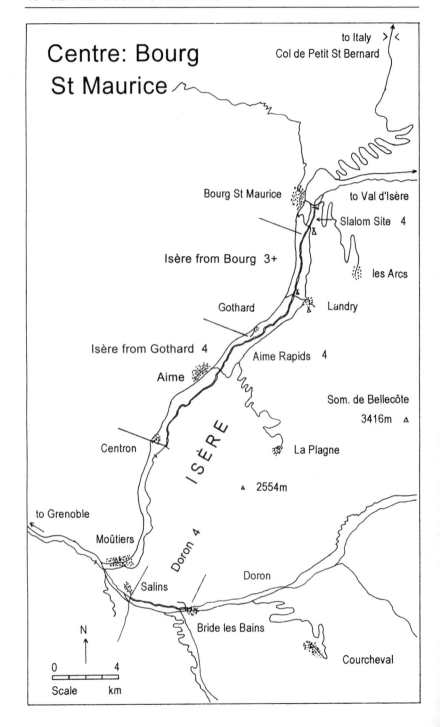

Centre: Bourg St Maurice

to Italy

Col de Petit St Bernard

Bourg St Maurice

to Val d'Isère

Slalom Site 4

Isère from Bourg 3+

les Arcs

Gothard

Landry

Isère from Gothard 4

Aime Rapids 4

Aime

Som. de Bellecôte

3416m

ISÈRE

Centron

La Plagne

2554m

to Grenoble

Moûtiers

Doron 4

Doron

Salins

Bride les Bains

Courcheval

N

0   4

Scale   km

Centre: Bourg St Maurice

The Runs

Name of run	Class	Stars	Scen	Km	cumecs	Notes
Isère from Bourg	3+	★★	⊛	8	20	a fine training run
Isère from Gothard	4	★★★	⊛⊛	11	20	a classic
Doron	4	★★	⊛⊛	4	10	continuous

The Centre

Bourg St Maurice is a famous venue for the World Whiter Wate Canoeing Championships and the area is well known for its winter skiing. The Isère is dam controlled so offers a reliable flow all summer, a world class slalom course, and 19 km of classic white water.

On the River

The headwaters of the Isère are captured for HEP by a sophisticated system of dams and tunnels which feed these back into the river at Bourg St Maurice. The flow from the dam is controlled so that it normally provides a good level for canoeing and rafting on the river downstream. This section of the Isère starts with the famous slalom course, then has one of the classic Alpine paddles which includes the notorious Aime rapids. This run is traditionally done as one long trip, but we suggest that it is better considered as two separate runs.

Below Centron, another series of dams capture the flow of the Isère, so that apart from the Doron, there is little else to interest the river runner in the area. Note though, that just over the pass into Italy is the Aosta valley (the river Dora Baltea, class 4) that is well worth considering for a day visit in late summer.

Bourg St Maurice is a popular training centre for more advanced kayakers, but the paddling here is limitted and we suggest that there are better centres to start at if this is a first trip to the Alps, or for a group of mixed ability.

Part of the appeal of Bourg St Maurice is that it is such a famous site for international canoeing. To camp here in the summer when one of the French competitions is taking place is quite an experience: sponsored teams from all the main cities in France with their own vehicles and cheering supporters; and in the evening, barbecues competing with the smell of fibreglass repairs, laughter and singing.

Commercial Rafting

This is one of the big centres in the Alps for rafting with many companies offering a wide variety of activities and trips on the Isère and Doron; and also day trips on the Dora Baltea over in Italy. 'Initiation' trips usually finish at Gothard or Aime, but the classic trip, and one that we can highly recommend, is the full 19 km from Bourg St Maurice to Centron.

Off the River

Bourg St Maurice offers everything you would expect from a well developed Alpine resort with a full range of facilities and activities on offer. It is surrounded by modern ski resorts - Val d'Isère, Tignes, Les Arcs and La Plagne, who work hard to attract summer visitors. The main lifts in these resorts are open in the summer months, so there is plenty of scope for mountain walks, parapents, and mountain biking (many lifts take bikes). Most resorts also have a summer luge run where you hurtle down a concrete chute on a little trolley - almost as exhilarating as a good kayak run! Tignes is only a short drive up the valley and has summer skiing high up on the glaciers with glorious views of the surrounding mountains. Several new Via Ferratas have been built in the last few years. Ask at the tourist offices for leaflets and more information on any of these activities.

Down in the valley, the cycle route alongside the river from Bourg St Maurice to Aime makes a very pleasant trip - it has a beautifully smooth surface and is also popular for roller skating.

If you're not tired of driving, then the route over the Col du Petit St Bernard into Italy is particularly scenic, not difficult, and gives some magnificent views of the Mont Blanc from near Courmayeur.

Bourg has a fine selection of all types of restaurants, whilst for more traditional french cooking we recommend the hotel in the middle of Landry village.

Campsites

Camping is often possible adjacent to the Slalom Site, on both banks of the river - usually when competitions are taking place, which is quite frequent in the summer months. Please enquire at the Canoe School building next to the bridge. Facilities are a little Spartan, but at least this is mirrored in the price.

A more luxurious alternative, but still within walking distance of river and town is just up the road at the Centre Renouveau. At Landry, 'le Eden' is a large riverside site with 130 emplacements just upstream of the bridge; whilst in the village is 'les Guilles' - a small, quiet, family-run site in an old orchard.

Museum Dauphinois

We invite you to visit this famous museum if you would like to discover more about the people, history, and culture of the Dauphinois Alps.

Musee Dauphinois
30 rue Maurice Gignoux
38031 Grenoble
Tel: 04 76 85 19 00

Ten minutes from the autoroute through Grenoble.
Pick up a leaflet from any Tourist Information Office.

Hospitals:
Bourg St Maurice (see map of Isère from Bourg) and Môutiers.
Telephone 18 in case of accident (fire/ambulance/rescue).

Maps
IGN TOP100 sheet 53 covers this and the surrounding area so is our recommended 'best buy'. If you are staying in the area and need more detail then IGN TOP25 sheet no. 3532ET, covers the upper Isère, and sheet 3532OT the lower river and the Doron.

Tourist Offices   **www.savoie-tourisme.com**
Bourg St Maurice, Tel: 04 79 07 04 92.   www.lesarcs.com

Rafting Operators
Many - please consult the Tourist Office.

Kayak schools / clubs / shops
Club Canoe-Kayak de Haute-Isère,
73700 Bourg St Maurice, tel: 04 79 07 33 20.

Bourg St Maurice slalom course.   *Sue Richardson*

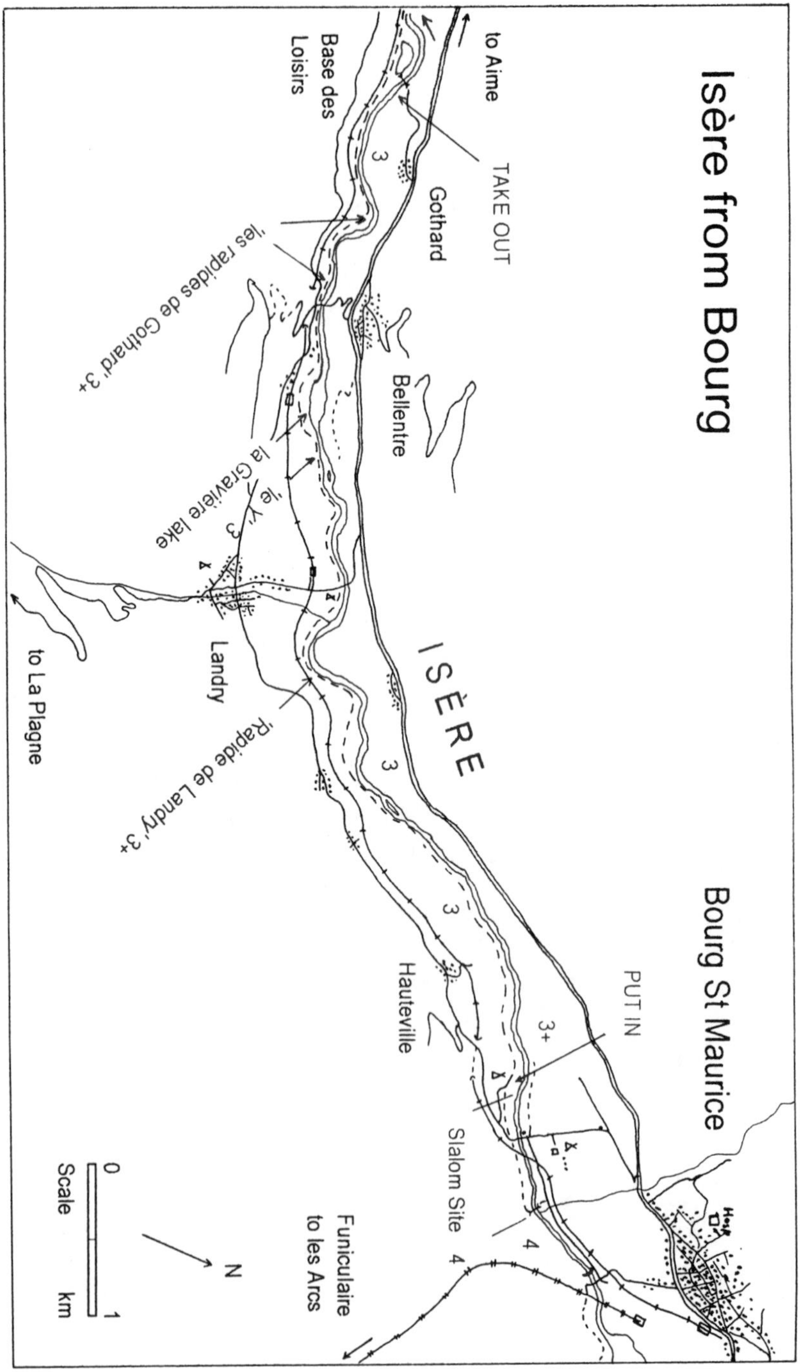

Isère from Bourg

to Aime

TAKE OUT

Base des
Loisirs

Gothard

3

'les rapides de Gothard' 3+

Bellentre

'le Y' 3

'la Gravière lake

Landry

to La Plagne

'Rapide de Landry' 3+

I S È R E

3

Hauteville

3

3

PUT IN

3+

Bourg St Maurice

Slalom Site

Funiculaire
to les Arcs

4

4

Scale

0   1

N

km

Isère from Bourg St Maurice

From:	Bourg St Maurice	Difficulty:	3+
To:	Gothard	Gradient:	10 m/km
Distance:	8 km	WW Stars:	★★
Time:	1½ hours	Scenery:	⊕
Best months:	May to Sept	Flow:	25 cumecs = MW
Bank support:	good	Gauge:	Slalom site
Water temp:	cold	Ass. runs:	Isère from Gothard
Water quality:	average		

Summary

Classic white water, fast and powerful but nothing too serious. Convenient access and assured water flow.

Special Points

Can get crowded at busy periods - look out for rafts!

Rafting

This is the most popular stretch of the river for 'initiation' - for those who want a short safe introduction to the joys of rafting. We think that most people are better booking the full run that finishes at Centron and it really makes an excellent raft trip with a pleasant variety of white water and scenery. Besides rafts, it is also possible to book smaller 2 man inflatable kayaks - 'le hot dog', or to try your hand at hydro-speeding ('nage en eau vive').

Access and Logistics

The main road up the valley makes shuttles fast and easy. The smooth and beautifully graded cycle track along the left bank (built for the 1987 world championships) makes a cycle shuttle a real pleasure - one friend of ours carried roller blades in his boat and then skated back for the car!

Put in on the left bank at the bottom of the slalom course. Take out on the right bank at Gothard - if you're waiting for your shuttle you can have an ice cream and swim in the 'Base de Loisirs' on the other bank - this is a nice warm lake and rolling practice is allowed except from 1200 to 1600. There is normally plenty of parking at both put-in and take-out.

The kayak school by the slalom course normally displays the times and planned flows from the dam. The white gauge at the bridge shows the flow in cumecs at the time.

Note that paddling is restricted to **0930 to 1900** each day - the river is reserved for fishing outside those hours. This regulation does not apply to the slalom course but access is regulated before and during competitions.

The Run

In the summer months the flow is regulated so it is normally between 15 and 30 cumecs - between 20 and 30 is an ideal level. More than 30 cumecs and the run becomes a class 4-. The river is wide in most places with a fast current making for a big bouncy enjoyable ride with a few big eddies in which to rest. This is a good introduction to alpine big water paddling for the confident intermediate paddler, particularly if they have a good roll. The banks are wooded so there is a minor hazard from trees in the water, but anything dangerous is normally cleared by the rafting companies so this is a relatively safe run - one paddler described it as 'sanitised'!

Those looking for a harder start can put in just below the barrage: 500m of roller coaster class 4 leads down to the slalom course which is fast, furious, and fun, but often busy.

Two thirds of the way down this run, just before Bellentre, the river runs through a small lake formed by gravel workings, which the local kayak schools use for initiation. If you're fresh out to the Alps and feeling nervous about putting on below the slalom course, then we recommend you follow their example and spend a morning here practising and running 'le Y' the friendly rapid that flows into the lake - there's also normally a nice warm pool for rolling practice. (Ask at the kayak school for how to get access to 'la Gravière' by road).

Playing kayak polo on la Gravière lake on the Isère.   *Peter Knowles*

Description

Take a minute to read the information board at the put-in which should tell you of any changes to the run.

The start takes you straight into big powerful class 3+ white water. If you're feeling a little nervous then take reassurance that it's fairly steady class 3 for the next 3 km giving you time to get in tempo with the river - lots of little waves for those who enjoy playing - and perhaps time to admire the surrounding mountains and church towers through the trees.

At the **'Rapide de Landry'** the river steepens up for a 100m forming a toboggan run of small haystacks - just good bouncy fun!   About 600m after the bridge to Landry the river branches around a small island and immediately after is **'le Y'** - a long, but straight-forward, class 3 rapid that leads down to the gravel workings and the lake. As noted earlier, this is a fine little training spot.

Shortly after the lake is the bridge to Bellentre (access if required just upstream on the right) and 200m below here are **'les rapides de Gothard'** - two class 3+ drops that create some nice big play waves at the right flow.   A few hundred more metres brings you to the footbridge at **Gothard** - take out here on the right bank upstream of the bridge.   There are ice creams and cold beers over the bridge at the 'Base des Loisirs'.

Note that the next section, which includes the infamous Aime rapids, is much harder - if you have any doubts, then we recommend that you build up confidence and skill by repeating this first section.

Rupert soon discovered that white water river
running was a total immersion experience

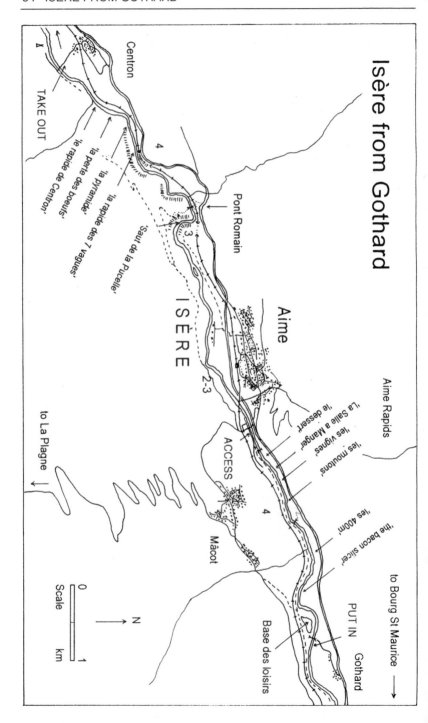

Isère from Gothard

Isère from Gothard

From:	Gothard	Difficulty:	**4**
To:	Centron	Gradient:	10 m/km
Distance:	11 km	WW Stars:	★★★
Time:	2 hours	Scenery:	✿✿
Best months:	May to Sept.	Flow:	25 cumecs = MW
Bank support:	reasonable	Gauge:	Slalom site
Water temp:	cold	Ass. runs:	Isère from Bourg
Water quality:	average/poor		

Summary

Powerful, classic, white water, and a scenic gorge. A justifiably popular run with assured water flow.

Special points

Can get crowded at busy periods - look out for rafts!

Rafting

This is the second half of the full trip that starts from Bourg St Maurice and finishes at Centron - an excellent and highly recommended raft trip that offers a pleasant variety of white water and scenery.

Access and Logistics

The 4 km down to Aime have a smooth cycle track along the left bank which allows easy inspection of the Aime rapids if required. The final scenic gorge above Centron can be viewed from the main highway on your drive up the valley. The put-in at Gothard and the take-out at Centron are both sign-posted off the highway. If you want to get away from the main raft hordes, then you could take out 300m upstream of Centron bridge on the opposite (left) bank where there is a quiet picnic site. Please see previous section for details of water flows, gauge, etc.

The Run

In the summer months the flow is regulated so there is normally a release of between 15 and 30 cumecs from the dam - around 25 is an ideal level, more than 30 cumecs and the run becomes a class 4+. Small streams joining the Isère probably add another 5 cumecs.

This run can be split into 3 sections. For the first 4 km, the river retains the character of the run down from Bourg St Maurice - but is much steeper and harder with the Aime rapids, the doom of many a white water racer (the international white water race course starts at Bourg and finishes at Centron). Below Aime the river reverts to a more natural state, wide and shallow in places with wooded banks, and class 3 down to the gorge section. This final gorge is natural, wild and scenic and forms a fine climax to the run.

Description

If you're starting at Gothard then put in on the right bank just upstream of the bridge. About 600m of class 3 takes you around the bend by the 'Base des Loisirs' and then shortly after this the current speeds up and you're in the first of the **Aime rapids**.

These rapids are probably not as bad as their legendary reputation - or how they were in the past. These days the river is sculpted and artificially constrained to make a better race course; anything really nasty has been bulldozed away - purists claim that the river has been ruined and sanitised in the interests of competition and safety (a view that seems to change following a swim!). The Aime rapids are now formidable without being ferocious, and daunting without being too dangerous. The water is fast and powerful, with big waves, crunching stoppers, and there are some holes you might not want to be in (but don't worry - a raft will knock you out!). Lines are usually fairly obvious and eddies well defined, however, so strong, confident paddling should see you through.

The lead-in rapid is **'the bacon slicer'** and then after a few hundred metres is **'les 400m'** (what an imaginative name!). This is a fine series of big blocks, eddies, shoots and surf waves. Half-way down the rapid a small stream comes in from the left and the **'Aime hole'** lurks below on the left - often marked by camera vultures hovering on the bank.

'les moutons' follows 100m after the **footbridge** (which roughly marks the half way point) - a superb rapid marked by a huge boulder in the middle at the top - most people take the left route and then head right. This leads you down to **'les vignes'** where the rapid curves round in an S bend. **'La Salle à Manger'** follows and this white water treat naturally finishes with **'le dessert'**.

A new wooden footbridge marks the approach to **Aime** and the various rafting bases on the left bank (also a couple of cafe/bars if you need a reassuring drink or ice cream). Some 300m brings you down to the road bridge and official take-out spot for kayaks on the left bank.

The next 3 km are relatively flat, wide and shallow and gives a welcome chance to drift along and enjoy the scenery. Usual advice here is to keep broadly to the left of the river.

A big right-hand bend heralds a dramatic change in the character of the river as it flows into a narrow, picturesque gorge. The river is constrained by sheer rock cliffs which create turbulent head-wall rapids and swirly eddies. The narrowest part is only some 5 m wide and is called the **'Saut de la Pucelle'** (the virgin's leap). This spectacular gorge can feel quite scary and committing, but in fact the paddling is relatively easy - no more than class 3 at normal water levels.

Easy water continues under the **'Pont Romain'** (not Roman!) and on for the next 1 km, as the river descends deeper into a fine wooded gorge, wild and pathless. As the river descends, so the tempo increases and you come to the final series of class 4 rapids **'la rapide des 7 vagues'**, **'la pyramide'** (on the left bend as you come out of the gorge) , **'la perte des boeufs' and 'le rapide de Centron'** (these follow closely). It's worth treating these with respect: they haven't been tamed by bulldozers, there are a few nasty holes and pour-overs, and there's no nice track along the bank.

A few hundred metres brings you to the picnic site and monument on the left bank and then a little further on the right is the rafters' **take-out**, upstream of the bridge. There is a pleasant outdoor café/bar just below the bridge on the right so take out here if you fancy a celebratory ice cream or drink whilst you await your shuttle. Note that 1.5 km downstream is a dangerous barrage which captures almost all of the water for HEP.

Lesser Classics

Doron

From:	Brides les Bains	Difficulty:	**4**
To:	Salins les Thermes	Gradient:	18 m/km
Distance:	4 km	WW Stars:	★★
Time:	½ hour	Scenery:	✹✹
Best months:	June-Sept	Flow:	10 cumecs = MW
Bank support:	reasonable	Gauge:	Bridge above put-in.
Water temp:	cold	Ass. runs:	Isère
Water quality:	average / poor		

Summary

An exciting paddle, very continuous, which never drops below class 4-. Local rafters treat this river with respect - it's more dangerous than the grade indicates with potential hazard from undercuts and trees. Rocks are sharp and a swim is likely to be quite nasty!

The Doron usually has good levels throughout the summer, depending on snow and glacial melt. It flows through a wooded gorge and a footpath follows the left bank. Put in by the swimming pool in the middle of Brides les Bains (an 'awfully nice' town). A start further upstream, just above the town, adds 600m of class 5 toboggan run. Take out by the bridge above Salins, next to a lay-by and 'les trois vallees' raft base. Below here the river is canalised, urban, with steep banks (but no weirs) and a possible alternative take-out for ice creams in town would be at the confluence with the Isère in Moûtiers - where a gravel dredger may give you a free big scoop!

There is a gauge on the Doron, on the next bridge up from the rafting put-in (by a big manicured lawn!): The local rafters do it up to 130cm, when it is probably class 4+; At 85-90cm, it is a full-on class 4; At 70cm it is fun but not so pushy; and we are told that the river is still runnable at 60cm.

Other runs

In summary: very limited. Reputedly there are some 3 km of class 2 on the Isère above Bourg St Maurice. The river below Centron has most of its water captured for HEP and there are no sections that can be recommended. The Doron above Brides les Bains has some steep, tree-infested sections of hard paddling and scouting. Its tributary, the Boron de Champagny is said to have some 6 km of class 4 and 5 down from Laissonay.

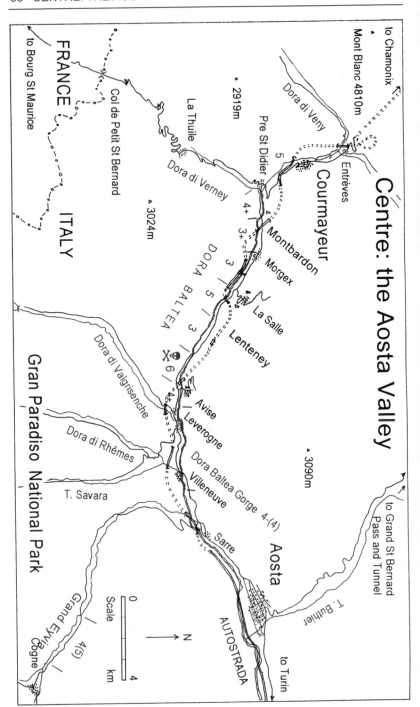

Centre: the Aosta Valley

Centre: the Aosta Valley

The Runs

Name of run	Class	Stars	Scen	Km	cumecs	Notes
Dora Baltea Gorge	3+ (4)	★★★	✿✿	6	30	Lots of interest
Dora from Pre-St Didier	4+	★	✿	2	20	Powerful
Dora from Montbardon	3+	★	✿✿	5	20	Continuous
Dora from La Salle	5	★★	✿	2	25	Technical
Dora from Lenteney	3	★	✿	3	25	Cold but fun
Canyon de l'inferno	4+	★★★	✿✿	2	30	Impressive
Grand Eyvia	4	★★	✿✿	4	15	Varied

The Aosta valley is a famous tourist area with magnificent mountain scenery. It's a main transit route through the Alps and is less than an hour's drive from Chamonix by the new tunnel and about an hour from Bourg St Maurice by the Petit St Bernard Pass.

On the River
A quick glance at the map and you will see that the Aosta valley is surrounded by mountain peaks and glaciers - Mont Blanc, the Matterhorn, Monte Rosa, and Grand Paradiso. With all this glacial melt water you can be assured of high water flows - the problem is that for much of the time most runs have too much water, so these rivers are usually **only at their best in late summer**.

The main river, the Dora Baltea, is a river of kayakers' wild tales, some major epics, and a few fatalities. Early in the summer, the river is usually in full spate from the melting glaciers - a huge volume (up to 200 cumecs), very fast, very cold, and no eddies: even local kayakers avoid the river and drive elsewhere for their paddling. Usually though, by the end of July the main run on the Dora Baltea Gorge from Leverogne to Villeneuve is runnable and can be recommended.

Note that sadly most of the tributaries and other sections of the Dora Baltea are now unrunnable and/or have many dangerous barrages. Older guide books should not be relied on as floods in recent years, and subsequent remedial work, have changed many rivers.

Commercial Rafting
Rafting is confined to the Dora Baltea. We highly recommend the main run from Leverogne to Villeneuve - this has all the things that make for a good raft trip and the World Rafting Championships were held here in 1994. Rafting is also offered on other sections of the upper Dora Baltea but these runs have less to recommend them.

Off the River
The Aosta valley is one of the main tourist areas in the Alps, famous for magnificent mountain scenery, Roman remains, numerous castles, religious art, and medieval villages.

To the south of the valley is the Grand Paradiso National Park - a beautiful area for mountain walking. If you like your mountain scenery the easy way then one of the most stunning cable car rides in the world is the journey over the Alps from Courmayeur to Chamonix reaching a height of 3842 m at the Aiguille de Midi - this obviously isn't cheap. If you're feeling poor then admire the vista of Mont Blanc from near Entreves, close to the Mont Blanc tunnel entrance; or better still, take the cable car from here up to Mont Chetif - you can take your mountain bike and have a great ride down to the valley of the Dora di Veny.

The town of Aosta was founded by the Romans and has many remains including a particularly fine bridge - well worth a stroll, as indeed are many of the old villages. One of our favourite villages is La Salle, partly for the pizzas in la Macina restaurant! The Aosta valley is paradise for those who like home made ice cream - a popular stop for most river runners is the ice cream parlour next to the pharmacy on the main road out of Morgex as you drive down the valley. Another thing to try is the local Fontino cheese that smells like wet suit boots but has a fine flavour (make sure you bite into the right package).

Campsites

Campsites in the Aosta valley are often crowded and relatively expensive (twice the price of their French counterparts). The site we recommend to friends for their honeymoon is 'Camping du Parc' at St Didier - what an evocative name! - the reality is that you are next to the main highway: devotees of diesel trucks will love the smell and roar of engines as climb the hill!

More pleasantly situated is 'Arc en Ciel' on the minor road on the north side of the valley between Pre-St Didier and Morgex. Another site in a fine setting in the heart of the gorge is the small one at Avise. Ian Beecroft recommends 'Camping la Pineta' at Aymarilles near Villeneuve (Tel: 069 902101).

Hospitals

Aosta. Dial 113 for Police and rescue services.

Maps

Detailed topographical maps are limited - our recommended best buy for paddlers is the beautiful 1:115,000 tourist map that can be obtained free from main tourist offices.

Tourist Offices

Aosta. Tel: 0165 236627, Fax: 0165 34657.   www.regione.vda.it/turismo
Also Tourist Offices in Courmayeur,   www.courmayeur.net
Villeneuve and other main towns.   www.granparadiso.org

Rafting Operators

'Rafting Aventure', Villeneuve,. Tel: 0165 95082.   www.aventure@aostanet.com
''Morgex Rafting', Morgex. Tel: 0165 800088.   www.rafting.it
'Totem Adventure' Pre-Saint Didier. Tel: 0165 876 77 www.totemadventure.com

Kayak schools / clubs / shops

Canoa Club Monte Bianco, Aosta. Tel: 0336 391303.

Dora Baltea looking upstream from Morgex bridge.   *Peter Knowles*

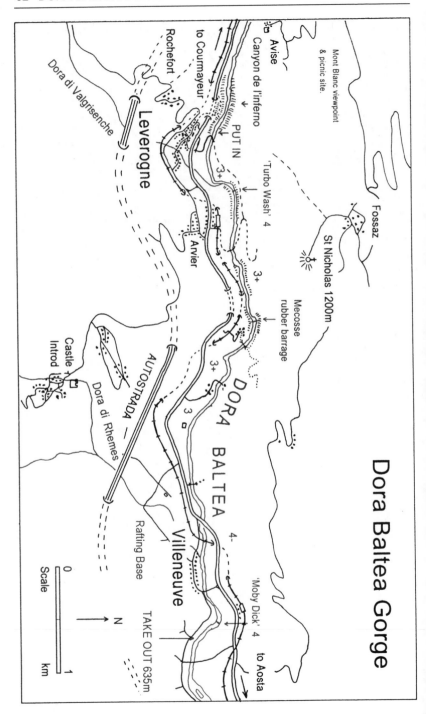

Dora Baltea Gorge

Dora Baltea Gorge

From:	Leverogne	Difficulty:	**3+ (4)**
To:	Villeneuve	Gradient:	11 m/km
Distance:	6 km	WW Stars:	★★
Time:	1½ hours	Scenery:	⊕⊕
Best months:	August to Sept	Flow:	30 cumecs = LW
Bank support:	reasonable	Gauge:	none
Water temp:	cold	Ass. runs:	Canyon de l'inferno
Water Quality:	average		

Summary
Big water but surprisingly friendly. Lots of variety, white water interest, and scenic gorges. This is the best section of the Dora Baltea and is at its best in **late summer** when water levels are low.

Special points
This run is dangerous in high water conditions - e.g. June and July. The old weir at Mecosse has now been replaced by an inflatable barrage.

The river
See centre notes. Upstream of Villeneuve the Dora Baltea runs through a spectacular gorge that can be divided into three sections: the upper gorge down to Avise is class 6 and has a 12m fall (see inset), the 'Canyon de l'inferno' that follows is class 4+ and described as a 'lesser classic' later; the lower Gorge is the classic run and is described here. Be sure to put on at the right place!

Rafting
This has become a popular raft run in the last few years and Villeneuve hosted the World Rafting Championships in 1994. We recommend this as an excellent rafting trip in low to medium flows.

Access and Logistics
We recommend a scout of 'Moby Dick' rapid, upstream of the take out in Villeneuve. Occasional glimpses of the run can be obtained from the main road, however to see the river at its scenic best just walk down to the put-in.

The recommended **put-in** is down a small private road opposite the village of Leverogne. Driving down the valley, this is the first turn off the main road (not the motorway) about 400m after the tunnel. Drive down this as far as the entrance to the wood yard to unload. This narrow road is used by trucks and rafting trailers so vehicles are best parked at the take-out, or on the opposite side of the main highway 200m up the road. Carry boats about 400m down the road to put in by the bridge.

If you're waiting for your shuttle, we recommend a short stroll around the village of Leverogne - quiet, unspoilt and photogenic.

The usual **take-out** is on the right bank downstream of Villeneuve next to a small fishing lake where there is plenty of parking.

There is no gauge on this stretch so we recommend that you talk to one of the local rafting companies who are normally very happy to advise on water levels and any new hazards. For most of the time the main highway is out of sight of the river, but it is in fact never more than a kilometre away so there is reasonable access in case of emergency.

The Run

Until recent years, this was a little-known run. Few paddlers realised that hidden from the highway was this secret gorge and fine paddle. Guide books either missed it out, or made it appear much harder by suggesting a start further upstream.

The river here is emerging from the main gorge so has lost quite a lot of its gradient: it's not the fast, furious torrent that you see further upstream; it's also had time to warm up a little and for much of the glacial silt to settle out. So, in low water conditions this is a relatively friendly run, with lots of variety, white water interest and is surprisingly scenic. Key features are: long bouncy rapids, a picturesque, green, foliage-hung gorge, big waves for surfing, large boulders and eddies and no boring stretches.

In medium flow levels, around 60 cumecs, the river naturally becomes much harder, class 4+(5), and quite a bit of the interest is washed out. In high flows you don't want to be here! In low water flows we recommend more expert paddlers consider putting on 2 km further upstream at Avise and running the spectacular 'Canyon de l'inferno' - see 'Lesser classics'.

Dora Baltea Gorge, hydro-speeds and safety kayaker   *Sue Richardson*

Description

Put in on the left bank upstream from the bridge - looking upstream from the bridge is a fine view of the last stretch of the **'Canyon de l'inferno'**. Immediately downstream from the put-in is a beautiful sheer-sided gorge with the rock walls draped in green foliage and a waterfall splashing into the river and showering passing paddlers. Swirly class 3 water takes you through the gorge and then the valley opens out a little with vineyards on the left and a glimpse of the main road up on the right.

The river bends first left and then right with low cliffs on the right - shortly after the bend is a class 3+ rapid, **'Turbo Wash'** - land left to inspect and portage if necessary. Class 3 paddling then takes you down to a concrete road bridge and shortly after, the river again swings left and then right. A second low gorge follows with a series of play waves that will tempt you to stay here for the rest of the day.

After this second gorge the river bends slightly left: there is a built up wall on the left, cliffs on the right, and the river can be seen about to bend sharply right - this is the approach to the **Mecosse Rubber Barrage** - a 2m diameter rubber tube that is fixed to the bed of the river. Eddy out on the left to inspect this. In normal summer conditions it lies flaccid and harmless on the bed of the river, out of sight, and the run then is a straight forward class 3 rapid - just avoid the obvious water intake on the right. If however, the tube is inflated and erect, then you should treat this with caution and portage left if necessary.

There is about 100m of bouncy water and then a green metal footbridge and a path leads up to the small hamlet of **Mecosse**. There's a mill outflow on the bend and then another good play section with looping waves. This ends with a rusty metal road bridge to a farm and about 500m further a big outflow from a HEP plant. The valley now opens up with distant views of snow clad mountains, a castle on the hill ahead, and a water outflow on the right is warning of a low weir which forms a stopper/play wave. Just below, a picturesque, old, roofed, wooden bridge spans the river.

Soon after, civilisation starts to impinge on the senses with the main road bridge and shortly after the railway. Just below the railway bridge is a small weir that forms a 'play stopper' that is usually shot right. The **Dora di Rhêmes** enters here on the right and then a big long bouncy rapid follows and takes you down to the town of **Villeneuve** (this is the start of the World Rafting Championship slalom course).

'Moby Dick' rapid is under the next main road bridge. This changes from year to year so should be scouted in advance. In medium and high flows it often forms a huge 'whale size' hole that swallows rafts and humans without a hiccup! Fast, bouncy water continues around the bend giving a fine finale to the run. Land right about 200m upstream of the next bridge.

It is possible to paddle on down another 3 km to Sarre, but we have not paddled this ourselves - those we have talked to who have run it are unenthusiastic, describing it as canalised with several sewage outfalls and broken weirs.

Location: The Italian Alps, close to the banks of the Dora Baltea

It was one of those summers when we didn't really have the money to go paddling but we were going to make it to the Alps, come what may. The plan was to live cheap and sleep rough.

Images of bivies with Alpine views and lush vegetation, very quickly gave way to a gravel car park, a concrete lay-by, progressing to our very own self contained dry mud ruts left by a JCB. Excavator. Eventually at 1.0. a.m the police found us and moved us on.

In the dark of that night we searched for a new spot. We stumbled upon an ideal field, except for the 20° slope. With the car tucked away off road behind a bush we were soon out for the count, dreaming of the day's epics.

As night drew on, the dreams became unusually vivid: the rush of the water, the boat rising up and over the waves, and the cold water hitting me in the face. In fact, it felt a little more akin to being on a raft than in a kayak and then suddenly I awoke: I was on the move.

As I sat up the water gushed in, into my sleeping bag, my hair was wet. It was at this point that the reality struck. In the dark I had put my air bed down in an irrigation channel and I was moving fast downhill in the direction of the Dora Baltea! Madly groping at clumps of grass I managed to stop myself, only to see Matthew and Adrian rush by still asleep - to be woken up as they collided with each other at the bottom - fortunately it was only a six inch weir!

Mark Herriott

Ranulph had never encountered such wild fluctuations in river levels before......

Lesser Classics

Dora Baltea from Pre-St Didier ('Fontina')

From:	Pre St Didier	Difficulty:	**4+** (5) (low water)
To:	Montbardon	Gradient:	30 m/km
Distance:	2 km	WW Stars:	★
Time:	½ hour	Scenery:	⊕
Best months:	Aug-Sept	Flow:	20 cumecs = LW
Bank support:	reasonable	Gauge:	none

Summary

Powerful, grey water, very cold and continuous. Big waves and holes. No one seems enthusiastic about this stretch but it is popular training run for local paddlers because it is short and an easy shuttle. Put in near the swimming pool of Pre St Didier on the Dora di Verney. There is one class 5 rapid near the start, then a km of mainly class 4. We recommend that you continue on past Montbardon and take out at Morgex, 200m upstream of the bridge on the right.

Dora Baltea from Montbardon

From:	Montbardon	Difficulty:	**3+** (low water)
To:	La Salle	Gradient:	17 m/km
Distance:	5 km	WW Stars:	★
Time:	1 hour	Scenery:	⊕⊕

Summary

Still powerful, grey water, very cold and continuous, but this is easier water. Banks are canalised for much of the run and there are not a lot of eddies or much potential for playing - just fast and fairly furious. The second half from Morgex is slightly easier - class 3. (Trainee rafters do this half first and then do the upper stretch). This section is usually OK in medium water levels, but check with the rafting base in Morgex.

Driving up the valley take the first small turn off left after crossing the river and just before 'Camping du Parc'; an archway then leads under the railway and a short track takes you down to the river and the put in.

2km below Morgex is a dangerous weir, 50m upstream is a wooden bridge - land here and scout/portage on the left bank. Take out next to the 'Meuble Bar Mirage' on the main road near the turn off for la Salle. A photogenic weir is 1 km downstream.

Dora Baltea from La Salle

From:	la Salle	Difficulty:	**5 (low water)**
To:	Lenteney Waterfall	Gradient:	30 m/km
Distance:	2 km	WW Stars:	★★
Time:	1 hour	Scenery:	✦

Summary

Described at 'nice, technical, Alpine paddling' the whole 2km of this run are best first scouted on foot. Put in above or below the highly photogenic curved weir just downstream of La Salle. 500m downstream are two small, but dangerous weirs with powerful tow-backs - scout and portage right. Take out at the famous Lenteney Waterfall which comes in from the right.

Dora Baltea from Lenteney Waterfall

From:	Lenteney Waterfall	Difficulty:	**3+ (low water)**
To:	Equilivaz Bridge	Gradient:	20 m/km
Distance:	3 km	WW Stars:	★
Time:	1 hour	Scenery:	✦

Summary

A fairly straight forward, fun paddle. The first kilometre or so is the hardest - always reassuring to know! Put in at Centenny Waterfall. 'Martino's Rapid' is the crux of the run and is 1km after the first bridge.

Make sure you take out on the right upstream of the main road bridge, or 500m downstream on the left. If you go past the railway bridge then panic and stop immediately - downstream is death and destruction! (see inset).

The Runaz Falls.

The steepest and hardest section of the Dora Baltea is where it falls through a steep, hidden gorge just upstream of Runaz and Avise, including one 12m fall. This has been explored, and where possible, paddled by a local team of experts with climbers in support.

It's a really difficult place to get a sight of - best view is probably from the shoulder of the hill at the top of the road opposite that zig zags up the valley side from Avise (to a fine picnic and barbeque site). To get a closer look, take a walk along the old road around the road tunnel just upstream of Runaz - you can get the occasional glimpse and hear the roar of the falls. Those with a head for heights can scramble up above this old road to some fine remains of the Roman highway up the valley. This scene was the subject of a romantic painting by Turner in the 19th century. In this fascinating crux point of the valley there is the old Roman road, the Napoleonic road, a 20th century road tunnel, a 19th century railway tunnel, and deep in the bowels of the mountain, a tunnel for the new Autostrada.

Dora Baltea 'Canyon de l'inferno'

From:	Avise	Difficulty:	4+ (low water)
To:	Leverogne	Gradient:	20 m/km
Distance:	2 km	WW Stars:	☆☆★
Time:	½ hour	Scenery:	⊛⊛
Best months:	Aug-Sept	Flow:	30 cumecs = LW
Bank support:	None	Gauge:	none

Summary

Named after a local wine - very powerful and with a surprising depth! - this impressive, sheer sided gorge can be viewed from the track around the outside of the road tunnel. Put in on the left bank downstream of the bridge to Avise: a faint path winds down from near the bridge. A short easy warm-up section takes you under a medieval bridge and then you should break out on the right after the HEP outlet to scout the first big rapid. Almost continuous big rapids lead from here into the gorge and onwards to the put-in for the main run from Leverogne - any swim could be a long one!

Grand Eyvia

From:	Cretaz	Difficulty:	4
To:	road bridge	Gradient:	20 m/km
Distance:	4 km	WW Stars:	★★
Time:	1½ hrs	Scenery:	⊛⊛
Best months:	Aug-Sept	Flow:	20 cumecs = MW
Bank support:	reasonable	Gauge:	none

Summary

Floods in recent years have changed this river but it's still a fine run in a beautiful Alpine valley. This is melt water from the glaciers of the Grand Paradiso so levels will be much higher in late afternoon. The two tributaries, the Valnontey and the Urtier, join at **Cretaz**, 1 km below **Cogne**, to make the Grand Eyvia. From the confluence there is a steep little 700 m long gorge, mainly class 4, with a couple of little drops that might be 5. Put in above or below this section, depending how you feel, and take out upstream of the main road bridge on the right. Below here is another more serious gorge, 1 km of class 5 (6), finishing at a barrage: this should be carefully scouted if you plan to run it.

If you have the time, check out the two tributaries: the **Urtier** has a fine little class 5 gorge, 3 km from Lillaz; the **Valnontey** is 2.5 km of continuous class 5 - a beautiful hike in the afternoon!

Jochen's Seventh Sense

It was the standard Jochen Schweizer situation. At least 30 experts from the Alpiner Kayak Club were standing around the Quare Falls on the Sesia River and apart from Jochen, nobody fancied the idea running this ugly looking rapid.

I broke into the eddy where Jochen was preparing to get into his boat and I asked him what he was up to. "I'm going to run the slot on the left. I think you can get behind the waterfall if you are careful - do you think you could organise a safety-line in there? I thought it a strange place to set up a safety line but I took my throw-rope and some carabiners and walked down to the falls.

I saw Peter Lintner sounding the depth of the boiling pot with his paddle. Knowing Peter, I felt that this was not a good sign. Jochen came back looking at the drop again. It was a high water route, a 12ft slot fall into a boiling pot of questionable depth. We indicated that we were ready and Jochan set off.

Jochen's kayak dived into the pot like an arrow and I just saw a quick shadow from my point of view behind the fall. Then there was silence......... he had disappeared out of sight underwater, and unknown to us, he was stuck in a hole between some rocks like a fountain-pen in its cap. For endless seconds nobody saw anything. I yelled at Wolfgang, who was standing outside in the eddy, and asked him if he was able to see anything. "No", he shouted. Then I looked around behind the falls again and could just see Jochen's rear grab loop sticking out from under the water. He had slammed into the rocks and got pushed backwards into the falls, with a ton of water on his back. I groped for the grab loop, clipped in the carabiner and Wolfgang dragged on the rope. At the same moment Jochen, after about 15 very long seconds, tried desperately to get out of his boat. He diverted some water pressure, and that, together with the combined forces of the rescue team enabled us to drag the kayak free.

Jochen was still in his boat, dangling unconscious from the cockpit. Somebody ripped his helmet off and he came to. We assessed his injuries: both knees were seriously damaged, and so we started the difficult carry up the cliff to the road. Although in agony, he could still laugh when Haibach called him a fat pig. He was transported to Milan and flown out to Munich where he had an operation the next day.

I had never seen a freak accident like this before and I was struck by the cold brutality of the fine line between success and death. Jochen's good sense, perhaps a 'seventh sense' had positioned me in the only place to realise the situation and be able to help - if he hadn't taken the trouble to ask me to stand behind the fall, then I wouldn't have seen the end grab and he would certainly have drowned.

Three weeks later, released out of hospital, Jochen told his story, a rather heroic one, in a live show on a Munich TV-station, saying he had rescued himself by deliberately breaking his knees ....which is what we threatened to do when we saw him next!

Marcus Schmid

Other runs

The Dora Baltea has been paddled from **Courmayeur** to Pre St Didier in very low water - 4.5 km of class 5 with a gradient of 35 m/km - probably better 'paddled' in a local bar. A possible run for mountain lovers is the 2-3 km on the **Dora di Veny** from near Freney to Pertud, class 3(4) - a fast, cold, aquatic toboggan run in awesome scenery.

If you are here in spate conditions (you should really be elsewhere) then local kayakers recommend a run on the **lower Dora Baltea** from the Nus motor way exit to Chatillon - described as 'like the Grand Canyon' with huge three metre waves. Make sure you take out at Chatillon, because a dangerous gorge follows.

The **Dora de Thuile** can be paddled for some 3km of class 3 above the village of la Thuile - it's impossible below here.

The **Chiusella** is the next valley to the south of the Aosta. It has a steep beautiful section of class 5 & 6 that starred in one of Sean Baker's films. For the more humble paddler there is 7km of class 4 from Succinto to Drussaco that usually runs in May and June. A neighbouring valley to this is the **Soana** - described as one of the best runs in Italy, this has 8km of class 4 above the confluence with the Orc, but again needs good water levels - usually May and June.

Special thanks to Roberto Chilosi

Grand Eyvia   *Matt Funnell*

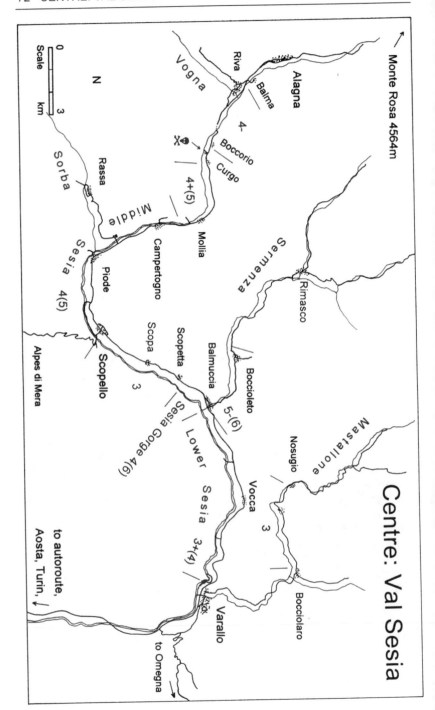

Centre: Val Sesia

Centre: Val Sesia

The Runs

Name of run	Class	Stars	Scen	Km	cumecs	Notes
Middle Sesia	4 (5)	★★★	✿✿	9	15	2 portages
Lower Sesia	3+ (4+)	★★	✿✿	9	20	a fine run
Sermenza	5- (6)	★★★	✿✿	6	10	several portages
Sesia - from Balma	4-	★★	✿✿	4	10	fast and shallow
- from Curgo	4+ (5-)	★★★	✿✿	3	10	fast and steep
- from Scopello	3	★★	✿	5	15	fast and shallow
Sesia Gorge	4 (6)	★★	✿✿✿	2	10 = LW	Best in low water

The Centre

The Sesia is a relatively unspoilt valley draining the south east slopes of the Monte Rosa. It offers some of Italy's best white water in very beautiful surroundings and is at its best in late spring and early summer.

The centre is about 15 hours drive from Calais - see 'driving from the U.K. If coming via the Aosta valley then it is better to use the Italian motor ways where possible, rather than local roads - note that the A26 autostrada north towards the Sesia is signed "Gravellona Toce". Turning off the auto route and driving up the Sesia valley is like entering another world and stepping back in time two centuries.

The Sesia valley is fairly convenient for Milan and Turin so the main road up the valley can be exciting on Friday and Sunday evenings in the summer months!

On the River

Paddling friends threatened physical violence if we included the Sesia valley in this book! - here's an incredibly beautiful river system that is unlike anything else in the Alps: turquoise green, clear water flowing between granite boulders and falls (the reason why the water is so clear). Ask kayakers what the Sesia valley reminds them of and you get replies like: Idaho, Costa Rica, Nepal, or Southern China - this is because the valley is such a jungle green and the river so clear. The difference is that the runs here are shorter and more intense, with some highly photogenic falls. It's mainly a centre for kayakers who enjoy steep class 4 & 5, but there are a several easier runs for the intermediate paddler.

Apart from one small dam on the Sermenza, the Sesia and its tributaries are beautifully unspoilt natural flowing rivers, and the valley has been suggested for protection similar to the American Wild and Scenic rivers. River runners can give support and help by spending their tourist income wisely, supporting local businesses and communities. Reliance on natural flow means that the rivers are at their best in **May and June** - come here in a drought in August and you will be disappointed, but in low water there are still some short runs..

The valley seems to have its own **micro-climate** with rain showers common in the afternoons: this relatively abundant rainfall makes it very green, with luxuriant deciduous trees climbing the valley sides and just the granite cliffs and the occasional church tower showing through the trees. The river also has a history of floods, normally in the Autumn so there may be major changes to rapids from year to year. Note that because of these floods, **water levels are hard to judge** - appearances can be deceptive and what looks like a low level to most paddlers is usually medium flow. Its well worth asking for advice at one of the kayak schools in the valley

The Sesia and its tributaries are popular for angling and so paddling is restricted to the hours 10.00 a.m. to 6.00 p.m. Access points for the main runs often have parking places and are normally sign-posted off the highway with yellow signs: **'imbarco'** is put-in, **'sbarco'** is take-out. A recreational race and rally is usually held each year on the third weekend in June.

To the north of the Sesia valley are the difficult rivers of the Piedmont and Tessin regions, the Anza, Verzasca, Cannobino, St Bernardino, etc. which flow into Lake Maggiore. These are a little comparable in character to the Sermenza so if you like this river and have the time you might want to consider heading on to this area - see the Piedmont Guidebook.

Commercial Rafting

Rafting and hydro-speeding take place on the lower Sesia which is a fine run, but the season is usually short, the river normally being too shallow for rafting by August.

Off the River

Recommended activity here has to be exploring some of the villages in the side valleys - all these villages have that feeling of traditional, proud communities with solid, well maintained houses, many of them having frescoes on the end walls and intricate wood carving. Decorated churches dominate every village and many hilltops, and small shrines line the roads and paths. Rassa (up the Sorba valley) is particularly picturesque, but for a true mountain village you should take a one hour hike up from Alagna to the hidden Otro valley and the wooden houses of the Walser people, a German speaking community who have lived in this high remote spot underneath Monte Rosa for seven centuries. Mountain Guides can be hired for high mountain walking and visits to glaciers.

For the **mountain biker** there is a very pleasant ride, mainly single track, fun but not too challenging, on the right hand side of the river from Mollia to Scopello through meadows and woodland with good views of the river (note that the path down from Quare goes off through the meadows beside the church). Most of the side valleys such as the Sermenza have little traffic and it's very pleasant to explore these by cycle. For the more adventurous there two ski areas at Alagna and the Alpe di Mera (above Scopello) that have downhill descents of over 1000m. For the wealthy adventurer one local mountain bike company even offers 'Heli-biking'!

Varallo is the main town of the valley, and is a pleasant place to stroll and shop - there's a thriving market on Tuesdays (local speciality is the toma cheese).   The town is famous for the Sacro Monte built in the 14th century high above the town as a 'New Jerusalem' with 44 decorated chapels.   Materialistic river runners may be more interested in the ice cream shops and Pizza restaurants - we recommend "la Sfinge" that has a balcony overlooking the Mastallone.   Another good restaurant is "la Rana" in Boccioleto.   Further up the valley there is an excellent pizzeria at the campsite at Campertogno and we can highly recommend the "Union" restaurant in Alagna.

Campsites
There are several campsites in the valley but most of them cater for fixed site caravans so we do not recommend them.   The campsite at **Campertogno**, just downstream of the bridge, "Il Gatto & la Volpe" is run by a keen kayaker 'Alberto' and is highly recommended. Tel 0163 77377. www.ilgattoelavolpe.it

The **Scuola di canoa della Valsesia** is on a really beautiful site approx. 7 km upstream of Varallo but at the time of writing the camping license had been suspended. **'Freeflow'** is another kayak school run by Italian champion Francesco Salvetto that often bases itself in the Sesia valley.   Camping at most of these sites works out around 6 euros per head per night.

Hospital
There is a small hospital in Varallo.   Dial 113 for Police and rescue services.

Maps
Two excellent free maps are available from Tourist Offices - a 1:85,000 tourist map and a rivers map 'Carta Fluviale' that shows all the rivers and grades of difficulty. IGC 1:50.000 sheet 10, Monte Rosa, is the official topographic map that covers most of the area but is neither up to date or accurate.

Tourist Offices
Varallo Tel: 0163 51280.   www.valsesia.com
Also offices in Scopello and Alagna.

Rafting Operators & Kayak schools
Scuola di canoa della Valsesia, Isola, Tel: 0163 53089.

Monrosa, Balmuccia, Tel: 0163 75298   www.monrosarafting.it
Freeflow Kayaks   www.freeflowkayak.com
Hidronica, Scopa, tel: 0163 73501   www.hidronica.com
Eddyline, Campertogno, tel: 0163 775111   www.eddyline.it
Rafting Valsesia, Vocca, tel: 0163 560957   www.rafting@rafting.it

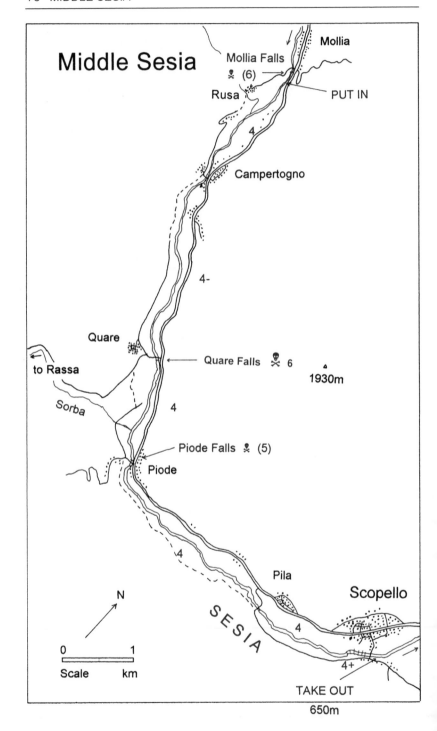

Middle Sesia

From:	Mollia	Difficulty:	**4 (6) 2 portages**
To:	Scopello	Gradient:	25 m/km
Distance:	9 km	WW Stars:	★★★
Time:	2 hours	Scenery:	✦✦✦
Best months:	May - June	Flow:	15 cumecs = MW
Bank support:	reasonable	Gauge:	no
Water temp:	cool	Ass. runs:	upper Sesia,
Water Quality:	good		Sesia from Scopello.

Summary
Clear turquoise water, green mountain sides, historic villages, white boulder rapids one after another, and two dramatic falls, make for non-stop action and a memorable run which we highly recommend.

Special points
Rapids change from year to year owing to floods.

Rafting
This section is not normally rafted commercially.

Access and Logistics
The usual take-out for this run is on the river right over the bridge in Scopello and some 200m downstream of the car park. Whilst you are here, have a look at the rapids above the bridge.

On your drive up the valley stop in the village of Piode to inspect the falls here. Also stop and inspect the class 6 falls just below Quare bridge and scout the approach rapid down through the bridge. You may if you wish also view the river at Campertogno and this will give you a good idea of the general standard and style of the rapids.

The put-in at Mollia is downstream of some pretty terrifying class 6 falls. Park in the village to view these (the old lady here sells excellent honey). The "embarco" is some 200m downstream and just has room for two cars to be unloaded. A faint path descends steeply to the river.

Note that there is a really pleasant, fun mountain bike ride down paths on the right hand side of the valley, through woods and meadows with good views of the river. Rusa is an especially pretty village.

The Run
This is the classic run on the Sesia and one that stays in the memory long after the event. The falls at Quare bridge and Piode are the highlights of the run, and make highly photogenic backdrops, but the rest of the river is non-stop action, with fairly continuous white water, never dropping below class 3 and with only small eddies.

The rock is smooth, water-worn granite, making bouldery rapids which change from year to year.

Quotes we had from this run were:

- *"We were on the go all the time. The scenery was great but we rarely had time to look at it"*
- *"Feels more intimidating than it actually is"*
- *"Exciting, forgiving, but I guess it would be a rough swim"*

In medium and high water levels this is a real blast, and quite daunting: and at least half a grade harder. At really low water levels it's probably slightly easier, maybe 4-. but still a fun paddle which holds its interest.

Description

The put-in below the falls at **Mollia** takes you straight into non-stop white water action. Little shoots, giant boulders, great eddy-hopping, all the way down to **Campertogno** where a big bouncy rapid takes you down through the town.

The action continues, but perhaps slightly easier, for the next two kilometres down to **Quare bridge**. These rapids change from year to year, but can normally be scouted on the hop by dodging from eddy to eddy. The rapid approaching the bridge often has a huge undercut boulder lying in wait at the bottom, to trap or capsize the unwary - just above the evil **class 6 falls** that follow! So whilst it is possible to paddle this approach rapid and portage the falls over the rocks on the left, the safer option is to land well above the bridge and portage along the road about 100m to where a faint path descends to the river.

Another kilometre of good white water brings you down to **Piode**. Either land on the left well before the falls and portage up to the road (the bar on the bridge has cold beer and cappuccinos, the delicatessen across the road specialises in palma ham and toma cheese rolls) then cross the bridge and put in by the car park on the other side. Or, land on the left just before the falls and carry along the rock ledges under the bridge. The **Piode falls** have been shot by a slot in the centre, but if you get the approach line wrong, then the consequences don't bear thinking about.

This is the place to take a quick check on adrenaline levels and how you feel - below here the action improves and the river probably becomes a little bit harder. Just below Piode is a more gorge like section of bedrock rapids that climax in "Hugo's Hole" - the valley opens out and a short pool gives a brief opportunity for a fast rescue before being swept down some more bouldery rapids that continue to the old pack horse bridge at **Pila**.

Slightly easier water then continues for a kilometre to a car park on the right above the town of **Scopello**. This car park is the start of the Masters race in the World Down River Championships. A long rapid (perhaps 4+) runs down into the town and this is then followed by the big rapid that you can see from the road bridge in Scopello - dramatic, photogenic and a great climax to the run. Take out on the beach on the right about 300m below the bridge, a few minutes walk from a celebration drink or ice cream.

Middle Sesia   Jerry Tracey

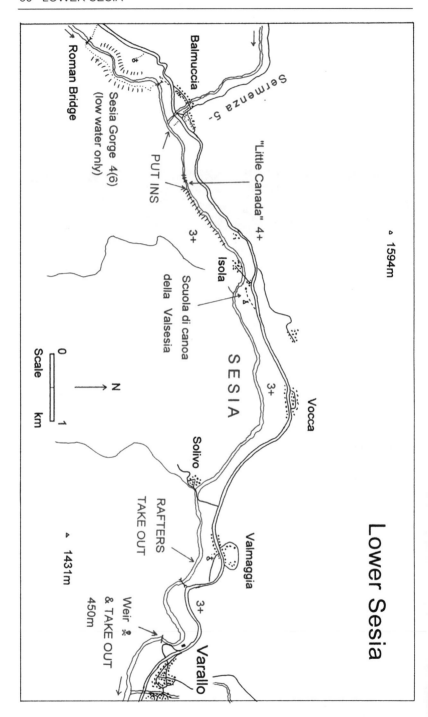

Lower Sesia

Lower Sesia

From:	Balmuccia	Difficulty:	3+ (4+)
To:	Varallo	Gradient:	11 m/km
Distance:	9 km	WW Stars:	★★
Time:	2 hours	Scenery:	❀❀
Best months:	May - June	Flow:	20 cumecs = MW
Bank support:	limited	Gauge:	no
Water temp:	cool	Ass. runs:	Sesia Gorge.
Water Quality:	average		Sermenza

Summary
A river that looks like as if it should be in the Himalayas: lots of boulder rapids, friendly and fun, clear blue water, white beaches and green valley sides. An ideal run for both intermediates and experts with lots of white water interest.

Special points
Rapids change from year to year owing to floods.

Rafting
This is a delightful uncrowded rafting run that we can recommend with confidence providing there is sufficient water. Many trips start below "Little Canada" but there are plenty of other fun white water rapids. Several companies also offer hydro-speeding, but this is not as popular here in Italy as it is in France. Rafting runs normally finish at Valmaggia where there is a safer and more convenient take out than Varallo.

Access and Logistics
The main put-in is just below the confluence with the Sermenza, reached down a short path from the main road junction at Balmuccia, where there is plenty of parking space. Alternatively, if you ask, you may be able to put in at Monrosa's rafting base approached through the centre of the village where there is a large car park, toilets, café, etc. There is an alternative put-in just below 'little Canada' rapid which is 1 km below Balmuccia, so we suggest that you stop on your way up the valley to scout this and decide how brave you feel. The rapid is next to a large lay-by and is signposted 'embarco' - apparently the rocks here are a favourite basking place for local snakes, so watch your step!

   The recommended and most convenient take-out is just downstream of the church in Valmaggia down the side road opposite the bar. If you decide to take out in Varallo then check this out in advance as the weir would be very dangerous if you shot it by mistake.

The Run
This run has one major rapid one kilometre below Balmuccia, usually class 4, that is known by paddlers as 'little Canada' but officially it's called 'Rapide di Balmuccia'. This rapid changes from year to year and can be class 5 at certain water levels so many paddlers put on just below.

The other rapids on the run are big and bouldery, very much in the style of the Grand Canyon of the Colorado, and again they change from year to year. There may be one or two class 4 rapids, but otherwise the run is fairly steady class 3 and 3+ with pools after most rapids in which to recover. These rapids are friendly and fun with an eddy behind almost every boulder, and a little play wave alongside. The rock is smooth water-worn granite - a paddler's delight.

Lift your eyes from the river and you will see green wooded hillsides rising to the sky, broken by granite cliffs, making a rugged wild landscape more like some jungle clad valley in the wilds of the Himalayas. Just a couple of bridges and the occasional church tower poke up above the trees to remind you that this is really Italy.

Catch this river after heavy rain and it really is like the Grand Canyon with some huge waves for surfing and some holes and pour-overs you'll be happy to miss. In low water levels this is still a pleasant run, but the best part is definitely the first 3 km down to Isola, where the river is more constricted in a semi-gorge. There are no gauges on the river so for advice on river levels we recommend calling in at one of the kayak schools.

Description

If you put in at Balmuccia then you only have one kilometre and two class 3 rapids before 'little Canada'. The name is apt - this ramp of white water in a granite canyon with tree-lined mountain sides is very reminiscent of rapids in Canada. In some water levels this is a straight-forward, adrenaline-pumping shoot; at other times it can be quite technical with one or more undercut boulders. At high water levels kayaks come out of the shoot like corks from a champagne bottle: the problem then is the turbulent water in the canyon below.

At normal levels the Canyon below the rapid is fairly flat. If you put in below the rapid then you have a dramatic start with a seal launch off a sloping rock ledge into the maws of the canyon - spectacular but quite safe! Take a minute to look back upstream at the surging white torrent of "little Canada" crashing into the deep green waters of the gorge - even more dramatic from a viewpoint at water level.

The next two kilometres are excellent paddling with the general standard at 3+, rapid following rapid, all bouldery with little holes, shoots, play waves, and normally a choice of routes. On one bigger rapid the river just disappears out of site over a horizon line, but is in fact a straight-forward big shoot, with big, bouncy, exploding waves. There's nothing too serious and normally a pool below each rapid in which to recover. There's just you and the river, woods, cliffs and sky - somewhere hidden in the trees is the highway, but you would never guess it.

A picturesque church overlooks the river and bridge at **Isola** and a long 3+ rapid leads you down past the campsite and canoe school. Below here the valley widens out and the river relaxes a little - still lots of rapids, a few class 3+, but most of them class 3 with class 2 water in between. In 1995 there was one big rapid about half-way down where the current flowed onto big blocks on the right bank: this might have been a class 4-, but by the time you read this, one of the regular floods will probably have changed it and made another.

The next bridge marks the return to civilisation, but not the end of the rapids - these continue down to **Valmaggia**, marked by an impressive church on a rock outcrop overlooking the river. The recommended take-out is on the left just past the church.

You could continue down to Varallo but you will have to take out above the dangerous weir, so check this out in advance if you want to do this. There is another kilometre of good class 3 white water with at least two big rapids - a big old mill building on the left is warning of the approach to the **weir.** Below the weir, the river continues as mainly class 3, but it has many more weirs so cannot be recommended.

Lesser Classics

Sermenza

From:	Piaggiogna	Difficulty:	5- (6) several portages
To:	Balmuccia	Gradient:	30 m/km
Distance:	6 km	WW Stars:	★★★
Time:	3 hours	Scenery:	⊕⊕
Best months:	May to June	Flow:	10 cumecs = MW
Bank support:	very limited	Gauge:	none

Summary
The lower gorges of the Sermenza is one of the best high-end runs in the Alps - when it has water (normally good levels in Spring, but flows in May and June will be less). It offers gradient combined with volume, spectacular drops, little gorges of a jungle-like nature, and makes a memorable climax to any trip to the Val Sesia.

Water flow is controlled by a reservoir upstream at Rimasco and there is normally a release mid-week from about 10 a.m. onwards. A new micro HEP system has its outfall above Piaggogna, so the kilometre upstream from there is normally dry. The bottom gorge and water levels can be inspected on the drive up the valley. Park considerately on the road at Piaggogna (about 1.5 km above Boccioleto) and carry your boat down the path that zigzags through this ancient village to put in at the old stone bridge.

There is only a few hundred metres of easier water in which to limber uo before the river gets harder with two class 4 drops on blind corners leading into a steep combination of falls starting with a 5m drop. The triple drop that follows is class 6 and usually portaged. This and the rapids that follow were changed by the 1993 floods so be cautious of what any old dog paddlers tell you! Final rapid of this steep upper section is 'Sawmill Falls' a huge 8m long slide with a monster stopper at the bottom.

A footbridge and path leads up to Boccioleto and then below here is a continuous gorge with many exciting rapids, and three exceptional ones that are class 5. If you portage once then you tend to portage them all. Below here is a more open valley and easier water for about 1.5 km. This brings you down to a little canyon, class 5-, which is often under-estimated - a swim here could be fatal - and we recommend setting up safety cover for the first drop after the entrance rapid. Below here, within the gorge are some roller coaster rapids that look bad, but aren't and these take you down through Balmuccia to the confluence with the Sesia. Take out here, or better still continue on to the campsite.

Upper Sesia from Balma

From:	Balma	Difficulty:	**4-**
To:	Boccorio	Gradient:	15 m/km
Distance:	4 km	WW Stars:	★★
Time:	1 hour	Scenery:	⊛⊛
Best months:	June to Aug	Flow:	10 cumecs = MW
Bank support:	reasonable	Gauge:	none

Summary
Much of this run can be viewed from the road. The Sesia can be paddled from Alagna but flood damage and construction work means that this is now a messy run with a lot of rubbish in the river. We recommend a put-in at the bridge to Balma, a small turn off the main road at the top end of Riva village. The run from here is fast, shallow and continuous and will keep you on your toes. It's at its best in medium-low water levels. Scout the take-out at Boccario on your way up the valley - God help you if you miss it! If you wish, you can portage about 700m down the road around the falls to the next section - a pleasant bar in the village offers sustenance.

Upper Sesia from Curgo

From:	Curgo	Difficulty:	**4+ (5-)**
To:	Mollia	Gradient:	25 m/km
Distance:	3 km	WW Stars:	★★★
Time:	1 hour	Scenery:	⊛⊛
Best months:	May to July	Flow:	10 cumecs = MW
Bank support:	reasonable	Gauge:	none

Summary
This is a cracking, steep run that in low water levels is a hard, exhilarating, technical paddle with a couple of the rapids deserving a 5- rating. At medium to high levels it becomes a very continuous, mind blowing class 4+ (5), and if you take a swim ..... aagh! This is the course of the "Kayak Alpin Sprint" event held in June each year. Scout the take-out at Mollia on your way up the valley so you don't end up running the falls there by mistake. The put-in is signed off the road down a small path, about 100m below the small turn off up to the houses that comprise Curgo (300m further up the road, past the falls, is the bridge to Buzzo and another 300m would bring you to Boccario). Beware of construction debris in the river.

Middle Sesia from Scopello

From:	Scopello	Difficulty:	**3**
To:	Scopetta	Gradient:	15 m/km
Distance:	5 km	WW Stars:	★★
Time:	1 hour	Scenery:	⊕
Best months:	May to June	Flow:	10 cumecs = LW
Bank support:	limited	Gauge:	none

Summary

To be honest we missed this out of the last edition as paddlers in the bar were disparaging about it. Well, we were pleasantly surprised when we ran it for this edition. It formed the main part of the World Down River Racing Championship course in 2002 where Juniors started at Scopello. and Seniors just above Scopello.

The river flows in a wide bouldery valley with several channels which may be too shallow in low water. With luck, these channels will have been consolidated by a bulldozer so that you have a pleasant. class 3 bimble, more technical and continuous than the lower Sesia, but slightly easier. Take out above the Roman Bridge and walk up to the road.

Playing on the Sesia Gorge   *Gianluca Ricci*

Sesia Gorge

From:	Scopetta	Difficulty:	**4 (5)** one portage
To:	Balmuccia	Gradient:	15 m/km
Distance:	2 km	WW Stars:	★★
Time:	1 hour	Scenery:	❀❀
Best months:	July to Aug	Flow:	10 cumecs = LW
Bank support:	very limited	Gauge:	none

Summary

A fine little gorge with that usual feeling of commitment, challenge and inaccessibility that paddling in these places evokes. It is usually paddled in low water conditions when it is at its best - at higher levels someone described it as "a lot of portaging for not much white water". Park at the "embarco" near the caravan site on the down river side of Scopetta and follow the path down to the superb old '**Roman Bridge**' (great for photos). If you wish, there's a pleasant scramble along the left side of the river so you can scout as far as the class 6 drop.

A bouncy photogenic rapid leads down to the Roman bridge and you can put in either above or below this. Approx. 200m below is a tight little drop; then it's straight forward paddling for about 700m to "the evil one" a class 6 - where the river channels into a narrow slot and undercut. Land above on the beach left and portage for about 100m up and over the rock ledges.

After this, provided that the rapids haven't changed too much, it's class 3 and 4 paddling to the end of the gorge and then down to the usual access point at Balmuccia. If you do get into difficulties, note that there is a footpath in the trees high up on the right bank.

Other runs

There are many other steep runs in the area that rely on good water levels - usually in the early summer or after rain. These include the **upper Sermenza**, the **Mastallone**, the Egua, the Vogna, the Sessera, and a superb run, the **Sorba**. Francesco Salvatore advises that the 2km run on the upper Sorba from the Haidi restaurant to Rassa bridge is "amazing and probably the most difficult run in the Sesia Valley". These harder runs are really outside the scope of this guide book, but are detailed in German and Swiss guidebooks. It is also quite a famous area for waterfalls, as can be seen by some of the photographs in this book.

If river levels are really high then make a special note of the middle section of the **Mastallone**. This needs a lot of water, so makes a fine fast **class 3 bimble** when most other runs are too big and hairy - put in at No Suggio and take out at the picnic site and footbridge above Bocciolara.

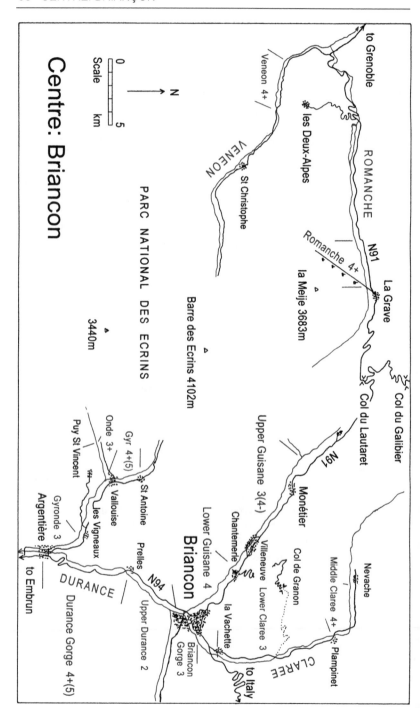

Centre: Briancon

Centre: Briançon

The Runs

Name of run	Class	Stars	Scen	Km	cumecs	Notes
Upper Guisane	3 (4-)	★★	✦✦	11	10	fast and scenic
Lower Guisane	4	★★★	✦✦	6	15	1 portage, great run!
Romanche	4+	★★	✦✦	5	25	full-on late season
Durance Gorge	4 (5)	★★★	✦✦✦	8	15	a mini-expedition
Briançon Gorge	3	★★★	✦✦	2	10	fine little paddle
Upper Durance	2	★	✦	7	30	confidence builder
Middle Clarée	4	★★	✦✦	4	5	fast and furious
Lower Claree	3	★★	✦✦	12	10	beautiful valley
Gyr	4+(5)	★★★	✦	3	15	"flat out"
Onde	3+	★★	✦✦	3	5	best early season
Gyronde	3+	★	✦✦	6	20	good training
Vénéon	4+(5)	★★★	✦✦	4	20	A hard alpine gem

The Centre

This is one of our favourite centres in the Alps because there is a wide choice of excellent white water, great scenery, and lots of interesting things to do and see. Briançon itself is the highest town in Europe and was an old market centre and defensive fulcrum for the southern Alps - the impressive fortifications of the old town 'Cité Vauban' are well worth a visit. High up on the ridges above the town are forts and gun emplacements from the 18th Century, built to defend the frontier with Italy, which is only a few kilometres away. To the south-west are the spectacular mountains of the National Park des Écrins.

In the last twenty years the town and surroundings have seen considerable development and it is now the bottom station for the major ski resort of Serre Chevalier. Several other smaller ski resorts are close by and over the border in Italy. In the town are all the facilities that you could want or expect, including a good choice of restaurants and bars!

Briançon is situated at the junction of four valleys so makes a natural centre for kayaking. and if you don't wish to move centres it can also be used as a base for paddling the runs of the lower Durance - less than an hour's drive away.

On the River

This area is justifiably popular with river runners - it has a good choice of fine white water. in beautiful mountain valleys. The upper and lower Guisane are the most popular runs and almost always have enough water to paddle. If you are here in early summer, then the Clarée is a fine run in a particularly beautiful valley. Later in the summer when many of the runs are past their best, then the Romanche and Vénéon come into their own.

We have included the Gyronde and its two short tributaries, the Gyr and the Onde. in this centre although these could just as well have been grouped with the lower Durance and Guil in the Guillestre centre.

Note that standard French river regulations apply, displayed at most access points: **paddling is normally only allowed between 9.30 a.m. and 6.0 p.m.** and is prohibited on the weekends at the beginning and end of the fishing season (usually the second Saturday in March to the third Sunday in September).

Commercial Rafting

All the main runs and many of the minor ones are commercially rafted. Most are fairly challenging so this is a good centre for anyone looking for more active runs.

Off the River

If you want a change from river bashing then this is an excellent centre! There are all the activities that you would expect in a well developed resort from tennis to rock climbing. including summer 'luge' runs - where you hurtle down a toboggan run on a little trolley - with a group of kayakers this is always a great laugh as the biggest mouth invariably gets injured! Another unusual activity is **Via Ferrata,** which are rock scrambling routes along dramatic cliffs - protected by steel cables and with iron ladders in places: a qualified guide is recommended if you are not a climber. For more sedate car excursions the mountain passes can be recommended - the Col de Granon. Col du Galibier and the Col d'Izoard are all spectacular.   The valley of the Clarée is particularly beautiful and worth exploring. There is, of course, excellent mountain walking in abundance!

Mountain Biking

The valleys and ridges surrounding Briançon are great for mountain biking. For the mellow cyclist there are good tracks along the valley bottoms close to the rivers and with frequent bars - the 'Navette' bus service that runs up the beautiful Clarée valley carries bikes and makes an excellent day's excursion.

Those with loftier aspirations can explore the old military roadways that snake along the tops of ridges, connecting the old fortifications overlooking Italy. One of our favourite run is to persuade someone to drive the bikes and ourselves up to the top of the Col de Granon, 2413m, and then to come down the other side into the Clarée valley. If you're planning a trip like this one then we recommend that you buy a 1:25,000 topo map and take suitable safety gear.

Another favourite is to take the bikes up on the ski lifts at Serre Chevalier or Puy St Vincent and to then come whooping down the red runs! In each resort there is normally one lift that remains open in the summer that will take you to the top of the mountain - and bikes are welcome. Mountain bikes can be hired in many places and you can also hire special 'piste bikes' with balloon wheels for careering down the ski runs.

Summer Skiing

Just an hour's drive from Briançon is one of the largest summer ski areas in Europe, on the Mont de Lans glacier above the resort of Les Deux Alpes. High up on the glacier above 3000m is a ski area with 6 lifts and about a dozen ski runs - this feels as if it's on the top of the world and of course the mountain views are truly outstanding!

This is so high that the skiing is surprisingly good but you do need to be up there really early to make the most of the snow conditions. This is a truly fantastic day, but naturally doesn't come cheap - about £20 for an all day lift ticket. Note that the glacier can perhaps be more easily accessed by the téléphérique from La Grave.

Campsites

There are numerous well equipped campsites in the area with riverside ones in Briançon, between Prelles and Briançon on the Durance, on the Guisane at Chantmerle and le Casset, and on the Clarée at La Vachette. There is some beautiful 'wild camping', for those with their own toilet facilities, at the very top of the Guisane valley (not suitable for large groups) above le Casset, also regulated wild camping in the upper Clarée valley.

To cover the lower Durance and Guil from the same base, we suggest that you consider the campsite at **Argentière**, which is next to the slalom course on the Durance and only a short walk from the town centre - this is deservedly popular with kayak groups. One of our favourite campsites , and ideal for families and smaller groups. is 'Les Vaudois', situated in pine woods on the banks of the Gyronde below Les Vigneaux.

Hospital:

Briançon - see map of lower Guisane. Also Grenoble.
Telephone 18 in case of accident (fire/ambulance/rescue).

Maps

IGN TOP100 sheet 54 'Genoble-Gap', covers this and neighbouring centres so is our recommended 'best buy'. IGN TOP25 sheet no. 3636OT Briançon, covers most of the area and is worth buying if you need more detail.

Tourist Offices

Briançon:. Tel: 04 92 21 08 50.
Serre Chevalier: Tel: 04 92 24 98 98.

www.ot-briancon.fr
www.serre-chevalier.

Rafting Operators

'Serre Che Eaux-Vives: Tel: 04 92 24 79 00   www.serreche-eauxvives.com.
Canoe-Kayak Club Briançonnais, (see map). Tel: 04 92 20 17 56.
'No limit' is based in La Grave specialise in the Romanche Tel: 04 76 79 91 93.
'Ecrins Eaux-Vives' are the specialists on the Gyronde and Gyr, and are based in Les Vigneaux Tel: 04 92 23 11 94.
'Vénéon Eaux-Vives' have a base below St Christophe. Tel: 04 76 80 23 99.

Kayak schools / clubs

Centre Régional de Formation Canoe Kayak (FFCK) is a national centre, equivalent to Glenmore Lodge or Nantahala Centre.
05120 l'Argentière la Bessée, Tel: 04 92 23 09 89.
Canoe-Kayak Club Briançonnais, (see map) Tel: 04 92 20 17 56.

Via Ferratas

A 'Via Ferrata' is a like an easy rock climb or scramble, but you are protected by clipping yourself onto a permanent wire cable. They use a lot of metal bolts, staples, rungs, and ladders to make the scramble fun, relatively safe, and to make the most of the features of the cliff (so for example the Via Ferrata at Les Vigneux has a ladder that leads you up and over a big dramatic rock nose, with the village several hundred metres down between your legs.). All this metal horrifies the purist climber but more pragmatic, fun-loving, active types, just love them - however you do need a head for heights!

In the last ten years these have really taken off in the French Alps, with over twenty to choose from in Durance Valley. The tourist offices have information brochures and can arrange a local guide - recommended and quite cheap. Each Via Ferrata is different - some come out on the top of a mountain, some follow a natural line, some are very artificial (the one in the Durance Gorge is like this). Some are long - one climbs the 300m cliffs above the Romanche - some are short - there is a training one on the cliffs just above Artgentière that is a great one to start on.

The via ferrata in the Durance Gorge is one of the harder ones and you just love it or hate it - as Pete Hennessy describes:

"I went up the new Via Ferrata in the Durance Gorge - and got terrified! There were two of us, and neither of us are proper climbers. I'd done a different Via Ferrata before and loved it - but the one in the Durance Gorge seems designed to terrify, and it succeeded. Most of it is on metal rungs up vertical faces - but it was the traverses that we found scariest, and I didn't particularly enjoy the climbing bits because they were too artificial, with great long lines of ladders. The via ferrata is directly below the pipeline and crosses over the river - which looks loads easier from the climb - and I would rather do the paddle than the climb any day!

The Via Ferrata that we really did enjoy starts on the back road from Vallouise to Briancon, behind the small village of Les Vigneaux - it's mostly Diff or V. Diff climbing, takes around 3 hours (going very slowly), is fun, scenic, and follows more of a natural line on the rock."

Via Ferrata above Les Vigneaux   *Sue Richardson*

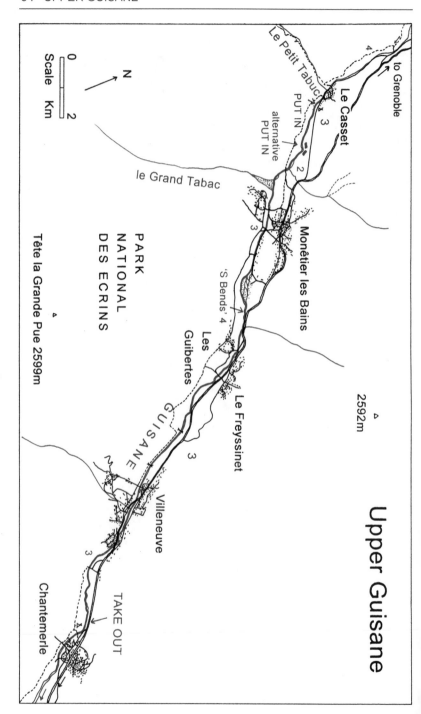

Upper Guisane

Upper Guisane

From:	Le Casset	Difficulty:	**3 (4-)**
To:	Chantemerle	Gradient:	15 m/km
Distance:	11 km	WW Stars:	★★
Time:	2 hours	Scenery:	✹✹
Best months:	May - July	Flow:	10 cumecs = MW
Bank support:	reasonable	Gauge:	Le Casset
Water Temp:	cold	Ass. runs:	lower Guisane,
Water Quality:	good		Romanche, Vénéon.

Summary

Fast flowing "non-stop" paddle in a scenic high Alpine valley.

Special points - none

The River

The Guisane rises near the Col de Lauteret and flows in a classic U-shaped alpine valley down to join the Durance at Briançon. The valley forms the northern border of the National Park des Écrins and there is some excellent scenery in the top part of this run - huge cliff faces, 3000m high mountain peaks and hanging glaciers. In the foreground. lush green alpine meadows border this turquoise river. After a rain shower the scent of wild flowers competes with the heady smell of pine trees drying out in the hot summer sunshine.

The villages on the lower half of this run form the ski resort of Serre Chevalier - developed mainly in the last 15 years. This is a good example of how modern development does not have to ruin a river - good planning. careful landscaping and new sewage systems mean that this is now a pleasanter river to paddle than it was ten years ago and a great tourist asset.

Rafting

Several companies offer trips on this upper section of the Guisane, normally starting at Monêtier. This is an ideal first-time run and is particularly good for mini rafts and le "hot dogging". Some companies also do tubing trips and hydro-speeding.

Access and Logistics

On the drive up the valley we suggest that you stop to inspect the "S bend" rapid just upstream from Les Guibertes; this is visible from the main road which runs close to the river at this point - a small stream acts as a landmark.

Best put-in for most groups is probably next to the lake that is visible as you drive down the minor road to Le Casset - you can usually drive down a track to the river side. For the more confident. a start at the campsite or in the middle of the village of Le Casset adds another kilometre of interesting paddling. For those looking for an easier start, we recommend putting on below the "S bend" rapid at les Guiberts. There is good egress, if required. at many points on the run.

Take out just upstream of Chantmerle in the small eddy just below the bridge to the campsite. There is convenient parking here by the roadside. For large, or less confident. groups we recommend a safer take-out at the gravel workings 200m upstream - reached by a rough track.

The Run

The Guisane is mainly fed by melting glaciers - so water levels depend on both sunshine and rainfall. On a hot summer day. the volume could double and the maximum flow will be in late afternoon - this needs to be borne in mind when planning your run.

The run is still possible at high water levels (when the lower Guisane would be too dangerous). but at bank-high levels it will be a very continuous class 4, and a great run for the experienced. Tributary streams probably treble the volume from the start to the end of the run so that flow figures aren't that meaningful. There is a gauge at le Casset: 50 cm equates to medium water level. 100 would be high. The local rafting companies are happy to advise on water levels and any special hazards; the company "H2O" have an office just by the take-out at Chantmerle.

The river above Le Casset is a tight fast mountain stream. two metres wide, with considerable tree hazards. that has been run from above Le Lauzet, class 4 (5). Note that there is some beautiful wild camping here at the top end of the valley and we highly recommend the restaurant at les Boussardes.

Description

Le Casset is a small picturesque village and we suggest that you allow some time to stroll around - there is a good display on the Park National des Écrins and a cafe by the riverside where you can have a coffee and croissant whilst you wait for your shuttle. One of the nearby attractions in the park. and a favourite afternoon hike, is to view the Casset glacier, only a few kilometres from the village. The melt-water from this forms Le Petit Tabuc stream that roars down to join the Guisane in the middle of the village and so doubles its flow - this would be a wild aquatic bob-sleigh run! If you put in just below this confluence then you're straight into fast continuous class 3, with tree-lined banks.

The fast water eases off after a kilometre to class 2 as the river winds through some gravel beds - this is probably a better place to put in if you are large group. From here. the river is quite fast but still only class 2, as it winds through the gravel beds. The Tabuc stream comes galloping in from the right. and shortly afterwards you go under the first of the three bridges in **Monêtier-les-Bains**. The river continues as class 2 and 3 with good mountain views all around and about 1km below Monêtier it winds through some more gravel beds. Shortly after, the river appreciably narrows as it comes close to the main highway - the approach to **"S bend"** rapid.

This is normally a fairly straight-forward class 4- but is 250m long. Each year the roadside is built-up and sharp rocks wash into the river and change the rapid - in some years there is an eddy on the left to set up protection, in other years the rapid is more continuous. Any swim though. can be long. rough, and cold. There is a reasonable portage on the left bank. A road bridge crosses the river about 500m below the rapid and marks the small village of Les Guibertes and this makes a convenient alternative put in (on the river right) for the less confident paddler.

Onde.

Iain Penketh

Ubaye Gorge.

Peter Knowle

Slot and drop', Durance Gorge.

Mark Pedley

Estellié rapid, Verdon, rescue from a syphon.

Peter Knowles

Chateau Queyras, view from the take-out.

Peter Knowle

The river continues as class 3 with some fine, fast flowing paddling. After 1.5km there is a sharp right bend next to the road that signals a low weir that can normally be shot with no problems. The next kilometre through the town of Villeneuve shows a fascinating change of character and scenery. The river flows past people's back gardens: old ladies are pruning roses and families having barbecues as you eddy-out under their balconies. Small channels lead off to old mills - now converted into smart restaurants. Everywhere people watch and wave. At the end of the village there is a blind right hand bend - look out for a sluice gate on the left that can trap the unwary.

After the town the river adopts a more natural course with shady wooded banks and dippers bobbing off boulders. The river continues class 3 down under another bridge and then eases off as it winds through some gravel beds. The end of this gravel section makes a good take-out (and salvage spot!) for groups with less experienced paddlers - the start of the campsite can be glimpsed on the right bank, and if you land on the left amongst gravel and bushes, a rough track leads to the main road.

Just downstream from here, the river speeds up as it passes the campsite on the right. Immediately after the bridge, break out left for the usual, most convenient, but last take-out. next to the road.

If you are continuing on the lower Guisane. the next bridge (for a ski-tow) is after about 300m, then land right before the next bridge/tunnel (ski lift above) to inspect "Shelob's weir" that lurks in the dark below - see description for 'lower Guisane'.

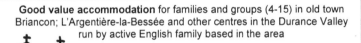

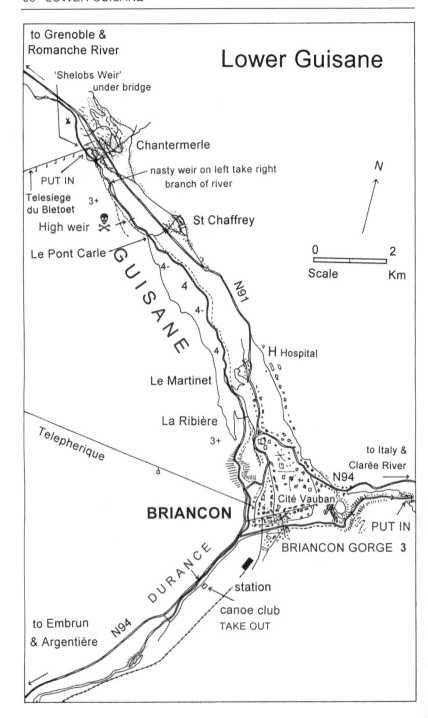

to Grenoble &
Romanche River

'Shelobs Weir'
under bridge

Lower Guisane

Chantermerle

nasty weir on left take right
branch of river

PUT IN

Telesiege
du Bletoet   3+

High weir ☠

St Chaffrey

Le Pont Carle

G U I S A N E

N

0   2
Scale   Km

N91

4-
4
4-

4   H Hospital

Le Martinet

Telepherique

La Ribière

3+

to Italy &
Clarée River
N94

Cité Vauban

BRIANCON

PUT IN
BRIANCON GORGE 3

station

canoe club
TAKE OUT

D U R A N C E

to Embrun
& Argentière

N94

Lower Guisane

From:	Chantmerle	Difficulty:	**4** (1 portage)
To:	Briancon Canoe Club	Gradient:	24 m/km
Distance:	6 km	WW Stars:	★★★
Time:	2 hours	Scenery:	⊕
Best months:	May to July.	Volume:	15 cumecs = MW
Bank support:	reasonable	Gauge:	none
Water temp:	cool	Ass. runs:	upper Guisane, Claree.
Water Quality:	average		upper Durance.

Summary
A "brilliant paddle" that for many people epitomises the rivers of the French Alps. A fast, steep, continuous run in a wooded gorge.

Special points
Two weirs and hazard from trees. The reputation of this run attracts many paddlers who are not ready for it and who often end up having minor epics!

The River
The French call this "La basse Guisane" - the river no longer bimbles about in a flat bottomed Alpine valley, but discovers it's strength and power and carves itself a steep-sided valley (almost a gorge) as it descends to join the valley of the Durance. The town of Briancon is next to the river at the end of the run, but you are never aware of it until you go under the last bridge. For most of this paddle you have a feeling of real isolation - all you have is the river dropping away in front of you, and the warm scent of pine woods on either bank. In reality though, is that there is a good trail in the trees along the bank - a popular Sunday walk with local people - who will enjoy your embarrassment if you take a swim!

Rafting
French rafters describe this run as "raft sportive" - this is a technical fast, exciting descent. It's a pretty intense experience which requires a lot of manoeuvring. People describe it as "pure exhilaration" and a "brilliant river for rafting", but this is definitely not the river for your any nervous first time rafter!

Commercial operators normally offer trips all summer from May through to September. Depending on water levels and your experience, it is also possible to book mini raft and hydro-speed trips.

Access and Logistics
If you are unsure about this run then we recommend that you drive to the bridge at Le Martinet and scout the 1.5 km upstream from here - the steepest and most difficult section of the river. Note that the river that you see near the Put-in and take-out is relatively easy. A good mountain bike trail follows the river and this is a fun way to inspect it.

We recommend that you **put in** just downstream of the weir under the tunnel/bridge where the Telesiege du Bletonet crosses the river. Drive to the centre of Chantemerle and then take the first minor road down to the river on the downstream side of the main ski lifts - opposite the Yeti Pub (which we recommend). There is a minor road here on the right bank and room to park, with a small hidden eddy 30m downstream to put in at. Note that there is reasonable egress in case of need at most of the bridges that cross the river.

The best **take out** is one kilometre downstream of the town of Briancon at the Canoe Club on the left bank, or at a lay-by next to the main road on the opposite bank, or upstream by the bridge.

The Run

This is a run that will delight the confident paddler - or strike terror in the nervous! The middle section is continuous class 4 water: fast, powerful, and steep. Numerous boulders create interesting rapids - most have more than one route down, but all require positive paddling and good river reading skills.   The more expert paddler will revel in "eddy hopping" - dodging from behind one small boulder down to the next. There are no reassuring pools in which to get your breath back and if you're the kind of paddler who likes nice big obvious eddies and plenty of time to make moves, you're going to be disappointed and maybe terrified - as someone put it "this is a pin ball machine for the inexperienced"

Jim Barbour, one of the veterans of English kayaking described this in his cockney accent as "a handsome river" - if Jim had ever made it out to the Himalayas he might have compared it with the Marsyandi, another classic river for eddy-hopping.

Lower Gusiane, hydro-speeds on 'Shelob's weir'   *Peter Knowles*

Local paddlers reckon that this river is best at medium flows. In higher water this is a class 4+ run - continuous, committing and serious if you take a swim. Water flows normally increase later in the day due to snow melt. At the time of writing, there was no gauge on the river, but staff at the Kayak Club, or from one of the local rafting companies, are very happy to give you up to date advice on water levels and new hazards.

Description

We recommend putting in 30m downstream of the wide concrete bridge that takes the "Telesiege du Bletonet" over the river. Just under this bridge is "Shelob's weir" - sharp rocks and jagged concrete, with an evil sluice gate river left, and underwater stanchions and debris below centre. This poses obvious dangers - with local knowledge this may perhaps be shot, but several kayakers have been impaled, so be warned and wary!

From the put-in the river is a fairly steady class 3+, giving time to get used to the water. After about 500m the river branches: **keep right** (the left branch takes you over a small vertical weir with a vicious tow-back). About another 500m of class 3+ brings you to the **Big weir** - the river slows off a little and flattens out just before it. Land in plenty of time on the right bank to portage this 3m drop (there should be several warning signs above the weir).

This weir is now a mess of rough concrete, rock, and reinforcing steel bars - not nice and not recommended! Below the weir, the river stays a nice bimbly class 3 for another 500m down to the next bridge, **Le Pont Carle.** Don't be deceived by this, the river very soon becomes a grade harder and if you're not happy, then this is your last good place for stopping.

The next 2.5km is the crux of the run. The river visibly steepens up, then eases for some 600m, just to deceive you, before it becomes even faster and steeper. This is exhilarating, "handsome" paddling, tight break outs, boulder drops, eddy hopping, scouting on the move - non-stop action and a swim here is likely to be fairly rough. The next bridge **Le Martinet** signals the start of easier paddling and time perhaps to play more.

The river continues on at class 3+ down through another bridge, Le Ribiere, and then curves through a scenic gorge. Time to relax and admire the tall mature pine trees that cover both hillsides. On warm summer afternoons, savour the scent of pine as it wafts over the blue river - so evocative of the South of France. You round a bend, and into sight come views of distant hillsides on the far side of the Durance valley - followed immediately by the main road bridge.

There is an old weir just below this main road bridge, however with an obvious shoot on the left. There is a possible take out on the right just below the bridge. The river course downstream has been channelled and shaped to make an artificial slalom course - however Stuart Woodward warns that there is some risk of injury to boats and bodies from sharp concrete slabs and reinforcement bars - so perhaps not the place to have a last play. You then paddle down through the middle of Briancon with tall apartment buildings on either side. About 500m below the main road bridge you come to the surrealistic blue and yellow bridge of the telecabine with a small take out next to the big car park. Below here, the river is fast bouncy class 2 and joins the Durance after 300m and then about 1km further on you will see the Canoe Club on the left bank, with a rafting ramp just downstream.

Weather requirements for paddling

Romanche

Julie Rowan

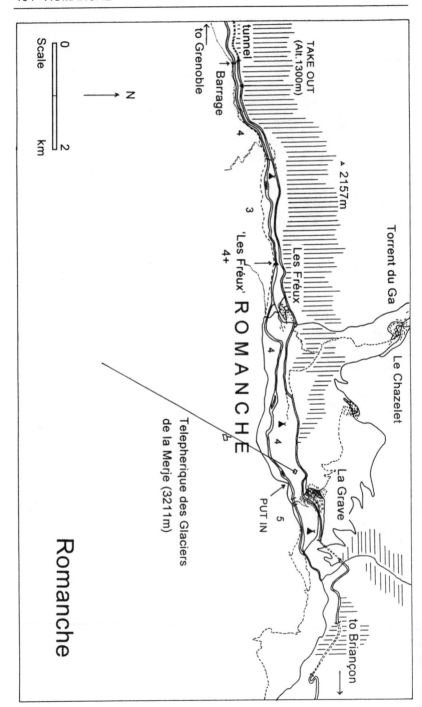

Romanche

Romanche

From:	La Grave	Difficulty:	**4+**
To:	Barrage before tunnel	Gradient:	24 m/km
Distance:	5 km	WW Stars:	★★
Time:	1 hour	Scenery:	⊕⊕
Best months:	July - October	Flow:	25 cumecs=MW
Bank support:	reasonable	Gauge:	none
Water temp:	very cold	Ass. runs:	upper Guisane,
Water quality:	good		Veneon.

Summary
A fantastic, powerful 'full-on' paddle: fast, steep, icy cold, in a one of the most dramatic and scenic valleys in the Alps. Guaranteed water flow even in late summer.

Special points
Very continuous and very cold. Potential tree hazard.

The River
Most kayakers driving up this grave-toned, steep-sided valley on the way to Briançon have probably been excited and fascinated by the river down below. We can remember stopping the car and looking deep into the gloomy depths of the magnificent abyss, labelled 'Gorge de l'infernet' on our map, and wondering if any of the river, that we could hear roaring below us, was runnable. The short answer is that most of the river is not: this is a powerful, steep river flowing through one of the most impressive and deepest valleys in the French Alps. Only two relatively short sections are normally runnable, both in the Combe de Malaval, and the second only late in the summer, when water levels are more reasonable - the Romanche is fed by most of the glaciers on the north side of the Massif des Écrins - this means it has plenty of water all summer but like all glacial rivers, it is icy cold!

Rafting
The Romanche river has been commercially rafted on a regular basis only in the last few years. This is a fast and furious challenge - a more intense and powerful trip than anything else in the area and definitely not one for "softies"! The company "No Limits" has an office in la Grave and are the local specialists.

Access and Logistics
This river is a short and scenic drive over the Col du Lautaret from the upper Guisane. As it's a glacial melt river, it's probably best planned as **morning paddle** when levels are low. The Véneon river is fairly close and makes a convenient paddle in the afternoon. There is no gauge on the river but 'No Limits' will be able to advise on water levels.

Short sections of the river can be glimpsed from the main highway, RN91, but it is best scouted by turning off the main road in the small village of **les Fréaux** and driving over the bridge there. If you stop just over this bridge, you can walk 500m down a path on the left bank to the inspect the rapid that is the climax of the run. From the bridge drive upstream on the minor road on the left side of the valley. A class 5 rapid can be seen just downstream of the next stone bridge (now closed) up the valley. The usual **put-in** is just downstream of this rapid. There is reasonable egress at many points, normally best to the left bank where there is a road or path.

Take out at the ramp above the barrage just upstream of the tunnel on the main highway.

The Run

This run compares to the lower Guisane in high water, or the Gyr. But, when you might be bumping and scraping down the Guisane in late summer - the Romanche will still give you a powerful big-water paddle that some paddlers have said deserves a 3 star rating. Deviants will like this run because it is little known and has sensational surroundings. This is a fast, furious, and enjoyable paddle, and has some stunning views if you crane your neck to look upward, with waterfalls crashing down the valley sides from the glaciers above.

There is potentially a considerable tree hazard - if however, the river is being rafted, then the local company 'No limits' will probably have cleared most of the more dangerous hazards, but check with them before putting on, or alternatively scout the most difficult sections from the bank.

The Alpes-Dauphine guide suggests that further upstream on the Romanche there is some 4 km of easier paddling, class 2-3, from Pied du Col to Villar d'Arêne. Also some long sections of easier paddling on the lower river downstream towards Grenoble.

Description

Put in just below the class 5 rapid below the old bridge. This rapid has changed in recent years with a central boulder sieve and metal bars protruding under water, waiting to impale any foolhardy kayaker. There is almost a km of paddling upstream of here, so keen paddlers will put on at the campsite bridge. Below the rapid is fast, solid, very cold water, class 3+. The pace is fast and furious with no pools and no big break-outs. You need 'on the move' route-finding skills and fast reactions to avoid the odd tree sweeper.

A tributary, La Ga, comes in on the right and then the river speeds up a bit, through the road bridge at Les Fréaux, and about 500m below is the **"Les Fréaux"**, a class 4+ rapid that forms the climax of the run. This can be quite tricky and is especially worth scouting (from the left bank) at low flows.

One kilometre brings you to another campsite on the right and the river now eases down to class 3 for another kilometre. There is chance to relax and look about and upwards at sheer cliffs, hanging glaciers and mountain tops some 2000m above. The last km gives some really enjoyable class 3+ water that leads down to the finish of the run.

Take out at the ramp above the barrage. Note that at medium and high levels the water flows over the top of the barrage and can take with it boats, gear and bodies.

The **lower Romanche**   downstream to the lake is class 5(6) and only occasionally attempted in very low water conditions in late summer (normally by local experts) - if you interested then make sure you put in below the outflow from the Hydro plant and scout every metre of the run beforehand - there are numerous boulder chokes and a big dangerous drop at the finish into the lake at the bottom. There have been several near fatalities on this run.....

Pont-en-Royans   *Victor Cassieu*

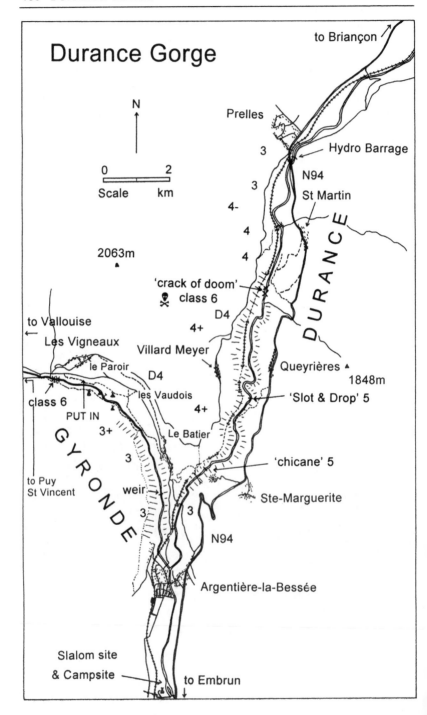

Durance Gorge

N

0   2
Scale   km

2063m

to Briançon

Prelles

3

Hydro Barrage

3

N94

St Martin

4-

4

4

DURANCE

'crack of doom'
☠ class 6

D4

to Vallouise
Les Vigneaux

4+

Villard Meyer

le Paroir

D4

Queyrières ▲

1848m

class 6

les Vaudois

'Slot & Drop' 5

PUT IN

4+

3+

Le Batier

3

'chicane' 5

to Puy
St Vincent

weir

Ste-Marguerite

GYRONDE

3

3

N94

Argentière-la-Bessée

Slalom site
& Campsite

to Embrun

Durance Gorge

From:	Prelles	Difficulty:	**4** (5) difficult portages
To:	Argentière	Gradient:	22 m/km
Distance:	8 km	WW Stars:	★★★
Time:	4 hours	Scenery:	✿✿
Best months:	June to Sept	Flow:	15 cumecs = MW
Bank support:	No	Gauge:	see note
Water temp:	cool	Ass. runs:	upper Durance
Water quality:	average		Gyronde

Summary
A mini-expedition. A challenging run in a spectacular and committing gorge. Seize the opportunity if water levels are right!

Special points
A committing gorge with very limited access. An un-navigable and dangerous fall at the start of the gorge requires a delicate and **dangerous portage** across scree slopes above the river - you need a head for heights and this could be especially dangerous in bad weather. Water levels may change without warning due to releases from the Hydro barrage upstream at Prelles.

The River
The Durance is the major river of the region and by the time it arrives at Prelles it always has a good flow, but in the summer months almost all this water is channelled off at the barrage at Prelles down a tunnel and pipeline to a big hydro station in Argentière. Like most gorges, you wouldn't want to be paddling this in high water, but it's quite difficult getting the right level - early in the season there is too much water - later on most of the flow has been diverted, so there is not enough water.

Rafting
There is no commercial rafting on this section of the river although it would probably make a great raft run if it didn't have such a hard portage.

Access and Logistics
Tantalising glimpses of this gorge can be had as you drive along the main highway, the N94, between Argentière and Briançon. A more spectacular view is obtained if you turn off the N94 close to the small village of Ste-Marguerite and drive up the small road that goes off to a small radio tower and viewpoint just above where the pipeline swoops over the gorge. There are also good panoramic views from the minor road on the other side of the valley (a fine cycle ride), but none of these distant views give you a really good look into the crux of the gorge below - this has to remain a mystery, only to be divulged to the intrepid kayakers who dare enter the maws of the canyon!

Well. that isn't strictly true: there are a couple of rough paths that wind down from the road. hundreds of metres above - you certainly see the odd fisherman, and there is the railway line, so in case of emergency you should be able to scramble out somewhere. as long as you don't mind abandoning your boat! In the event of a casualty needing evacuation, then you're almost guaranteed an epic. It is fairly easy. and probably a good idea, to view the entrance to the gorge and the start of the portage - park in St Martin and follow the footpath down to the river where there are some old mine workings.

There is an easy put in on the left bank. downstream of the bridge at Prelles - but to reach here you have to solve a magic mystery maze set by the traffic engineers (take the turn off the new road maked 'St Martin' and then double back on yourself. Most paddlers take out at the slalom and camp site 1.5 km downstream of Argentière. but it is possible to take out in the middle of the town on the left just downstream of the bridge.

The Run

This is a spectacular and committing run. with huge boulders, shoots and staircase rapids. most with pools at the bottom - super paddling! The difficulty is very dependent on water levels and we have heard it called everything from an easy class 4 up to class 6! In high flows, you just wouldn't want to be here; in medium-high flows. however. this is an immensely satisfying class 4 with several class 4+ rapids. In low water the river is easier and less satisfying, a technical 4- with just a few rapids that merit a 4+ rating. One paddler commented *"this is a grade 4 river with a grade 5 portage"*!

This portage at the entrance to the gorge is the key feature of the run and it is essential that you break-out on the right before the gorge - to be swept down the rapid below would probably be fatal.

Water levels have to be assessed by inspection as there is no gauge. Some indication may be had from the viewpoint high above the gorge and then look downstream from the bridge at Prelles - if the river looks full and fast with no rocks showing then it is only for the big volume expert. Less than this then it's worth looking at the first rapid downstream - if this has rocks prominent and clearly defined eddies (and makes a good warm up) then you can expect medium levels and an exciting class 4+ run. If the river looks a total bump and scrape, then don't bother. Somewhere between these last two then it is probably low water, but still a worthwhile run. Remember when assessing the flow that the river will be constrained by the narrow gorge walls.

Note that this is an adventurous mini-expedition and you should be suitably equipped with full safety gear.

Durance Gorge looking upstream from Ste-Marguerite   *Peter Knowles*

Description

The run starts off fairly easy with one kilometre of class 3 as a nice warm up. As you come to an old bridge, the pace quickens with a couple of class 4 rapids - these are a test piece: anyone struggling here should not continue, but walk back to the road. The river then eases again as you approach the entrance to the gorge. A highly dangerous fall is just below and you need to **break out right before the entrance to the gorge,** just upstream of a sheer rock wall on your left; this is 30m or so below the entrance to the railway tunnel, now over-grown and not clearly visible from the river. You may be tempted to make one last eddy - not a good idea: you might make it, but will your partner?

So there you are, hanging on by your finger nails in the last little micro-eddy before the entrance to hell. Scramble out, shrug nonchalantly, and find the portage path which is fairly obvious, but delicate and potentially dangerous in places as it traverses scree slopes above the river - to slip and lose a kayak would be disastrous so we recommend doubling up carry the boats on the difficult sections. You pass the rapid we're making all the fuss about, **'Crack of Doom'**, just below you - the whole river appears to flow down a constriction less than a metre wide, also blocked by a tree trunk! This portage is approximately 500m long and brings you out at a good put-in where the river bends by some trees and a grassy area - a beautiful lunch spot with a great sense of isolation that feels as remote as some Himalayan rivers. Young tigers with no time for beauty may prefer to put in a little way upstream and run the short section of class 5 downstream of 'Crack of Doom'.

Below here, the river is quite wide and open as it flows deep in the gorge; huge boulders create staircase rapids, normally with pools or slower sections below in which to sort out any problems. Most of these rapids can usually be run by scouting from the eddies.

After about 1.5 km there is a long railway embankment on the right and then a further 500m later are the remains of a wooden structure on a rock in the middle of the river - keep to the right of this and land on the large shingle beach on the right to scout (and portage?) the next rapid. Just below, the rivers narrows and sweeps you into the infamous **'Slot and drop'** rapid .   The slot is a short constriction immediately followed by a 3-4m drop. This rapid changes from year to year - in 2002 the river must have scoured out the bed above and below the slot and most of the water appears to syphon under the central rock of the drop. At good paddling levels there is now a serious risk of getting wedged on the drop, so the whole rapid is usually portaged on the right bank - about 200m with a difficult scramble down to the river..

Back on the river the difficulty now eases somewhat, though with still plenty of rapids to maintain interest and some nice play waves and eddy lines behind big boulders. The gorge appears to deepen and the cliffs close in - however, it's reassuring to know that most of the major white water is now behind you. There are three distinct rapids after Slot and Drop, (in high water these merge into one long class 5!) before you come to the final rapid of real note **'Chicane'**, just under the cable bridges of the Via Ferrata and before the huge pipeline that arches over the river. The river goes around a blind bend to the right and the river is blocked by a massive boulder - this is badly under-cut (even though there is a cushion wave against the upstream face) and there have been some real epics here.

There are two routes available, but either or both are usually blocked with tree debris so we strongly recommend landing on the river left before the first blind bend and scrambling over some huge boulders to check out the exit.

From here on, it's a mellow class 3 run, just one surprise rapid at 3+ to keep you on your toes, down to the confluence with the Gyronde and the town of **Argentière**. Downstream from the town bridge look out for a big pipe arching over the river - underneath this is a small weir which in low water has a nasty tow-back, and dragon teeth, metal spikes. However, there is a safe easy shoot on the left. At very high flows this makes a super surf wave. **Take out** at the Slalom site and campsite 1km downstream of the town on the right bank. There is a café and bar here for celebration drinks.

Durance Gorge - portaging around the 'Crack of Doom'   *Peter Knowles*

Lesser Classics

Briançon Gorge, Upper Durance

From:	Le Fontenil	Difficulty:	3
To:	Briançon Canoe Club	Gradient:	25 m/km
Distance:	2 km	WW Stars:	★★★
Time:	½ hour	Scenery:	⊛⊛
Best months:	May to June	Flow:	10 cumecs = MW
Bank support:	limited	Gauge:	none

Summary

A fine little paddle if there is sufficient water - *'a nice introduction to technical paddling - steep and yet forgiving'*. The put-in at the bridge at le Fontenil is reached by a road that descends parallel to the N94 from the top end of the big parking place at Cite Vauban, the old fort of Briançon. Park near the bridge, 300m downstream is a barrage that can usually be shot by a shoot on the right.

From here starts a fine steep technical run through a pretty little gorge. After this, the river is canalised for a stretch and below the next road bridge are the remains of a rocky weir (this used to be dangerous so was blown up in 1994). Continue through the town and take out at the Canoe Club.

Perhaps the most dangerous thing about the run is the aggressive old Gardien of the boules court at the put in, note however that his run is much harder and committing in high flows - several university groups lost boats on this run in the high water conditions of 2001.

Upstream of this run is the infamous 'Malefoss' - a 2km stretch of class 5 in low water - paddlers have died on this section in high water - just looking at if cures most peoples constipation.

Upper Durance

From:	Briançon	Difficulty:	**2**
To:	Prelles	Gradient:	7 m/km
Distance:	7 km	WW Stars:	★
Time:	1 hour	Scenery:	⊛
Best months:	May to August	Flow:	30 cumecs = MW
Bank support:	reasonable	Gauge:	none

Summary

A very straight-forward paddle on fast moving water, suitable for beginners at medium levels and worth doing to build confidence, particularly if you are camping en-route.

For the put-in see the take-out for the Lower Guisane. We suggest you avoid the sewage outfall on river left after Briançon. Water quality is poor in low water flows so we do not recommend this run in late season. Take out well above the barrage at Prelles, river left.

Middle Clarée

From:	Névache	Difficulty:	**4**
To:	Plampinet	Gradient:	25 m/km
Distance:	4 km	WW Stars:	★★
Time:	1 hour	Scenery:	✤✤
Best months:	May to June	Flow:	5 cumecs = MW
Bank support:	reasonable	Gauge:	none

Summary

An exciting run that is faster than it looks. The best put-in is by the municipal campsite 1 km downstream from Névache. This gives you time for a little warm up on easier water down to, and after a small footbridge. Then follows a drop which is probably worth inspecting. Now follows a fast and furious kilometre of the main run, through a small wooded gorge down to the highway bridge. This is very fast, shallow water with sharp rocks where even to roll could be painful and a swim is likely to be serious.

After the road bridge the river eases-off to fast, bouncy class 3, but look out for a rock in river centre that has been known to hold trees in early season.

Two kilometres above Névache are some very scenic waterfalls - above them in the upper valley is some extreme hair boating.

Briancon Gorge - shoot near the start.   *Conor O'Neill*

Lower Clarée

From:	Plampinet	Difficulty:	3
To:	La Vachette	Gradient:	10 m/km
Distance:	12 km	WW Stars:	★★
Time:	2 hours	Scenery:	❀❀
Best months:	May to June	Flow:	10 cumecs = MW
Bank support:	limited	Gauge:	none
Water temp:	cold	Ass. Runs:	Upper Clarée
Water quality:	average		

Summary

A fast scenic run ideal for intermediate paddlers - recommended if you are here in early summer when the river has sufficient water levels (after mid-July you're probably out of luck). A major landslide in 1995 changed the course of the river through the wooded banks - there should be no major difficulties but trees are always a potential hazard. Most of this run is probably class 2 with just a few rapids somewhat harder. Note that there is beautiful wild camping in the upper valley - enquire and register in Névache (approx. 1 euro per head).

Gyr

From:	St Antoine	Difficulty:	4+ (5)
To:	Vallouise	Gradient:	27 m/km
Distance:	3 km	WW Stars:	★★★
Time:	20 minutes!	Scenery:	❀
Best months:	June to Sept	Flow:	15 cumecs = MW
Bank support:	reasonable	Gauge:	none

Summary

A non-stop aquatic toboggan run, fast and furious, with very few eddies! The river is fed by some of the major glaciers of the Massif des Écrins so you can be assured of adequate water levels, lower flows in the morning - raging torrent by late afternoon and ice cold.

Put in at the bridge by the swimming pool just below Pelvoux St Antoine and take out at the barrage just below Vallouise. Floods change the course of the river from year to year, diverting the river through the forested banks so trees are usually a major hazard. Also note that this river changes rapidly from day to day - we ran it in late July one year, with two local experts who had both independently run the river the previous week 'it's fine' they both said 'no major problems' - half way down, round a bend, and the river suddenly steepened and dropped out of sight - a brand new class 5 rapid which we had to run blind! A footpath follows the river reasonably closely on the right bank and you might like to consider a little bit of country walking to stretch your limbs before paddling!

Onde

From:	Les Grésourières	Difficulty:	3+
To:	Vallouise	Gradient:	27 m/km
Distance:	3 km	WW Stars:	★★
Time:	1 hour	Scenery:	✲✲
Best months:	May to July	Flow:	5 cumecs = MW
Bank support:	reasonable	Gauge:	none

Summary

Stuart Woodward reckons that this is one of his favourite early season river "when it's just a blast". It's a great little river with plenty of boulders, shoots, and eddies to provide technical interest. (If you like the Tryweryn in Wales, then you will probably like this). This little river tends to catch people out and many paddlers have lost boats on it in recent years - changes have perhaps made it slightly harder, especially so in higher flows when it needs respect and fast reactive paddling skills. Trees are a hazard. High mountains are all around making for fine scenery.

Drive to the put-in by taking the D504 that turns left in Vallouise and goes through the little village of Le Villard. Putting on at the bridge at Les Grésourières will give you a class 3 start - those looking for more excitement can drive up further for another kilometre or so, for some class 4 and 5. Take out at the road bridge where the D504 crosses the river - check this before paddling as there is a **dangerous barrage** just downstream at the confluence.

Gyronde, just below class 6 rapid.   *Mark Pedley*

Gyronde

From:	Les Vigneaux	Difficulty:	**3+** (1 weir)
To:	Argentière	Gradient:	16 m/km
Distance:	6 km	WW Stars:	★
Time:	2 hours	Scenery:	✸✸
Best months:	June to Sept	Flow:	20 cumecs = MW
Bank support:	limited	Gauge:	none
Water temp:	cold	Ass. Runs:	Gyr, Onde,
Water Quality:	poor		Middle Durance

Summary *(see 'Durance Gorge' for a map of this run.)*
The Gyr and the Onde join at the barrage just below Vallouise to form the Gyronde.
One kilometre below this is another barrage with a sewage outfall (normally
portaged right). More class 3 water, mainly canalised. brings you after 3.5 km to the
road bridge at **Les Vigneaux** with a **class 5 rapid** below which usually requires a
500m portage. We don't think this top section is pleasant or worth the hassle unless
you are continuing a run down the Gyr or the Onde - instead, we recommend that
you **start below Les Vigneaux** - take the first track down to the river opposite the
garage, just downstream of the village.

In July 2002 one of the tributary streams had a monstrous flood down it, so the
river is **now full of gravel** and it will probably take a year or two for this to wash
out and the river to become a good paddle again. The Gyronde normally has good
water levels throughout the summer (especially in the afternoons) and putting on
100m downstream of an old toilet block gives a pleasant, training run for the less
experienced paddler; put on further upstream if you want more excitement (a Dutch
paddler paddler died in a boulder entrapment in 2001), further downstream if you
want an easier class 3 start.

The river has pine woods and the 'Vaudois' campsite on both banks for the first
2 km and shortly after that it enters a fine little gorge. Paddling into any gorge you
always have that feeling of commitment, slight apprehension and anticipation -
'what's around the corner?' Well, in this case. somewhat unusually and about 500m
into the gorge. is a **weir** which should be inspected and normally portaged left. This
weir is very dangerous at high flows.

The gorge continues with straight-forward class 3 water down to the town of
Argentière and the confluence with the Durance. Downstream of the town bridge
look out for a big pipe arching over the river - underneath this is another small weir
which in low water has a nasty tow-back. and dragon teeth, metal spikes. However,
there is a safe easy shoot on the left. At very high flows this makes a super surf
wave. **Take out** at the Slalom site and campsite 1km downstream of the town.

Vénéon   *(by Mike Bruce)*

From:	Bourg d'Arud	Difficulty:	**4+** (5)
To:	Ougiers	Gradient:	23 m/km
Distance:	4 km	WW Stars:	★★
Time:	1 hour	Scenery:	✿✿
Best months:	July, August.	Flow;	20 cumecs = MW
Bank support:	Good	Gauge:	none
Water temp:	very cold	Ass. Runs:	Romanche, Bonne.
Water quality:	average.		

Summary

An Alpine gem! The Vénéon is fed by more glaciers than either the Romanche or the Gyr so has high flows and dam releases in late afternoons - the best time for a run is usually after 4 p.m. If you are coming from Briançon, then this river combines well with a morning run on the Romanche. Note that it is subject to flash floods after thunderstorms with automatic opening of the dam 3 km above Bourg d'Arud - accompanied by warning sirens.

The classic run starts just above the road bridge at Bourg d'Arud and finishes at the bridge just upstream of Les Ougiers. The next section is unrunnable and it is usually wiser to take out well upstream of the bridge, above the last rapid. All of the run can be inspected from the road and track on the right bank, but remember that river levels can change rapidly whilst you are on the water. There is a nasty man-made fall 600m after the put-in which should be inspected. Both main rapids start after footbridges.

Most of the rest of the Vénéon is class 5 and 6, but there is a 3 km section of class 2 and 3 from the Vénéon Eaux Vive base and campsite below St Christophe, which is good for training. There is another 4 km of class 4+ further up the valley from La Berarde which is best paddled in the morning.

Other Rivers

Over the border in Italy is the **Dora Riparia** - a river of many epic tales. If you are tempted to do it then do not trust any old articles or guide book descriptions. On the upper river, just after the town of Cesana Torinese is a new (2002) killer weir - in low flows the river goes under the weir, in high flows over the top - both suicidal to run, and of course, no eddies before ....

The Dora Riparia and another Italian river, the **Chisone**, normally only have sufficient water in May to June. For more information on these and other deviant paddles in the area check out the 'Alpes-Dauphine' guidebook. (Note the Torrent St Pierre above **Ailefroide** normally has water in July and August)

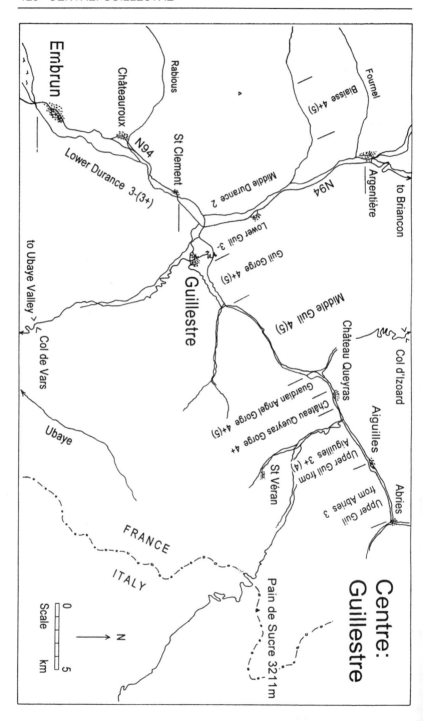

Centre:
Guillestre

Centre: Guillestre

The Runs

Name of run	Class	Stars	Scen	Km	cms	Notes
Lower Durance	3- (3+)	★★	✺✺	16	60	Big and bouncy
Middle Guil	4 (5)	★★★	✺✺	9	25	True classic
Middle Durance	2 (3)	★★	✺✺	19	40	Good intro.
Upper Guil - from Abries	3	★	✺✺	4	4	High Alpine valley
- from Aiguilles	3+ (4)	★★	✺✺	17	5	Fine little gorge
Château Queyras	4+	★★★	✺✺	1	7	Committing
Guardian Angel	4+ (5)	★★	✺✺	3	7	Much scouting
Guil Gorge	4+ (5)	★	✺✺	4	15	Russian Roulette?
Lower Guil	3-	★★	✺✺	7	25	Pretty and fun
Biaisse	5 (6)	★★★	✺✺	8	7	A gem

The Centre

This centre, consisting of the lower Durance and Guil valleys, has become a justifiably popular holiday centre for all kinds of outdoor sports. There is a good choice of paddling trips on some excellent rivers and a wide variety of alternative activities. This also makes it an ideal centre if you don't want to move base to paddle the Ubaye and the rivers around Briançon - less than an hour's drive away.

The area really developed as a major tourist centre after the early 1970s when the lower Durance was dammed below Embrun thus forming the large Lac de Serre-Ponçon. This warm lake has become almost an alternative to the Mediterranean as a summer destination for both windsurfers and sailors, whilst new ski resorts like Risoul, Vars, les Orres and Réallon cater for the winter visitor. Embrun is a pleasant large town with a good market and many old buildings, built on a bluff overlooking the valley. Guillestre is a smaller quaint old village that makes a more central base.

On the River

The Durance and the Guil are two of the most famous white water rivers of Europe. The Durance has good water levels throughout the summer, whilst most of the Guil is a natural flowing river in a spectacular valley with best water levels in early summer. These rivers of the southern Alps are pleasantly warm when compared with their northern counterparts and the best time to visit this region is June or early July - before the French school holidays.

The region quickly realised the commercial benefits of "le tourism d'eaux vive" and there has been careful development of access points to the rivers, with parking and often a café/bar. River running here can be terribly civilised - epitomised by a rest stop at the Rabioux (possibly the best known rapid in the Alps), relaxing in an armchair with an ice cream and a cappuccino, admiring the kayakers pirouetting on the wave and soaking up the ambience of the 'Bay Watch factor' on the beach. A unique experience is to take a barbecue and go and play by floodlight at the Rabioux - a fantastic kayak rodeo spot.

Note that standard French river regulations apply, displayed at most access points: boating is normally prohibited before 10.00 a.m. and after 6.0.p.m. and on the weekends at the beginning and end of the fishing season (usually the second Saturday in March to the third Sunday in September).

A catastrophic flood in June 2000 scoured the Guil valley and caused huge damage, cars, trucks and 3 piste bashers were swept away - two ended up in the reservoir and one was jammed underwater in the Chateau Queyras gorge.

Commercial Rafting

The lower Durance is probably the most popular rafting run in Europe, offering relatively warm, easy, big water in a scenic valley - ideal for the beginner. The Guil has some exciting and challenging raft runs, superb white water, and spectacular scenery. Worth a special mention is the run through the Château Queyras and Guardian Angel Gorges which is probably the most intense, fun rafting adventure in the whole of Europe!   If you're here as a 'shuttle bunny' or 'shuttle monkey' then this is a great place to mutiny and try your hand at rafting, 'le Hot-dog', or hydro-speeding - why should those kayakers, those 'river maggots', have all the fun?

Off the River

This is a great area to explore, by foot, cycle or car. Here's a few tempting ideas - local tourist offices will be able to help with more details.

* Hire a windsurfer or a sailboat on the warm waters of the lake at Embrun - or try your hand at kite surfing.
* Explore the beautiful alpine side valleys west of the Durance: the Fournel, Biasse, Rabious, that lead into the Parc National des Écrins.
* Hire mountain bikes and take these up the bubble lifts at Reallon or Risoul, to then come screaming down the mountain sides!
* Drive and walk up to the strange tunnel at the Col de Parpaillon (2645m) that goes over from Crevoux to the Ubaye valley (a rough jeep road - ideal for adventurous mountain bikers!).
* Explore the highest village in Europe, St Véran, 2040m.
* Drive up to the Col Agnel, 2744m, one of the highest passes in the Alps, and take a high mountain walk (and bag a 3000m peak like 'le Pain de Sucre'?).
* Explore the old fortress town of Mont Dauphin (really interesting English tours one day a week).
* Just relax on the beach down at the lakeside - warm water and sun.

Food and Drink

Best value for money and a favourite of paddlers for many years is 'Christian's Pizzeria behind the InterMarche supermarket by the bridge at Embrun - the pizzas are huge! More upmarket and serving excellent traditional food is the 'Hotel Marie' in the centre of Embrun.

Handy for a meal after a play session at the Raboux, we can recommend the family run, 'le Daupinoise' hotel in Chateauroux. 'La Creche' in Roche de Rame' is another recommended restaurant.   The Pizzeria in the middle of Argentière is pleasant and good value, but even better value are the take away pizzas from the wooden chalet just up the road from the campsite. Best snack bar in the valley with an innovative menu, has to 'Fido's' at the put in at St Clement.

Campsites

There are a huge number of campsites close to the lake below **Embrun**, but most are noisy and crowded - the one lakeside site we can recommend is run by the Embrun Sailing Club - Club Nautique Alpin, Base de Chadenas, is great for nautical families. tel: 04 92 43 00 12.

A better centre for most paddlers is probably **Guillestre**: 'St James les-pins' is a small, well-managed site and there are at least six other sites within walking distance of the town.

The campsite at the **Rabioux** rapid is a great location, with just a short in walk to one of the best play waves in Europe: but in recent years there have been many problems with large groups of noisy school kids (non kayakers), so most paddlers have avoided camping here. We hope the local Municipality will see sense and the long term potential of this site as a centre for international kayaking. So check the site out before camping here - a great site it the kids groups haven't taken it over.

An alternative riverside site in pine trees, and next to a warm lake, is the FFCK one. on the banks of the Durance near Mont Dauphin Gare (you need to be a member of a recognised club, BCU member, or similar). The campsite next to the slalom course at **Argentière** is another favourite choice for larger groups.

There are more family-orientated, riverside campsites at St Clément and St Crépin. If you are looking for a quieter. more primitive, campsite in beautiful surroundings then we suggest that you should explore one of the side valleys.

Hospital

Embrun - in the middle of the old town.
Telephone 18 in case of accident (fire/ambulance/rescue).

Maps

IGN TOP100 sheet 54 'Genoble-Gap', covers this and neighbouring centres so is our recommended 'best buy'. IGN TOP25 sheet no. 3537ET 'Guillestre', gives more detail at a scale of 1:25,000 and covers most of the lower Durance and the Guil so is probably worth buying if you're spending much time in this area. The tourist offices have a free river map in English to the lower Durance.

Tourist Offices

Embrun: Tel: 04 92 43 77 43   www.embrunais-serreponcon.net.
Guillestre: Tel: 04 92 45 04 37   www.pays-du-guil.com.
Queyras: Tel: 04 92 46 76 18   www.queyras.com.
Argentière la Bessée: Tel: 04 92 23 03 11   www.puysaintvincent.com.
Chateauroux: Tel: 04 92 43 43 74   www.chateauroux-alpes.net.

Rafting Operators

Over 10 companies - please obtain a current list from a local tourist office.
Queyras rafting specialise in the Guil -   www.queyraft.com

Kayak schools / clubs

Eau Vive Embrun. Tel: 04 92 43 09 18.

Kayak and rafting shops

Kayak and Outdoor, Embrun, (see map) Tel: 04 92 433 433.
Wonderland. (by the bridge in Embrun). Tel: 04 92 43 89 94.

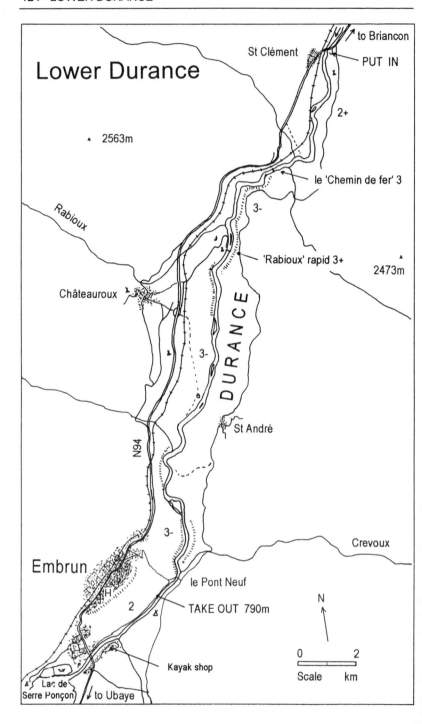

Lower Durance

to Briancon

St Clément

PUT IN

2+

le 'Chemin de fer' 3

2563m

Rabioux

3-

'Rabioux' rapid 3+

2473m

Châteauroux

D U R A N C E

3-

St André

N94

3-

Crevoux

3-

Embrun

le Pont Neuf

2

TAKE OUT 790m

N

Kayak shop

0   2

Lac de
Serre Ponçon   to Ubaye

Scale   km

Lower Durance

From:	St Clément	Difficulty:	**3- (3+)**
To:	Embrun	Gradient:	5 m/km
Distance:	16 km	WW Stars:	★★
Time:	2½ hours	Scenery:	❀❀
Best months:	June to Sept	Flow:	60 cumecs = MW
Bank support:	limited	Gauge:	1km above Embrun.
Water temp:	cool	Ass. runs:	middle Durance,
Water Quality:	average		lower Guil

Summary
A classic big water run justifiably popular with all species of river runner - big bouncy rapids and good scenery. A safe, fun trip with plenty of interest - notably the Rabioux rapid, a famous spot for rodeo and freestyle paddlers.

Special points
Can get crowded at peak periods.

The River
The Durance starts as a small stream above Briançon. By the time it reaches Embrun it is relatively large volume, and mature - this section is the river's last bit of fun before it is captured in the still green waters of the lake de Serre-Ponçon.

Rafting
This is probably the most popular raft run in the whole of Europe. It's an ideal trip for beginners, but the river has lots of interest so will also be enjoyed by more advanced rafters. It's also a popular river for 'le Hot Dog' - inflatable canoes holding one or two persons. There are very few rocks and if you take a flip it's usually a safe swim. If you do want to try swimming a river, then this is an ideal place to try hydro-speeding, 'le nage en eau vive' (sometimes called).

There are many companies offering different packages - one favourite is to pause at the Rabioux rapid to eat a picnic lunch and watch the fun. It's also possible to book a shorter raft trip starting or ending at the Rabioux rapid, but we strongly recommend the whole run - it's well worth it! If you're looking for some intense adventure, then it's possible to sign up for a session of 'Nage en eau vive' just swimming the Rabioux.

Access and Logistics
The usual **put-in** is at St Clément, on the left bank downstream of the bridge, clearly signposted off the road and with plenty of parking and a good snack bar. A pleasant alternative, if you would like a longer run, perhaps with a lunch at the Rabioux, is to start on the **lower Guil** and then paddle the 3 km down from the confluence.

The **Rabioux** has a good road to it and a large car park, so makes an alternative access point plus a fine vantage place for supporters - with beach, shady riverside bar, ice creams, and guaranteed entertainment (Rabioux is spelt on government publications with either an 's' or an 'x'). There is another possible access point La Pinéon on the left bank between the Rabioux and Embrun, but otherwise, it's a long climb up through woods and fields to any road.

The best **take-out** for kayakers is on the right bank 500m below le Pont Neuf where there is an access ramp and beach in low water. It is also possible to continue down into the warm waters of the lake and take out near the Kayak club where there is a large car park and a second even warmer lake for swimming and rolling practice. Rafting companies have their own agreed take-outs between le Pont Neuf and the lake.

The Run

This is a big, wide, natural river, the last remaining high volume run left in a natural state in the southern Alps. It does make a superb paddle, so spare a thought for all the other rivers that have been dammed, canalised, and diverted - sterilised and lost forever.

The lower Durance is a run that has a lot to offer all kinds and grades of paddler:

The aspiring intermediate will find this friendly and an ideal introduction to the joys of big water paddling - Fiona Firth described it as "a lovely, bouncy river with loads of wave trains and smaller play waves". There are few rocks, no nasty holes, just a big wide river with strange swirls, eddy lines, and wave trains to get used to. There's plenty of time to practise your roll, and if it does fail, swimming is almost fun (some paddlers even reckon it's quite warm!) Any hazards are normally very obvious: occasionally a fallen tree or drift wood in one of the big eddies. What catches out most newcomers are the big water eddy lines. The special hazard is rafts - at peak periods over 2000 people a day descend this stretch and that equals a lot of rafts. It pays to keep a wary look out upstream and not to loiter on the edge of eddies unless you like the idea of a big rubber massage.

The young tiger will want to catch every eddy, surf every wave, play in every little hole, and will get off the water knackered but satisfied.

The old hand can just drift sideways down 95% of the run, savouring the scents of hot sun on rocks, river and pine woods, relishing the fresh vistas at each new bend - wooded banks, sandstone cliffs glowing a warm orange in the late afternoon sun, huge lumps of mountain rising above the valley, and the occasional glimpse of a distant snow-tipped peak. There are few modern developments on the banks, roads are far away from the river, and for most of the 16 km there's just you and the river - civilisation seems far away.

The gauge at Le Pont Neuf is now broken, but there is a new one approx. one kilometre above the bridge at Embrun. The centimetre readings shown on this new gauge roughly correspond to the following:

gauge cm	typical month	level	cumecs	c.f.s.
200	May or June	flood	250	9000
110	June/July	high	100	3500
85	end of July	medium	60	2100
70	August	medium	55	1900
55	December	low	40	1400

New Gauge 1km above Embrun Bridge

This run is probably most fun for kayaking at medium to low levels and for rafting at medium to high levels. At medium levels there are more well defined eddies and play spots are better. At higher levels waves are larger, and wave trains longer. Even at low levels the river has a powerful current that seems to just whoosh you along. Note that the Rabbioux wave gets washed out at high levels.

Lower Durance, the play-wave on the Rabioux rapid.   *Mark Nichols*

Description

The put-in at **St Clément** is clearly sign-posted as "Base de sports d'eau vive" just by the bridge and it now has a large car park, Fido's snack bar (recommended), and steps down to the river - mainly of course for the thousands of rafters who descend this stretch. For the kayaker, there's a quite unique facility - an artificial pool next to a cafe, in which to practice your roll, and then slide down a fibreglass shoot and into a channel that takes you upstream, and then 'whoosh' down another little shoot into the river. Several small breakwaters have been built out into the river, to make small shoots and eddies - perfect for practice - and bringing you back to the steps and the cafe. This is a really imaginative development, free to use, ideal for big kids, great fun, and of course perfect for limbering up for the paddle to come.

As soon as you set off from the put-in, you leave the road and the noises of civilisation behind - there's just the wide river in front, wooded banks and distant hillsides. The river trundles with a helpful current, a very straightforward class 2+ and no big rapids for a while. After 3 km there is a big wide eroded stream bed on the left and 500m below on the right is the '**Chemin de fer**' rapid at the exit of the railway tunnel. The river bends right and the current piles up against the abutments of the railway embankment and creates some interesting swirls. Keep left if you want a less exciting run!

The current eases a little for the next 1.5 km down to 'Dead Dog Eddy' found on the left just before a cliff face - the river turns right and then left. The eddies on the left under the cliff are usually good for practice at breaking out. On the right 300m downstream is a large rocky beach at the confluence of the Rabioux stream which is the main landing and put-in for rafts. Land here if you want to scout the **Rabioux rapid**.

An island in the middle of the river leads down to the crux of the rapid - the right-hand channel normally gives the easier run, the left-hand one often has some good waves for surfing. Immediately below the island the river narrows and funnels close to some rocks on the left, forming one or more big holes and waves. This is a premier play spot for those who enjoy performing kayak acrobatics to an appreciative audience. You can eddy-out either right or left and then land on the beach for a rest and an ice cream. This is also the climax of any raft trip and there's usually a couple of professional photographers taking shots, besides a cluster of lesser camera vultures and beach lizards.

In our experience, this is a relatively safe spot to take a swim, but in high water conditions this could be a long one, taking you far downstream - note that after 400m cliffs come down to the river and there is no further access on the right bank. The main hazard, however, is probably being in a collision with another kayak, raft or swimmer!

Continuing on from the Rabioux the river is an easy class 3, sometimes class 2, with a powerful current to bowl you along. Several islands in the next few kilometres test your skills at route finding and the ancient Abbey Les Baumes can be seen through the trees to the right after 3 km. Look out for a long rapid on the left of the river, and be prepared to eddy out half way down on the left to catch a great surf. Some other long but easy wave train rapids give experts a chance to combine sight-seeing with a bit of surfing - do keep looking back upstream as there are some excellent vistas.

A small stream is on the right 200m before the little used egress point on the opposite bank that leads to the village of St André. Wooded banks, sandstone cliffs (good eddy spots for enders and cart wheels), more islands and easy rapids continue for the next 3 km, with almost no signs of civilisation. Then this suddenly changes as you come round a bend: the Crévoux stream comes in left, followed by the bridge, **le Pont Neuf**, cars and people. Be wary of the rapid below the bridge - the powerful current jets into an undercut rock on the right and creates some turbulent water which is ideal for stern dips and accidental swims.

Below here a small road now follows the right bank and it's possible to take out in several places on the right in the next 2 km. If continuing to the bridge or the lake, beware of the last little drop that might have been built out from the right bank just upstream of the main Embrun bridge. A classic trip - and time to celebrate!

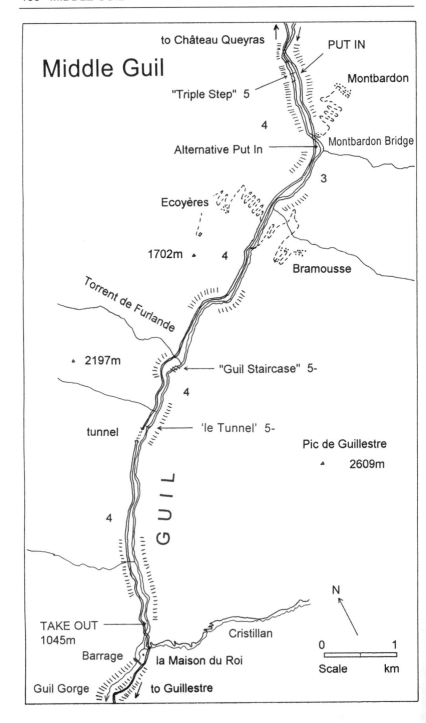

Middle Guil

to Château Queyras

PUT IN

Montbardon

"Triple Step" 5

4

Montbardon Bridge

Alternative Put In

3

Ecoyères

1702m   4

Bramousse

Torrent de Furlande

2197m

"Guil Staircase" 5-

4

'le Tunnel' 5-

Pic de Guillestre

2609m

tunnel

4

G U I L

TAKE OUT
1045m

Cristillan

Barrage

la Maison du Roi

Guil Gorge   to Guillestre

N

0   1

Scale   km

Middle Guil

From:	Triple Step	Difficulty:	**4** (5)
To:	Maison du Roi	Gradient:	23 m/km
Distance:	9 kms	WW Stars:	★★★
Time:	3 hours	Scenery:	❀❀
Best months:	May to July	Flow:	25 cumecs = MW
Bank support:	Limited	Gauge:	N94 road bridge
Water temp:	cool	Ass. runs:	Guardian Angel Gorge,
Water quality:	good		Guil Gorge.

Summary
Probably the best class 4 paddle in the southern Alps: continuous, fast water, like a non-stop slalom course. Easily scouted from the road alongside.

Special points
This is a popular angling river: please paddle in regulated times only - normally 9.30.a.m. to 6.00.p.m. in the summer- see signs at the main access points.

The River
The Guil is one of the most beautiful and least spoilt rivers in the French Alps - and certainly one of the best for white water. Much of the valley is protected as the Parc Naturel Regional du Queyras. There are no big glaciers feeding the headwaters so the flow of the river drops considerably from July onwards. In the right water levels local experts like to paddle most of the river as one run down from Abries to the Maison du Roi, some 25 km, most of which is class 4 or above.

Different water levels however, are best for different sections: the upper Guil is best in high water, when the two difficult sections just below, the Château Queyras Gorge and Guardian Angel Gorge, are dangerous. A dam at Maison du Roi, the take-out for the run on the middle Guil, normally diverts the water from the section below, the Guil Gorge, but the water comes back in again for the last few kilometres of the river - the section we call the lower Guil. The middle run of the Guil is normally considered as the classic run and is described here - the other shorter sections are described at the end of this chapter.

A phenomenally large flood in June 2000 caused huge damage to the Guil valley (see inset) and changed this run - but not as much as was feared. You will notice changes to some rapids, noticeably 'le Tunnel', however we are happy to report that the character and difficulty of the run is much the same as before.

Rafting
The Guil offers some of the most exciting rafting in the Alps - see article on page 37. The rafting season normally opens in the middle of May with trips on the upper Guil and then as water levels drop, so runs open up on the middle Guil and then the Château Queyras and Guardian Angel Gorges. Smaller rafts and one man 'hot-dogs' are used in late season. A plus point for the Guil is that the water temperature is quite user-friendly, varying between cool and warm.

Access and Logistics

The D902 road follows close by the river and makes access and road support easy. On your way up the valley we suggest that you stop just after the road tunnel to inspect 'Le Tunnel' and the 'Staircase' rapids.

We suggest a **put-in** just below the 'Triple Step' - there's limited parking on both sides of the road and starting here throws you straight into dramatic, class 4 action in a photogenic setting. A more mellow place to put in is at Montbardon bridge (there is a parking spot on the upstream side of the bridge river right) which gives you a kilometre or so of class 3 to warm up. The usual **take out** is at the parking spot upstream of the lake - take time to check the egress from the river, which although signed, is easily missed (and an interesting climb out if you do!).

The Run

Ask well-travelled paddlers what is their favourite river in the Alps, and this one would be top of many people's lists. Drop follows drop, follows drop - look back over your shoulder and you can see what looks like a staircase of small rapids disappearing upstream, flanked by the impressive rock walls of 'la Combe de Queyras'. Experts will probably do most of this run by eddy-hopping from boulder to boulder; one or two rapids, however, will still need scouting from the bank.

Many paddlers like to compare this run with the lower Guisane, both classics in the same area. We reckon that the Guil has the edge because it's longer, the scenery is more spectacular, the water warmer, and it has several rapids with their own strong personalities. The road alongside does detract from the experience a little, but this is more than made up for by the scope for scouting, and photography.

Those new to the river, often use those classic words "it looked o.k. from the road" and it's quite typical for a group of 6 paddlers to start from Triple Staircase, and only 2 reach to finish the whole run! So, if this is your first time, or you're a little doubtful about whether you want to do the whole run, or if you're short of time, then we recommend doing this run backwards - first putting in below 'Le Tunnel' and paddling the last 3 km down to the lake - a great section with nothing too serious plus the lake at the bottom in which to recover boats and bodies. This is a popular training run with clubs and kayak schools who often start by running the last rapid and then work their way up the river, building experience with each run.

Stuart Woodward makes the point that at low and medium levels this run offers a very structured run (unlike the more helter-skelter runs of say the lower Guisane, or the Onde) so it offers a good environment for practising river leadership skills. Although the road follows the river quite closely, egress to the highway can involve a tricky climb. Note that there is no path on the river left bank, which is quite wild.

The run is at its best for paddling at medium levels, but still in our opinion worth doing at low levels - don't be put off too much if it looks low from the road - it will be better on the water. At higher flows, this is obviously a river for experienced boaters who can decide and make their own lines, without relying on others.

Viewing the run on your drive up the road will give you the best idea of water levels and difficulty. The old gauge at Montbardon bridge is no longer reliable but there is a new gauge just downstream of where the N94 crosses the river and suggested levels are given in the following table:

gauge cm	typical month	level	cumecs	class.
100	April-May	very high	40	5
80	May	high	25	4+
60	June	medium	15	4
50	July	low	10	4-
40	August	too low	6	no

New Gauge below main N94 bridge

Description

The usual start is in the spectacular 'Combe du Queyras' where sheer rock cliffs shoot straight up for several hundred metres. Put in just below the '**Triple step**' rapid which is fairly obvious from the road. Rafts often shoot this, and it makes a very photogenic setting if any young tigers in your group are tempted - we should warn you that we've seen a kayaker shoot the main fall the **'Shower Curtain'** and then disappear from view completely for several minutes because he'd come up under the undercut ledge on the right! The top fall 100m above 'Triple step' is a class 5 with an undercut boulder and should be carefully inspected (The flood of 2000 changed this).

Non-stop action follows: there's another tasty rapid 100m downstream and a third "slotty" one before you come down to **Montbardon bridge** and the small settlement of la Chapelue. This is a more relaxed **alternative put-in** as the river eases off a bit for the next kilometre before the fun starts again. Three kilometres of wonderful white water take you past **le Pont de Bramousse** down to la Torrent de Furlande. a steep valley entering from the right.

Just below. is a landslide on the left and a graveyard of boulders and scree debris that forms the '**Guil Staircase**' (also known locally as 'the Labyrinth'), a long boulder garden that may be a class 5, depending on water level. This is worth scouting if you have not checked it out from the road on the way up. It changes from year to year and in 2002 it changed dramatically no less than 3 times. It often forms three distinct steps with the last one close to the road - and at times this last drop may form a headwall rapid with a dangerous undercut.

Just under a kilometre of paddling brings you to '**le Tunnel**', a difficult rapid next to the upstream entrance to the road tunnel.(prior to the flood of 2000 this was a nasty slot of a rapid called the 'Letter Box'). Neither rapid nor tunnel is obvious from the river so it's a good idea to have checked the break-out in advance and perhaps to be met by your bank support, if any. The difficulty and danger will depend on the water level, but most paddlers portage this rapid by a short well-worn path on the river right. The old road around the outside of the tunnel now makes a shady picnic and access point.

The last 3 km from here down to the dam normally has no nasty surprises and can usually be paddled by eddy hopping - it's an excellent stretch of white water that continues almost flat out down to the lake with two bigger drops a few hundred metres above the take out that attract the photographer. These make a magnificent finish to this unique run - one that will leave you both exhausted and elated! Don't let this elation make you miss the take out which is before the lake, on the last bit of a rapid. and there is no real eddy so it's easy to shoot past without noticing.

Lesser Classics

Middle Durance

From:	Argentière	Difficulty:	**2** (3)
To:	St Clement	Gradient:	5m/km
Distance:	19 km	WW Stars:	★★
Time:	3 hours	Scenery:	✹✹
Best months:	July to Sept.	Flow:	40 cumecs = MW
Bank support:	reasonable	Gauge:	none

Summary

A relatively easy, wide river with a fast current flowing over gravel beds and shingle rapids - class 2 apart from one long rapid. This makes a good introduction to the speed of larger Alpine rivers - the only hazards are likely to be a long cold swim and the occasional tree "sweeper" on outside bends where the current has undercut the shingle bank. Rock breakwaters are sometimes built to protect these banks and can create an occasional play wave for the enjoyment of the more experienced paddler, who will also enjoy the sharp eddy lines that are good for play moves. Best place to **put in** is a rafting ramp on the right and downstream side of the D104 road bridge downstream of the campsite at Argentière. It's easy to take out at any of the bridges en route.

3km downstream is the next road bridge, and after this, and just before Roche de Rame, is a long easy class 3 rapid with some big bouncy standing waves - all seemingly straight forward and great fun, except that lurking at the bottom is a big rock that forms a pour-over at high flows.

The Millennium Flood

In early June 2000 the Guil went ballistic. The area of the Queyras, from where the river flows, received six days of continuous torrential rain. The river at 70 - 80 cumecs is huge, grey and virtually unrunnable, but imagine it at the height of the flood when 1,000 cumecs was recorded through the dam at Maison-du-Roy! Debris and the shear force of the water destroyed the top section of this dam, ripping the steel gates apart. The river washed away 300 metres of road at Montbardon and also washed through a campsite leaving it as a gravel bed and moved rocks as big as our minibus.

An entire sawmill was washed into the river, leaving timber along the river banks for some 30 kilometres. Some time after the flood we discovered a bulldozer bucket or a piste basher wedged (above the narrows) in the famous Château Queyras Gorge - this, along with other debris has now been cleared by the French authorities.

Stuart Woodward

Middle Guil   *Peter Knowles*

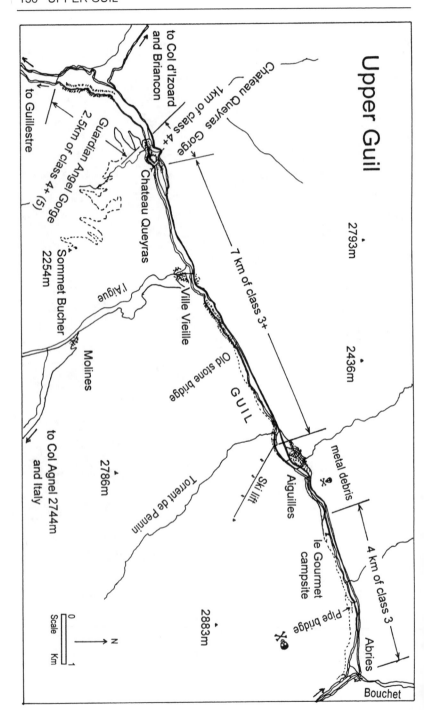

Upper Guil

to Col d'Izoard
and Briancon

Chateau Queyras Gorge
1km of class 4+

Guardian Angel Gorge
2.5km of class 4+ (5)

to Guillestre

Sommet Bucher
2254m

Chateau Queyras

l'Aigue

Ville Vieille

Molines

2793m

2436m

7 km of class 3+

Old stone bridge

G U I L

metal debris

Aiguilles

Ski lift

Torrent de Pennin

to Col Agnel 2744m
and Italy

2786m

le Gourmet
campsite

4 km of class 3

2883m

Pipe bridge

Abries

Bouchet

Scale
0 ——— 1
Km

N →

Upper Guil from Abries

From:	Abries	Difficulty:	3
To:	1.5km upstream of Aiguilles	Gradient:	13 m/km
Distance:	4 km	WW Stars:	★★
Time:	1 hour	Scenery:	✤✤✤
Best months:	May to July	Flow:	5 cumecs = MW
Bank support:	good	Gauge:	N94 road bridge

Summary
This is an ideal run for anyone looking for a relatively straight forward, fast, descent in a **beautiful high Alpine Valley** - you're up here at about 1500m and Stuart Woodward says *'note the fresh Alpine air - and bring your drycag!'*. It is best at high water levels, above 60 cm on the gauge at the N94 road bridge. (The river upstream of Abries is possible in high water levels from about 4km above l'Echalp) The road is close and the run should be inspected on your drive up the valley - especially the approach to the weir at the take out and the pipe bridge.

Put in at the remains of the old bridge, down the first rough track on the upstream outskirts of Abries, just above the confluence with the Bouchet (this almost doubles the volume). After 2km there is a **dangerous pipe bridge** which will need a short portage. Take out at the next bridge (where the road goes off to 'le Gournet' campsite) above a broken weir. The section below down to Aiguilles contains lots of metal debris and broken concrete pipe and is not recommended.

Upper Guil from Aiguilles

From:	Aiguilles	Difficulty:	3+
To:	Chateau Queyras	Gradient:	13 m/km
Distance:	7 km	WW Stars:	★★
Time:	2 hours	Scenery:	✤✤
Best months:	May to July	Flow:	5 cumecs = MW
Bank support:	limited	Gauge:	N94 road bridge

Summary
An interesting and varied paddle that includes a short gorge that is an ideal introduction to gorge paddling for those new to this deviant activity. It is best at high water levels, above 60 cm on the gauge at the N94 road bridge. **Put in** next to the ski lifts at Aiguilles and then there are 3km of easy class 3 paddling with beautiful high Alpine valley scenery down to an old stone bridge. This marks the 'entertaining paddle at good water levels. The road is some way above so there is that real feeling of commitment that such gorges inspire.

The valley widens out through the village of Ville Vielle and then 2km ahead the impressive fortress of Chateau Queyras can be seen guarding the valley. **Take out** here next to the ice cream stand. This last section makes a fine straight forward fast. big. bouncy run in high water, but beware. as there are few eddies in the final approach to the infamous Chateau Queyras Gorge!

Château Queyras Gorge - Guil

From:	Château Queyras	Difficulty:	**4+**
To:	bridge below	Gradient:	25m/km
Distance:	1 km	WW Stars:	★★★
Time:	½ hour	Scenery:	❀❀
Best months:	June to August	Flow:	7 cumecs = MW
Bank support:	No	Gauge:	N94 road bridge

Summary

A spectacular, infamous, sheer-sided gorge that looks horrendous, has been the site of many epics, and is the subject of many bar stories. *"Stiffen the sinews and summon up the blood"* wrote Terry Storry, and he's right - this is one of those runs which is guaranteed to get the adrenaline flowing just by looking at it! Almost everyone we know who has paddled this reckons that at low to medium levels it is easier than it looks - but the author is not convinced: I got well and truly trashed in the first stopper and the resulting "swim" was like being flushed down a toilet!

Note that the Millennium flood changed the gorge and at high water levels there is now a new re-circulating eddy and stopper on the left in an undercut (that you cannot see from above) that traps swimmers, and from where rescue is impossible - in 2001 there were two near fatalities.....

This run should be inspected beforehand in case a tree trunk (or raft!) is blocking it. Most of it can be viewed from a minor road on river left. Where the road and river separate is the end of the most difficult part.

The finish is where the river passes under a minor road bridge. The gauge at the N94 road bridge gives a good idea of river levels and the likely difficulty:

gauge cm	typical month	level	cumecs	class.
100	April-May	very high	12	Help!
80	May	high	12	5
60	June	medium	8	4+
50	July	low	5	4
40	August	very low	3	4

New Gauge below main N94 bridge

Guardian Angel Gorge - Guil (Gorge de L'Ange Gardien)

From:	bridge below Château Queyras	Difficulty:	**4+** (5)
To:	road below gorge	Gradient:	30 m/km
Distance:	2.5km	WW Stars:	★★
Time:	2½ hours	Scenery:	❀❀
Best months:	June to August	Flow:	7 cumecs = MW
Bank support:	limited	Gauge:	N94 road bridge

Summary

This is very different from the Château Queyras gorge. It's more like a Corsican river with many shoots and falls over, around, and under huge rocks. Most of the falls are difficult and if you're not with someone who knows the run well, most will need to be inspected from the bank before being shot. Inspection, safety cover, and portage, will involve a lot of scrambling around, and take time - frustrating if you are not mentally prepared.

The **put-in** is at the road bridge at the end of the Château Queyras gorge; then there is just over a km of easy water before the remains of an old foot bridge (washed away in the floods of 2000) marks the start of hostilities - if you do not like what you see ahead, now is the time to walk out up the path on the right. Once past here, the gorge is a 'river of no return' with cliffs dropping to the river - the only way out in the event of emergency is a rough fishermen's path on the right about half way down the gorge.

The gorge is just over a kilometre long, but feels much longer! After about 750m the cliffs on the left open out a little and you come to a class 5 drop where at medium and high levels most of the river flows into a big, horrible, hole centre and right - this is normally portaged at these levels. Note the rock high up on the skyline near the end of the gorge that looks like an angel - hence the name. Water levels and corresponding difficulty are the same as indicated for the Château Queyras gorge. This run finishes at a picnic site near where you rejoin the main road again, just past the remains of an old bridge.

If you intend to continue down the next section, the **middle Guil**, then make sure that you have scouted 'triple step' rapid, which immediately follows just after the next road bridge.

Guil Gorge

From:	Maison du Roi	Difficulty:	**4+** (6)
To:	Eygliers bridge	Gradient:	25 m/km
Distance:	4km	WW Stars:	★
Time:	3 hours	Scenery:	⊕⊕
Best months:	June to August	Flow:	15 cumecs = MW
Bank support:	no	Gauge:	no

Summary

This is an exceptionally committing gorge. The river level is controlled by the dam and normally there is insufficient water. There may be adequate water after rain but beware, because the dam sluices can open automatically at any time and a 20 cumecs wall of water will sweep down the river - some German kayakers died a few years ago when this happened. One local expert described running this section as *'a bit like Russian Roulette'*!

You can reach the **put-in** by scrambling down the bank near a lay-by after the first tunnel downstream of the dam. Throw ropes are needed to lower the boats. Once on, the river is class 3, then a class 4 rapid leads into a long section of class 5 & 6 that has to be portaged right. Steve Fullard says: *"this is a proper gorge with magnificent sheer sides - a forbidding, lonely place with no escape except down river"*. Note that normally once a year, the EDF will open the sluice gates fully to empty the lake - you might want to check with them by telephoning the number shown at the dam before doing this run.

Middle Guil, just below 'le Tunnel'   *Peter Knowles*

Lower Guil

From:	Eygliers bridge	Difficulty:	**3-**
To:	St Clement	Gradient:	10m/km
Distance:	7 km	WW Stars:	★★
Time:	1½ hours	Scenery:	❀❀
Best months:	June to Sept	Flow:	25 cumecs = MW
Bank support:	very good	Gauge:	N94 road bridge

Summary

A delightful little paddle under the towering cliffs of the old fortified town of Mont Dauphin that makes a friendly and ideal warm up for nervous paddlers perhaps new to the Alps. Clear blue water, white shingle. and the occasional big block that has fallen from the cliffs above, create nice little rapids with clearly defined eddies that almost justify a 3 star rating for the quality of the paddling. The water which was diverted by the dam at Maison de Roi is fed back into the river just above Eygliers bridge. so if levels are good for paddling the middle Guil, then they are normally also good for this stretch.

Put in at the bridge on the very minor narrow road from Guillestre to la Font d'Eygliers. From the N94, drive into the centre of Guillestre then turn left up the hill, signed 'Champ des Fer Parking'. Continue straight on past this, and then past a large Gites 'les Barnieres', the narrow lane levels out and then after another 600m brings you out at a panorama point. Park here for a few minutes and enjoy the magnificent view with the snow-covered Ecrins in the distance, Mont Dauphin, and the lower Guil carving its canyon below you (a fine panoramic walk sets off from here). You can see the narrow road down to the put in bridge as it hair pins below you - a grade 5 drive for mini buses with large trailers!

We recommend continuing this paddle on into the Durance to finish either at St Clement or at the Rabious, but if you want a really short paddle (2 km) then there is the possibility to take out on the left just after the N94 road bridge. Note that a gravel road follows the river on the right bank: locked gates bar the road to vehicles but this makes an easy and pleasant cycle shuttle or emergency egress at any time.

Biaisse

From:	Dormillouse	Difficulty:	**5** (6)
To:	Freissinières	Gradient:	30 m/km
Distance:	8 km	WW Stars:	★★★
Time:	4 hours	Scenery:	✿✿✿
Best months:	June-July	Flow:	7 cumecs = MW ?
Bank support:	reasonable	Gauge:	no

Summary

Josef Haas describes this as *"an absolute high point in this region blessed with so many gems"*. It is one of the hardest runs in the area and is also in a stunningly pretty valley with fine views (so it's always a beautiful river to come and check out, even if you're not too serious about running it!). Stuart Woodward makes the point that this is a very tight, fast, technical river only suitable for a small team of class 5 kayakers - "it requires re-active paddling, eddies are few and very small, there is a considerable tree hazard and you will probably have to portage at least once because of a tree blocking the river (no nice rafting company comes along to clear the river each year). If you're not sure that this is you, then don't even think about getting on the water"! Needless to say, this run is very dangerous in high water.

Access to the Biaisse is by following the D38 from where it branches off the N94 just north of La Roche-de-Rame until you come onto the D238 around Pallon, where the road runs by the river for a while. The **put-in** is at a car park at the end of the road at Dormillouse . About 1 km below the road bridge there is a class 6 fall - portage on the left by the road. The rest varies between class 3 and 5 depending on the level. At Fressinières there is long class 5 rapid which will need scouting and some protection. You can take out here, or continue to the campsite for a further 2.5 km of class 2 and 3. Stuart advises that if the level looks runnable at Fressinières and 'bump and scrape' at Dormillouse, then the level is probably about right.

Other rivers

There are many steep, smaller rivers and shorter 'creek runs' in this area that are normally best at higher flows in early season - we recommend the Alpes-Dauphine guide for more details. We recommend the **Bouchet**, 3 km at class 3+ from the junction with the Goulon down to the upper Guil at Abries.

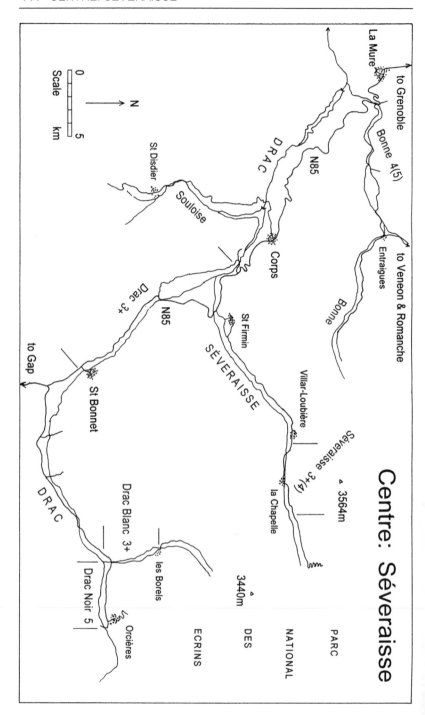

Centre: Séveraisse

The Runs

Name of run	Class	Stars	Scen	Km	cumecs	Notes
Séveraisse	3+ (4)	★★	❀❀❀	8	15	Scenic
Bonne	4 (6)	★★	❀❀	6	10	tight gorge
Drac Blanc	3+	★★	❀❀	4	10	fast and furious
Drac Noir	5	★	❀❀	5	10	tight and rocky
Drac	3+	★★	❀	20	30	high water run

The Centre

These are the rivers that drain the western slopes of the Park National des Écrins, the highest peaks of the southern Alps. The main river system is in fact the Drac, but the lower part of this river is now dammed so the classic river on this side of the mountains is the Séveraisse.

The valley of the Séveraisse is one of the most beautiful in the French Alps and it's a popular centre for French climbers, walkers, and lovers of mountain scenery, but it is relatively unknown to other nationalities. As it's around the other side of the mountains from the major river-running centre of the Durance, it's also little known amongst kayakers and rafters - it seems almost a shame to publicise it in a guide book!

If you're driving down from Britain, then the Séveraisse is en-route to the Guillestre and the Ubaye centres, is less than an hour's drive from Grenoble, and makes an enjoyable introduction to Alpine paddling.

On the River

This area offers a limited number of runs, but a surprising variety. The Séveraisse and the Drac are at their best in June and July, but the Bonne is good through to October.

Note that standard French river regulations apply, displayed at most access points: boating is normally prohibited before 10.00 a.m. and after 6.0 p.m. and on the weekend at the beginning and end of the fishing season (usually the second Saturday in March to the third Sunday in September).

Commercial Rafting

The Séveraisse and Drac both offer enjoyable, scenic, but limited runs. There is also some limited rafting on the Bonne. This is not a popular rafting centre so you will not be bumping into other rafts all the way down the river!

Off the River

The Séveraisse is a stunningly beautiful Alpine valley in which to relax. Most visitors staying here are keen outdoor folk, so are early to bed and early to rise - indeed we couldn't get a meal in a restaurant after 7.30 p.m in La Chapelle. St Firmin and La Chapelle have basic shops and a handful of restaurants and bars, but don't expect too much night life!

This is obviously a great base for mountain walking and it's well worth taking the car to the head of the valley and thinking about a walk as you sit on the terrace of the Chalet-Hotel du Giorberney admiring the mountain scenery over a drink. Because the valley is a cul-de-sac, the road isn't very busy and it's pleasant for cycling. The track on the left bank from le Bourg is a fun single track route for mountain bikes. If you're a rock climber then there are a couple of crags close to the valley bottom with well established climbing routes on them.

The la Mure mountain railway is a must for any train enthusiast and provides fine views of the lower Drac Gorges. The Museum Dauphinois in Grenoble is well worth a visit - a good idea for a wet day?

Campsites

The Séveraisse valley is so beautiful that it would be a shame to camp anywhere else. There are many sites up and down the valley, but we particularly recommend one of those by the riverside.

The site at le Bourg is pleasant, scenic and rustic, with private little clearings in the trees by the rivers. At la Chapelle, 'les Moulins', upstream of the village and by the bridge is an old favourite of paddlers, being just 5 minutes walk from bars, restaurants, and ice cream shops. There's another pleasant site near the take-out at Villar Loubière with shady clearings and good facilities, including tennis courts.

Hospital

Gap or Grenoble. Telephone 18 in case of accident (fire/ambulance/rescue).

Maps

IGN TOP100 sheet 54 'Genoble-Gap' covers this and neighbouring centres so is our recommended 'best buy'. IGN TOP25 sheet no. 3437OT, covers the Séveraisse and upper Drac in more detail.

Tourist Offices

Valgaudemar: Tel: 0492 49 09 35.   www.champsaur-valgaudemar.com
St Bonnet: Tel: 04 92 50 02 57.   www.saint-bonnet-en-chmapsaur.net.
La Mure: Tel: 04 76 81 05 71.

Rafting Operators

'Actions' specialise in the local rivers and in season have a base at La Chapelle.
Tel: 04 92 50 11 84.

Séveraisse looking upstream from la Chapelle. *Peter Knowles*

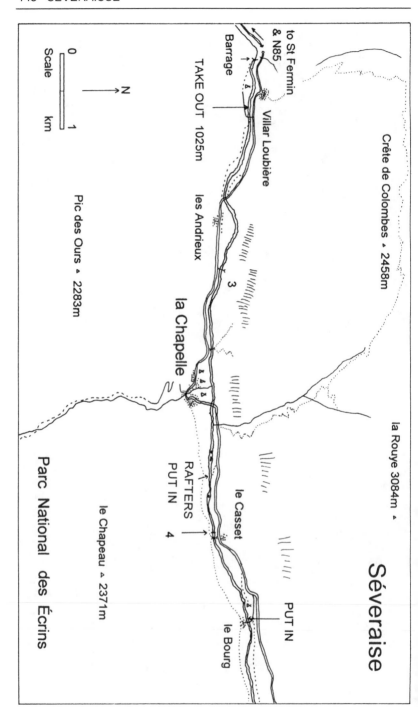

Séveraisse

From:	le Bourg	Difficulty:	**3+** (4)
To:	Villar Loubière	Gradient:	20 m/km
Distance:	8 km	WW Stars:	★★
Time:	1½ hours	Scenery:	✹✹✹
Best months:	June & July	Flow:	15 cumecs
Bank support:	reasonable	Gauge:	Villar Loubière
Water temp:	cold	Ass. runs:	Bonne, Drac.
Water quality:	good		

Summary
A fast enjoyable paddle in a stunningly beautiful valley.

Special points - none.

The River
The Séveraisse rises from, and drains many of the glaciers of the Parc National des Écrins, and its valley is surrounded by 3000m peaks. Although a relatively small river, the large glacial watershed means that it retains its flow better than comparable rivers and is still runnable in early August. Most of the flow is captured by a H.E.P. barrage at Villar Loubière (just below the take-out) and the water is then channelled back into the river near its confluence with the Drac.

Rafting
This is an exceptionally photogenic raft run. Runs are dependent on the water levels, so later in the season will be best late in the day when the river is high. The run is fast and continuous, good fun and has no special hazards, and is equally suitable for rafts, mini-rafts, and hot-dogs. The river gets too shallow for rafting around early August.

Access and Logistics
You have good views of the river as you drive up the valley. The usual put-in is just upstream of the bridge at le Bourg. The take-out is upstream of Villar Loubière where the road runs close to the river, and downstream of the bridge to the campsite. Stop at le Casset on your way up the valley if you want to scout the crux of this section - if you want to avoid this class 4 section there is an alternative put in used by the rafting companies 1km downstream of le Caset where a track runs down to the river.

The river is predominantly glacial melt so on a sunny day there will be a big variation in the flow, and because it takes quite a while for the water to flow down the valley: the peak flow normally occurs about midnight - this means that the best time to do a run is usually early evening, or, for the real keenies - sunrise!

There is a gauge by the bridge at Villar Loubière: locals reckon that 50 cm is a good level and roughly corresponds to 15 cumecs, 40 cm is a minimum for rafts, and 30 cm probably a minimum for kayaks.

The Run

Typical comments for this run are "pure dead brill" and "very friendly". It's a fast and continuous river with no bad nasties to worry about and it makes an excellent introduction to 'conveyor belt' alpine paddling. If you put in at la Chapelle then it is an easier run - class 3 for about 4.5 km down to the take-out.

We first ran this river in 1974, and being young and foolish we thought it would be fun to have a race down it on our airbeds. Our rolling ability didn't prove up-to-scratch and we lost our airbeds - penance was sleeping on the hard ground for the rest of the holiday!

Description

The usual put-in is just upstream of the bridge at **le Bourg**. (There are a couple of kilometres of 'interesting' paddling above here for any hair boaters in the party.) The kilometre down to the next bridge at **le Casset** is fast class 3+ with small eddies, boulders, drops and shoots. Just below the bridge at le Casset there is one section of about 50m of more difficult water, class 4, that can be portaged on the left bank if necessary.

Two kilometres of class 3+ water bring you down to the bridge at **la Chapelle** and from here the difficulty eases to class 3 down to **Villar Loubière**. Take out on the right about 100m downstream of the road bridge to the campsite.

Spot the difference!

1. The novice waterfall kayaker.   2. The expert waterfall kayaker.

Bonne - First drop below Pont du Prêtre. *Julie Rowan*

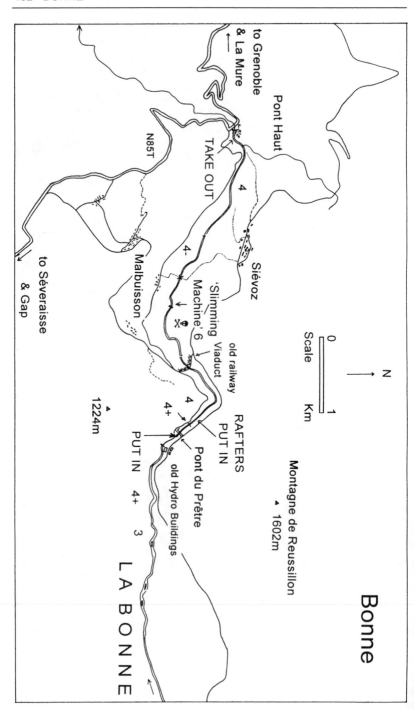

Bonne

LA BONNE

Bonne

From:	Pont du Prêtre	Difficulty:	**4 (6)**
To:	Pont Haut, RN85	Gradient:	25 m/km
Distance:	6 km	WW Stars:	★★
Time:	2 hours	Scenery:	✤✤
Best months:	July to Sept.	Flow:	10 cumecs = MW
Bank support:	No	Gauge:	Pont du Prêtre
Water temp:	cool	Ass. runs:	Séveraisse, Veneon.
Water quality:	good		

Summary
A beautiful, tight, committing gorge. Blue water, black rock and lush green vegetation. Very different from other rivers in this book.

Special Points
A considerable **tree hazard,** a powerful current, limited and small eddies, make this run only suitable for small groups of experienced paddlers.

The River
The Bonne is the next river valley north of the Séveraisse and in its upper valley it shares many similar features, including lovely clear water. What makes this river quite unique though, is that lower down the valley, on its way down to join the Drac, the rock strata causes the river to cut a knife edge slit of a gorge . This is a unique kind of gorge that brings a smile and a sparkle to the eyes of even the most blasé old river dog.

Rafting
Very tight and committing, but it is rafted by local specialists 'Actions' using rafts in July and then 'hotdogs' and hydrospeeds from August through until October. This is an adventurous trip for active people!

Access and Logistics
An old railway line runs along part of the valley and crosses high over the river on a viaduct. This has now been converted into a road and makes a great viewpoint for checking out the top stretch. Inspect this top section carefully and check out the top drop, because once on the river, you will probably not be able to stop in time if a tree is blocking this.

Put in just upstream of the Pont du Prêtre on the river left (upstream from here is an old H.E.P. plant and barrage) or downstream of the bridge and the first drop at the first layby on the river right. Take out at the Pont Haut, where the N85 crosses the river - a rough road goes steeply down to the river on the upstream, left hand bank.

The top section of the run, down to the viaduct, is committing and it would be difficult if not impossible to climb out of the gorge. At the viaduct, and below, it should be possible in emergency to scramble out in many places, through woods and fields.

The Run

One German kayaker said *"some of my most beautiful paddling memories are of the Bonne"*. This is unlike any other run we know in the Alps: another paddler put it, "it's like some Alpine version of the Spean Gorge" (in Scotland). It's a tight steep, V-shaped gorge with smooth rock walls running straight into a cleft of a river. As you can imagine from this, the water is channelled into a powerful current and there are not many break-outs, and never where you want them - this is short boat country and requires confident paddling! This is, however, a great fun run, and even at low water levels there are still a few play spots for looping.

The Bonne normally has too much water in early summer, so when other rivers are too low, this run is likely to be at a good level. There is a gauge under the bridge at the Pont du Prêtre (ignore the one a few metres downstream): between 70 and 80 cm is probably the ideal level for a run (80 cm = MW and is approx. 10 cumecs?). Over 100 cm and your mother is definitely not going to be happy with you, and you probably won't be either. Because the gorge is so narrow, it holds its water level and you can still have a good run in low water at the end of August.

If the level is 80 cm or above, then it's possible to put on further up the valley at Entraigues for 5km of class 3 warm-up - pleasant but rather uninspiring.

Note that in every description of this river, and from most paddlers we have talked to who have run it, **log jams of fallen trees** have been encountered, usually on the second half of the run below the viaduct.

Description

From the put-in at Pont du Prêtre it is fast water to the first drop about 100m downstream of the bridge - a class 4+, metre wide, blind slot which has a substantial stopper in high water. This may be blocked by a tree so it is best to inspect this beforehand. To scout or avoid this drop, use the rough path to the **alternative put in** (used by rafters) which starts below - follow a rough path that leads down from the first lay-by, 200m downstream of the bridge on the right side of the river.

From here it is a couple of hundred metres of paddling and then you're into the V-slot log flume that you could see from the old railway line and that continues to below the **viaduct**.

The river then widens out slightly, maybe 5m instead of 2m, still fast water but it now undergoes a change of character with densely wooded banks. Just over 1 km after the viaduct is the dangerous, **class 6, 'l'Infran'**. It's not obvious from the river and there are no good eddies immediately above, so you need to be alert to land in good time on the river right. One clue is the slate-like slabs of rock that slope towards the river on the river right. The crux is a 1.5 m drop through a very tight crevice. This is unrunnable at most water levels (it also acts as a natural tree collector) and it is normally portaged on the right. Take care - in 1995 a German kayaker slipped on the rocks whilst trying to help his friend and was killed. Ian Fairclough reports that it is fairly easy to scout this beforehand by walking up the north bank of the river from Malbuisson bridge. There's a super little seal launch just below.

About 500m below this crux rapid is the old stone arch bridge of **Malbuisson**, and a kilometre below here the river changes character yet again as it enters an area of soft shale deposits.   When we were here in 1994 there had been a landslide and it seemed that half a forest had been washed into the river, creating five log jams in the next kilometre - this detracted from an otherwise excellent run.

Take out left (just after a stream comes in right) before and in sight of the high bridge.   A track leads up to the main road and a bar/restaurant on the other side of the bridge.

Entrée du désert de la Grande Chartreuse   *Alexandre Debelle*

Lesser Classics

Drac Blanc

From:	Les Borels	Difficulty:	**3+**
To:	Confluence	Gradient:	26 m/km
Distance:	4 km	WW Stars:	★★
Time:	½ hour	Scenery:	⊕⊕
Best months:	June-July	Flow:	10 cumecs = MW
Bank support:	good	Gauge:	Take-out bridge

Summary *(Pat's Guide)*

This is a small river, but fast and furious without a break-out to be found. The put-in is upstream of the bridge where the road crosses the river above Les Borels. The run may be class 4 in higher water and it is certainly more fun than it looks, but it wouldn't be funny if someone went for a swim. It's basically a straight thrash with the last kilometre as class 2.

Take out at the road bridge just upstream of the confluence (below here, a barrage abstracts most of the water - there is a gauge at this bridge (river right) - at 80 cm tree branches will be right across the river.

Drac Noir

From:	Orcières	Difficulty:	**5**
To:	Confluence	Gradient:	30 m/km
Distance:	5 km	WW Stars:	★
Time:	2½ hours	Scenery:	⊕⊕
Best months:	June-July	Flow:	10 cumecs = MW
Bank support:	limited	Gauge:	see text

Summary (Pat's Guide)

This is totally different to the Drac Blanc. The upper and lower sections are tight, difficult, rocky, low volume class 5; whilst the middle part is gravel beds, with many islands, shallow easy water, but with desperate undergrowth hazards! We had a good level, but it was not flood conditions. There is a gauge on the river, but it's about half-way down the second class 5 section.

The put-in is at the road bridge by Orcières where the road goes up to Les Audibers (there is some harder paddling for hair boaters higher up). The water is immediately hard, and continues like that for about 500m down to the next bridge. Then starts the gravel section, which has little to recommend it except as a link to the next part of the river, in about 2 km distance.

A bridge, plus a stream dropping precipitously on the left, marks the next stage of the river, a section of over a kilometre of class 5 for which inspection is essential. Take out at the pipe bridge or at the confluence with the Drac Blanc.

Drac

From:	St Bonnet	Difficulty:	**3+**
To:	Lac du Sautet	Gradient:	10 m/km
Distance:	20 km	WW Stars:	★★
Time:	4 hours	Scenery:	✸
Best months:	May to July	Flow:	30 cumecs = MW
Bank support:	limited	Gauge:	Café du Drac

Summary (Pat's Guide)

This section of the Drac proper is well below the confluence of the Drac Noir and the Drac Blanc (the river between is flat and has most of its water abstracted). This is a large river, but even with a good water level it is rather shallow and it is not worth doing in low water. It normally has long sections of class 2 and 3 with no special hazards, but in high water (we paddled it when it was chocolate coloured), it goes up to a big bouncy class 4. It's a long paddle with the occasional wave or stopper that is worth playing on, and a fast current makes it a good run for beginners or a fine introduction to Alpine paddling.

If you get bored you can take out where the N85 crosses the river at the Café du Drac. This half way point is a good spot for lunch as it's a couple more hours gentle paddle down from here to the lake. Take out at the D457 road bridge, which turns off the N85 at le Motty. The river below here runs into a gorge and over a **7m barrage** before the lake so do not attempt to paddle beyond this bridge.

Other rivers

The **Vénéon** is the next valley north over the pass from the Bonne and is described under Briançon Centre. The **Souloise** is sometimes kayaked and rafted when river levels are good, normally in June, and is mainly class 4 with one portage. The **lower Séveraisse**, below the barrage at Villar Loubière, rarely has water in it but may be worth a trip - it's usually graded a class 3 & 4 and has some weirs.

If you are here in the area in spring or autumn when water levels are up, then there are several shorter, 'creek' style runs that are listed in the 'Alpes Dauphine' kayaking guidebook.

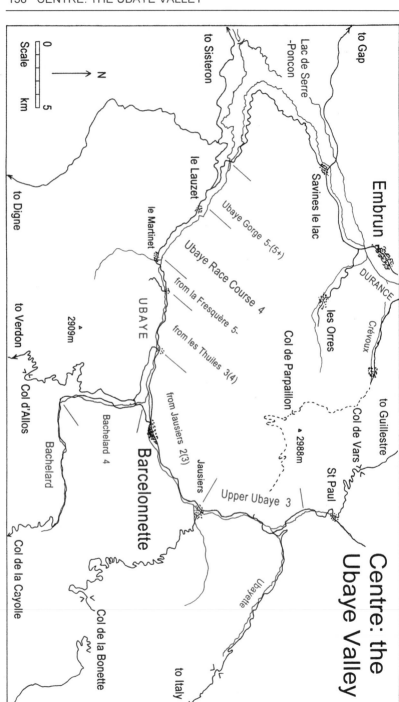

Centre: the Ubaye Valley

The Runs

Name of run	Class	Stars	Scen	Km	cumecs	Notes
Ubaye Race Course	4	★★★	❀❀	8	30	Justly popular
Upper Ubaye	3	★★	❀❀	13	10	recommended
Ubaye from Jausiers	2 (3)	★	❀	13	20	high water run ?
- from Les Thuiles	3 (4)	★★	❀	5	25	large open valley
- from La Fresquière	5	★★	❀❀	2.5	25	challenging run
Ubaye Gorge	5- (6)	★★★	❀❀❀	4	20	low water run
Le Bachelard	4	★★	❀❀	8	10	May-June

The Centre

The Ubaye is the only major river in the southern Alps which has not yet been dammed: it still flows natural and free, and so is a magnet for river runners. The valley is about an hour's drive from the lower Durance and you could drive across every day, but this seems a shame as this is a very different valley offering a wide choice of runs so it makes sense to stay here.

On the River

The source of the Ubaye is on the Italian border next to the headwaters of the Guil and it's navigable from above St Paul, giving over 60 km of white water at different classes of difficulty and in an unspoilt valley. A couple of the smaller tributaries of the river flow through shale deposits so unfortunately the water colour is often grey, although the temperature is almost warm.

Runs on the upper river are normally low by late summer, but the infamous Ubaye Gorge should then be at a good level. The Race Course is a justifiably popular classic run and was a 'must' for a full write up in this guide as was the main run on the upper Ubaye which makes an ideal trip for intermediates.

Note that standard French river regulations apply, displayed at most access points: boating is normally prohibited before 10.00 a.m. and after 6.0.p.m. and on the weekends at the beginning and end of the fishing season (usually the second Saturday in March to the third Sunday in September).

Commercial Rafting

Like its neighbour, the Guil, most sections of the river are rafted, depending on the water level at the time, so there is a very wide choice of runs at different levels of difficulty. The Race Course is the classic run and is very popular.

In low water conditions, the infamous Ubaye Gorge offers a class 5 run for the more experienced adventurer. The upper Ubaye is an excellent small volume trip for mini-rafts and les 'hot dogs'. The relatively warm water of the Ubaye makes it an attractive river for hydro-speeding.

Off the River

Barcelonnette is an old market town right at the centre of the valley with a thriving market, a host of specialist shops, a wide selection of bars, cafes and restaurants and a full programme of cultural events and entertainment: it must be one of the most active small towns in the whole region.

There are no less than 6 mountain passes, all offering magnificent scenery, within an hour's drive of Barcelonnette. These offer great scope for mountain walks and to members of the DMBC (Downhill Mountain Bikers Club). One of the least known, and for us the most interesting, is the old tunnel and pass over the Col de Parpaillon (2645m), a rough 4x4 track that may be best approached from the Embrun side.

A unique feature of the upper valley is the impressive old forts and gun emplacements that seem to have been built on every hill top and promontory to protect the invasion route from Italy - guided tours are offered by the local tourist office. Lower down the valley, we recommend a walk around the picturesque village of le Lauzet and down to the roman bridge. The side torrents flowing into the Ubaye offer some exhilarating canyoning.

Campsites

Barcelonnette is the most central base and has several campsites, all with good facilities. There are also sites close to the river both further upstream, and downstream at Les Thuiles. Having said this, our own preference as a base is Le Lauzet - probably because it's such a fine old village and has a mouth-watering baker, butcher, grocer and two good restaurants!

Our favourite site is at the end of the Race Course 'la Source' - this is run by the local farmer and his family and has a nice old fashioned, rural feel about it (including the facilities!). Larger groups will probably feel more at home at the municipal site in le Lauzet next to the small lake or at the other river-side site just upstream of the village 'les Bois des Hoches'.

Hospitals

Gap is probably the best choice. Also one in Embrun and a small one in Jausiers.
Telephone 18 in case of accident (fire/ambulance/rescue).

Maps

IGN Top100 sheet 54 'Grenoble-Gap' covers this and adjacent centres at a scale of 1:100.000 and is a best buy. If you are staying in the valley and want more detail for walks or bike rides then IGN TOP25 map sheet no. 3438ET, covers the lower valley and 3538ET the upper valley.

Tourist Offices

Barcelonnette, Tel: 04 92 81 04 71.
Jausiers:

www.ubaye.com
www.barcelonnette.com
www.jausiers.com

Rafting Operators

Many companies - please ask at the Tourist Office for an up-to-date list.

Kayak school and Guiding

Aqualibre, Méolans-Revel, tel: 92 81 90 96.

Shaun Baker on one of
the World's great
waterfall kayak descents
- on the lower Sorba in
the Val Sesia, in 1992.

Only half the fall is
shown on this famous
photograph.

Talking to Shaun he said
the trickiest part was to
clear and spin out of the
whirlpool / cauldron you
can see in the middle of
the drop - he just
managed to do this but
as you can see at the
bottom of the
photograph, this flipped
him so that he slid down
the bottom half of the
fall upside down.

He was very thankful
that he was wearing
body armour!

Philippe Fragnol

Lower Durance, playing on the way to Embrum.

Sue Richardso

Lower Durance, Rabioux rapid.   *Peter Knowles*

Lower Durance, ICCC armchair paddlers.   *Harry Wood*

Verdon pre-canyon.

Paul Mackenzie

Can a paddler influence things?

All over the Alps we are faced with the same scenario: dammed rivers and flooded valleys, followed by a barren river bed and parched vegetation. In most cases it is too late to do anything about these projects, but in some instances the final stone has not been laid, and the final word has not been said. What that final word is could depend on you.

In this we're not just talking about direct action like writing to the relevant authorities - although this too helps. The thing that will really make the difference at the end of the day is not how many people have written to how many politicians, but what the locals think and there are any number of ways in which we, as occasional visitors to an area can influence this.

It's simple things that will make a difference. If paddlers use a campsite, rather than dossing in a lay-by, then they are pumping money into the local economy (money that could always come from the sale of land to the electricity companies....) If we eat and drink in local pubs and cafes, if we buy our food from local shops rather than city supermarkets - the same thing is true. If we change discretely.... Then we become tourists that are welcomed rather than unwelcome parasites who are barely tolerated.

In country areas, small things can make a big difference.

-   The world is complete, it cannot be improved,
-   Those who would own it, will lose it,
-   Those who would change it will destroy it.   Lao Tse

Peter Bandtock

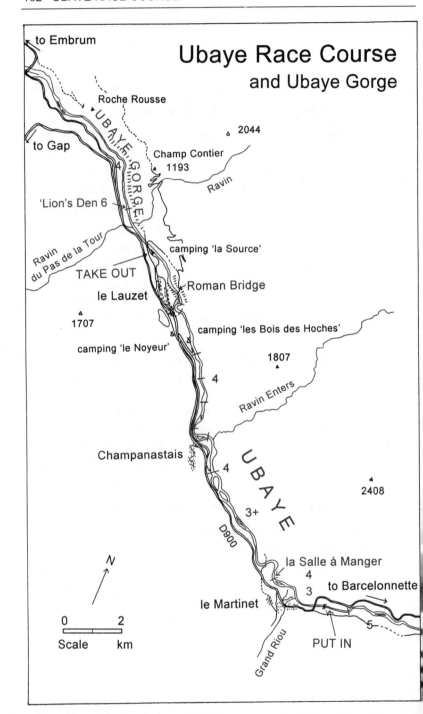

Ubaye Race Course
and Ubaye Gorge

to Embrum

Roche Rousse

to Gap

UBAYE GORGE

△ 2044

Champ Contier
1193

Ravin

'Lion's Den 6

Ravin
du Pas de la Tour

camping 'la Source'

TAKE OUT

Roman Bridge

le Lauzet

△
1707

camping 'les Bois des Hoches'

camping 'le Noyeur'

1807
▲

4

Ravin Enters

Champanastais

4

UBAYE

▲
2408

3+

D900

la Salle à Manger

N

4

to Barcelonnette

3

le Martinet

5

0   2

PUT IN

Scale   km

Grand Riou

Ubaye Race Course

From:	le Martinet	Difficulty:	**4**
To:	le Lauzet	Gradient:	15 m/km
Distance:	8 km	WW Stars:	★★★
Time:	2 hours	Scenery:	✹✹
Best months:	May - July	Volume:	30 cumecs = MW
Bank support:	reasonable	Gauge:	see note
Water temp:	almost warm	Ass. runs:	La Fresquière,
Water Quality:	average		Ubaye Gorge.

Summary
One of the classic white water race courses in Europe with a variety of large rapids. An unspoilt and natural flowing river in a beautiful valley.

Special points
A popular rafting run and may be crowded at peak periods.

The River
See Ubaye Centre notes.

Rafting
This is a classic raft run that is almost as popular as the lower Durance. It's slightly harder than the Durance and has more white water interest with a lot more named rapids. This makes an absolute stonker of a trip in early summer when levels are high but later on it can get a bit 'bump, scrape and bounce' and in our opinion the lower Durance is then a better run for rafts - the Ubaye then comes into its own for 'le hot-dog'.

Access and Logistics
The main highway up the valley, the D900, offers panoramic views of the river, and there are several places from where you can obtain a closer view, but there's really no need as there are no nasty rapids that need checking out in advance and why diminish the experience?

Put in by the old road bridge at le Martinet - this is clearly signposted off the new road. The take out is also signposted off the road at the bottom end of Le Lauzet: note that if you are loading boats then you can continue past the parking signs to the actual take out next to the riverside campsite 'la Source'.

The Run
This is a wide river and in medium and high flows the rapids are big and bouncy and there are some stoppers that you probably wouldn't want to play in (and some you would!). In higher flows it deserves a class 4+ rating. It compares well with the Isère. lines and eddies are fairly obvious but the power of the water requires positive paddling. At medium flows most of the river is class 3+ and easy 4, with just the named rapids lifting it to a class 4.

In many ways this run compares to a Himalayan river with lots of big boulders and ledges forming well defined eddies and play waves - so it makes a **great run for play boating** and we have come off this run after 4 hours of hard playing, absolutely knackered and content!

There are good views of wooded valley sides and distant hillsides and then at the end of the run the river narrows and it runs in a sheer-sided gorge, with the old roman bridge arching high overhead - a memorable and much photographed spot. It is a justifiably popular run and you have to accept that you are going to be sharing the river with other river users, and you need to keep a wary eye out for rafts if you are playing.

There is an old gauge on the bridge at le Martinet, but this is totally unreliable so you have to rely on your judgement, or consuit one of the rafting companies - what does it matter? - this is a run that is still fun at low flows!

Description

Put in on the left bank by the old bridge at le Martinet signposted off the road and normally busy with lots of raft groups getting ready. There's normally a couple of play waves here for limbering up on.

Just downstream of the bridge is the first big 'pumpy' rapid called 'la Salle à Manger' (the dining room) - presumably named after all the things that get eaten here. Easy water just below gives you a chance to digest and recover and if you really do have bad indigestion then the old footbridge just around the bend can be used for emergency egress to the road.

The river now settles down, but look out for the 'Tree lined avenue' a section which is fast and continuous. When you get the chance lift your eyes from the river - to the fresh vistas of mountain peaks at each bend. The next big rapid 'Champanastais' comes up when you see the small village on the hillside up on the left - after that. the major rapids come about every 500m. One notable one 'la Moustage' has a huge rock in the centre and can be viewed from the main road as you drive up the valley, but we have no intention of spoiling your fun by giving you a detailed description of all the rapids!

The run has a splendiferous finish as the river narrows into a gloomy, sheer sided. gorge with an old Roman bridge high above you. There are no significant rapids actually in the gorge, and then the campsite and take out follows 500m further on the left - take out exactly where a **water pipe** crosses the river. Go beyond the bridge and it's a river of no return, the dreaded Ubaye Gorge!

Ubaye Race Course approaching the Roman Bridge   *A.N.Rafting*

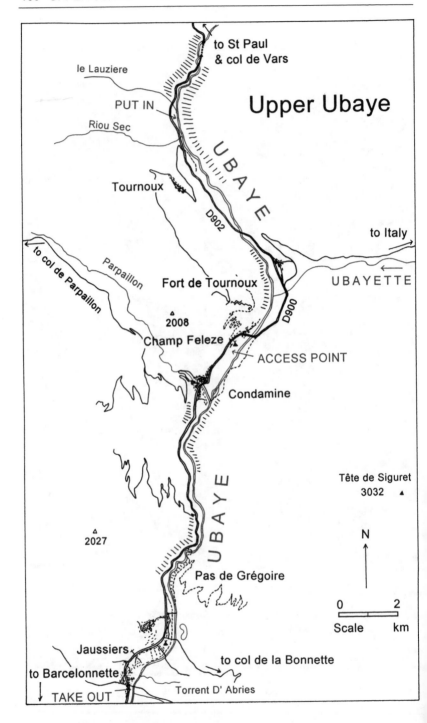

Upper Ubaye

From:	la Lauzière	Difficulty:	3
To:	Jausiers	Gradient:	12 m/km
Distance:	13 km	WW Stars:	★★
Time:	2½ hours	Scenery:	⊕⊕
Best months:	May - July	Flow:	10 cumecs = MW
Bank support:	good	Gauge:	no
Water temp:	cool	Ass. runs:	Ubaye from Jausiers
Water quality:	good		upper Guil

Summary
A fine small volume run for intermediate paddlers - one of the best in the area for training and progression.

Special Points - none

Rafting
This is a great little run in early summer when water levels are good - ideal for mini-rafts and hot-dogs.

Access and Logistics
If you are driving to this run from the Durance valley, then we recommend coming or going via Guillestre and the Col de Vars.

Put in for this run 2 km below St Paul. If water levels are low then there is an alternative access point below the confluence with the Ubayette, about 200m downstream of the main highway bridge (the D900) below the old Fort de Tournoux near the Champ Félèze campsite. The take-out is downstream of Jausiers at the Pont Barnuquel by a cross-roads and hotel on the outskirts of the town.

The River
Up here near the source, the Ubaye is fairly small volume and, as there are no major glaciers in its headwaters, water levels drop right down by August, however the Ubayette joins after 4 km and roughly doubles the flow.

The Run
In the past. before this guide book, this run has suffered from the "let's get in as high as we can" syndrome - people read that the run down from St Paul was called a grade 3-4. put in there, had an epic, and then been put off the rest of the run. It took the local rafting companies to identify la Lauzière to Jausiers as the ideal run and in our opinion they're absolutely right. None of this run drops below class 2, there are innumerable small class 3 rapids, lots of variety. and no nasty drops, weirs, or other hazards. that might need portaging. The scenery is pleasant and varied.

Even in low water, this is still an enjoyable run, but a little easier - you may, however. need to put in below the confluence of the Ubayette at Champ Félèze then making it an 8 km run.

We cannot recommend the Ubaye upstream of this run as a great deal of highway work has been done in recent years in the gorge below St Paul and there is all kinds of nasty debris in the river bed. The risks hardly seem worth the 2 km run. Note that 'sports de l'eau vive' are prohibited above St Paul.

Description

Two kilometre below St Paul is a picnic site where you can put in if you want a harder start straight into a rapid ('La Lauzière' is the small stream that comes in just above the picnic site). For many paddlers this makes for a bit of an intense start so for most people we recommend putting in where the road bridges the next stream down the valley and a track goes down to the river.

This allows a warm up as the river cuts through gravel bars, with fast water, and tree-lined banks, so beware of sweepers (trees fallen into the river). The difficulty then eases off for a while. The confluence with the **Ubayette** brings a welcome increase in volume and then on the right, the huge **Fort de Tournoux**, built in massive steps for hundreds of metres up the hillside.

The old ruined base station for the téléphérique to the fort is just downstream of the main highway bridge and this is now a 'centre d'eau vive'. There is a good access point to the river next to the 'Champ Félèze campsite. One kilometre of gravel bars brings you to the bridge at **la Condamine** and the start of some enjoyable class 3 water. This is followed shortly by 'la Rapide des Parisiens', 300m of boulders and small break-outs in a scenic little gorge. Another 2 km brings you to the 'Pas de Gregoire', another fine little gorge with a delightfully sinuous rapid and then another 1 km down to the outskirts of **Jausiers** and the first bridge. There are canalised banks and two more bridges through the town and then a jet black stream runs in from the left, just before the final bridge. **Take out** just below the bridge on the right, in some pine trees with a convenient café and bar just across the road.

Lesser Classics

Ubaye from Jausiers

From:	Jausiers	Difficulty:	**2** (3)
To:	Les Thuiles	Gradient:	8 m/km
Distance:	13 km	WW Stars:	★
Time:	3 hours	Scenery:	⊕
Best months:	June - July	Flow:	20 cumecs = MW
Bank support:	reasonable	Gauge:	no

Summary

Stuart Woodward recommends this as a high water run, finishing **at La Fabrique** after 7km. To continue to Les Thuiles has little to recommend it as it is canalised through Barcelonnette, with buildings, then gravel bars and sewage outlets below. There is one rapid at the 'Pont des David', the next bridge after the start (approx. 1 km), which is an easy class 3 and then it is straight-forward paddling down to La Fabrique. If you do continue on (Stuart Woodward says "C'est orrible") then the gravel beds finish about 1km before Les Thuiles and wooded banks commence - about half-way down this last kilometre is a **dangerous syphon on the river right.** Take out after this on the right before the bridge.

Ubaye from les Thuiles

From:	Les Thuiles	Difficulty:	**3** (4)
To:	La Fresquière	Gradient:	12 m/km
Distance:	5 km	WW Stars:	★★
Time:	1½ hours	Scenery:	⊕
Best months:	May - August	Flow:	25 cumecs = MW
Bank support:	reasonable	Gauge:	see note

Summary

Put in at the bridge just upstream of Les Thuiles. The rapid at the start is class 3+ in high water, but class 4 at lower levels, and you would be wise not to fall in as the water flows fast and shallow over sharp rocks! From here, the river is large and open, class 3. We recommend that you **take out at Rioclar 1km before La Fresquière.** The last section down to La Fresquière bridge is a technical class 4 in low water, with notable stoppers in higher water, raising the grade to 5-. The take out at La Fresquiere is not that easy to spot from the water - also to swim here, you risk being swept down the next section - sadly, one British kayaker was drowned in just this way. So consider the risk and scout this last section very carefully if you want to take out at la Fresquière.

Ubaye from la Fresquière

From:	La Fresquière	Difficulty:	**5**
To:	Le Martinet	Gradient:	22 m/km
Distance:	2.5 km	WW Stars:	★★
Time:	1 hour	Scenery:	❀❀
Best months:	June - August	Flow:	25 cumecs = MW
Bank support:	limited	Gauge:	see note

Summary

Below the bridge the river drops steeply. The first part of this section can all be viewed by walking down from the bridge. In high water the river is large, and drops over big boulders, leaving stoppers where you can't avoid them. In a little less water this becomes a good class 5 paddle, still big water, continuous, with big rocks, conspicuously small gaps and enormous stoppers. There is a second hard section near the end of the run which can be viewed from the road. It is technically difficult in low water and is probably then a hard class 4+. Note that this is a wide, powerful river, and, if you get pinned or trapped, people on the bank may not be able to reach you - **several fatalities have occurred on this section** and its difficulty should not be under-estimated, particularly at higher flows. The run finishes at the rafting centre on the left bank.

This run seems to change considerably every year - for example in the 1995 season there was a particular problem with trees stuck in and across several drops.

Ubaye Gorge

From:	le Lauzet	Difficulty:	**5- (6)**
To:	the lake	Gradient:	20 m/km
Distance:	4 km	WW Stars:	★★★
Time:	2 hours	Scenery:	❀❀❀
Best months:	August - Sept.	Flow:	20 cumecs = LW
Bank support:	limited	Gauge:	see note

Summary

An infamous gorge and one that kayakers love to talk about. Very spectacular and some hard paddling but not as committing as it might first appear. You can scramble down from the road to inspect the crux of the run and scouting, portages, and break-outs are all fairly reasonable.

We have seen this run called everything from class 4- to 6. The truth is that, like most serious gorges, **the difficulty depends on the water level.** In June this is an awesome maelstrom of white water, but by mid-August it's almost friendly and a fantastic and memorable run.

The start is very awe-inspiring as you paddle under the old railway bridge at le Lauzet between sheer rock walls, with the river bending out of sight. Relax, it's only class 3 for the first 500m past a spectacular waterfall cascading into the river on the right. A further 200m and the river narrows and obviously drops away. Land here to inspect the 'Lion's Den', the crux of the run. This is a very nasty, dangerous, class 6 drop which a few people have run (usually in higher water when the syphon is covered) however one person died here in 2000.

Immediately below is an easier rapid, class 5- in low water, and then the run becomes a hard class 4+ for the next kilometre - steep shoots, huge boulders, narrow drops, powerful water - all made more impressive by the sense of isolation down at the bottom of this magnificent gorge. After this, the difficulty eases to class 3 down to the lake. Chance to lie back in the warm waters of the lake and relax with the cold beer you had perhaps thoughtfully stuffed down the end of your friend's boat.

Ubaye from la Fresquière, kayak sinking!   *Robin Knapp*

Le Bachelard

From:	le Grand Pont	Difficulty:	4
To:	the Ubaye	Gradient:	24 m/km
Distance:	8 km	WW Stars:	★★
Time:	2 hours	Scenery:	⊕⊕
Best months:	May-June	Flow:	10 cumecs = MW
Bank support:	good	Gauge:	no

Summary

A small river in a pretty gorge with the road alongside. One writer called this "a ditch that only runs for one month a year", but others have told us that this is "an exciting, technical paddle, well worth running if there is sufficient water!"

Driving up the valley there are four bridges. The first three are quite low over the river, the fourth is high and called 'le Grand Pont'. Put in just upstream of this bridge; the tributary coming in on the right below is the Paluel and so the gorges downstream are called the 'Gorges de Paluel'. Above here is class 5 and 6 and paddling is prohibited. From the put-in to the third bridge is class 4. From there down is class 3 and 4. Take out on the right bank at the confluence with the Ubaye where there is a picnic site called 'les Graves'. Trees may be a hazard, but are normally cleared by the rafting companies in the main season.

Other rivers

The **Ubayette** is a steep bouldery torrent, with many portages. The last kilometre or so before the confluence is class 3 (4); above here, class 5 and 6. Locals warn of the remains of cables in the drops so this is probably best left to fully-wired paddlers, or those with hang-ups.

The **Stura di Demonte** is in Italy, just over the pass from the Ubayette. We've paddled it and checked it out: the bottom section of the river near Gaiola has 6 km of class 3 but in our opinion hardly merits the 80 km drive.

Ubaye Gorge, the drop below the 'Lion's den'. *Peter Knowles*

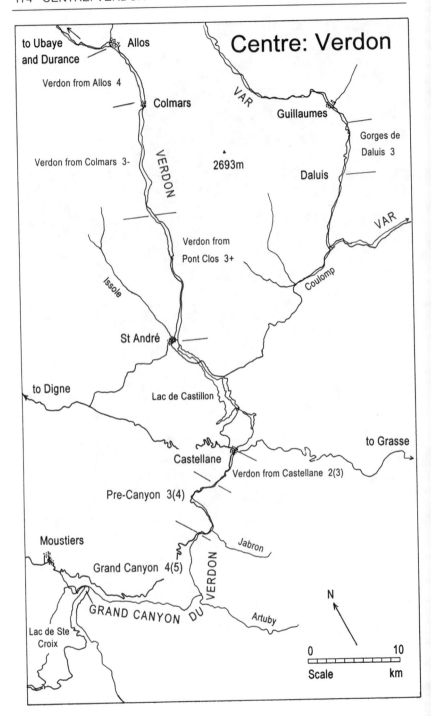

Centre: Verdon

to Ubaye and Durance

Allos

Verdon from Allos 4

Colmars

VAR

Guillaumes

VERDON

2693m

Gorges de Daluis 3

Daluis

VAR

Verdon from Pont Clos 3+

Issole

Coulomp

St André

to Digne

Lac de Castillon

to Grasse

Castellane

Verdon from Castellane 2(3)

Pre-Canyon 3(4)

Moustiers

Grand Canyon 4(5)

Jabron

VERDON

GRAND CANYON DU VERDON

Artuby

Lac de Ste Croix

N

0   10
Scale   km

Centre: Verdon

The Runs

Name of run	Class	Stars	Scen	Km	cumecs	Notes
Grand Canyon	4 (5)	★★★	❀❀❀	30	18	An expedition!
Pre-Canyon	3 (4)	★★★	❀❀	13	18	recommended
Verdon from Castellane	2 (3)	★	❀❀	6	18	Friendly
Upper Verdon from Allos	4	★	❀❀	7	7	Early season run
- from Colmars	3-	★	❀❀	15	10	Early season run
- from Pont Clos	3+	★★	❀❀	18	10	Early season run
Var - Gorges de Daluis	3	★	❀❀	7	10	Committing

The Centre

The Verdon is the most southerly major river system in the Alps and is less than 100 km from the Mediterranean, so snow melts early and the ideal time to paddle here is in May and June. However in the main summer months there are now **dam-controlled releases - usually twice a week** - for rafting below Castellane.

Much of this region of Haute-Provence is a limestone plateau, very arid and poor for farming and tourism has been a welcome boost for the local area. The landscape is quite different from the usual 'chocolate box' Alpine valleys:, instead, sweeping vistas of lavender fields, maquis scrub, hazy limestone hills and mellow villages. The star of the region is the stupendous 'Grand Canyon du Verdon', Europe's Grand Canyon and this is worth a visit even if you never get to paddle it. On or off the river, this is a fascinating area.

On the River

The first 40 km of the Verdon are typically Alpine in character and make for some enjoyable paddling in early summer. Below here, two barrages at Castellane now control the flow in the Grand Canyon downstream. There were plans in the 1970s to dam the Grand Canyon itself, but fortunately these were defeated by an international outcry and it survives as one of the natural wonders of Europe.

Below the Grand Canyon are the scenic 'Basses Gorges du Verdon', which used to provide fine touring paddling until they were drowned under various barrages - the flooded gorges and lakes are now popular for other water sports and are also fine for lazy exploration by kayak or canoe.

Note that standard French river regulations apply, displayed at most access points: boating is normally prohibited before 10.00 a.m. and after 6.0.p.m. and on the weekend at the beginning and end of the fishing season (usually the second Sat in March to the third Sunday in September).

Commercial Rafting

Most commercial rafting takes place on the pre-canyon section of the river from Castellane down to the start of the Grand Canyon. There is no rafting as such through the Grand Canyon but it is possible to take a guided trip in two-man inflatable canoes. An alternative is the Gorges de Daluis on the Var, which is a scenic and popular raft trip. There is also some rafting on the upper Verdon when water levels permit.

Off the River

In the summer months this is a major tourist area and so there are many activities available, from bungy jumping to horse riding. The star attraction of the area is the Grand Canyon and you should definitely plan to drive or cycle the 'Route des Cretes' along the canyon rim. We also recommend that you plan either a kayak trip through the canyon or a walk down into the heart of it at the Styx.

The Verdon is also famous for its rock climbing and there are some excellent routes just below the Route des Crêtes - easily accessible from la Palud, which makes a natural centre for exploring the area. Castellane is a small medieval market town with good services that makes a pleasant alternative centre. Mid-summer temperatures can reach 40°C so bear this in mind when making your plans.

Campsites

There are several high-class family campsites along the riverside downstream from Castellane with all facilities including swimming pools. However, outdoor-orientated river runners will probably feel more at home staying at one of the campsites in la Palud, displaying their rubber gear to all the lycra clad rock athletes and knobbly kneed walkers. Our favourite is the municipal site on the road towards Castellane, some 10 minutes walk from the village shops, restaurants, and bars. There are also a couple of farm campsites near la Palud.

Hospital

Digne. Telephone 18 in case of accident (fire/ambulance/rescue).

Maps

Michelin sheet 245 'Provence Côte d'Azur' covers the whole of this area at a scale of 1;200,000 and represents good value. Best detailed map of the Grand Canyon is the IGN TOP25 'Gorges du Verdon' sheet 3442OT at a scale of 1:25,000. There used to be a detailed full-colour guidebook to the Grand Canyon published by Roger Verdegen, but this is now out of print.

Tourist Offices

Castellane: B.P. 8, Rue Nationale, Tel: 04 92 83 61 14.

also: La Palud, Moustiers, Val d'Allos,

Colmars, St Andre, and St Julian.

www.parcduverdon.com

www.verdon.com

www.castellane.org

Rafting Operators

Check with the local tourist office for an up-to-date list of companies operating on the Verdon - note that for the Grand Canyon you need a qualified 'Guide Aquatique'.

Over at the Gorges de Daluis on the Var, the local company is: Azur Nature, Plan d'eau du Savé, F-06260 Puget-Theniers. Tel: 04 93 05 05 88.

Verdon Grand Canyon, view from Route des Crêtes.   *Robin Knapp*

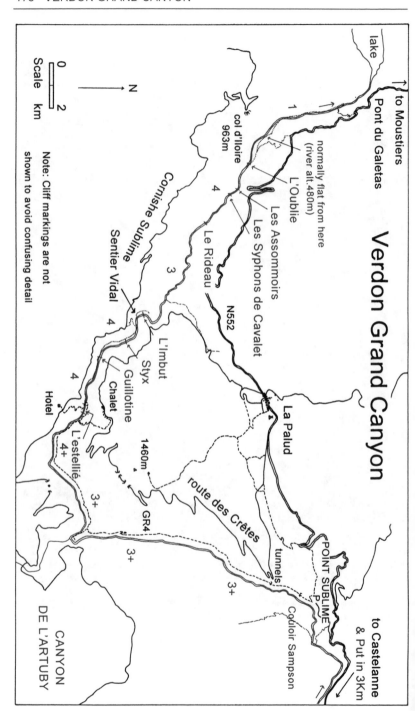

Verdon Grand Canyon

From:	Pont de Carajuan	Difficulty:	4 (5) some portages
To:	Pont de Galétas	Gradient:	4 m/km
Distance:	34 km	WW Stars:	★★★
Time:	9 hours	Scenery:	✹✹✹
Best months:	May to Sept	Flow:	18 cumecs = MW
Bank support:	very limited	Gauge:	no
Water temp:	warm	Ass. runs:	Verdon Pre-Canyon
Water quality:	good		

Summary
The 'Grand Canyon of Europe' - a spectacular limestone gorge, phenomenally deep and narrow, which makes a magnificent and memorable kayak expedition.

Special points
- A long and committing trip.
- Many **siphons** - not clearly visible (cause of numerous fatalities).
- Arduous - much scouting, rock scrambling and portaging.
- Risk of rock fall in storms.
- The river may flood and trap you in the canyon.

The River
For 30 km the Verdon cuts through the surrounding limestone plateau in a 500m deep, narrow canyon, with spectacular cliffs. Geographers theorise over how the Verdon came to cut such a unique canyon: most believe in antecedent drainage, but it has also been proposed that in places it was an underground river, whose roof subsequently collapsed.

What can be said with little argument, is that this is The Grand Canyon of Europe, obviously smaller than the Grand Canyon of the Colorado, but very comparable in terms of its awe-inspiring rock grandeur. There are no roads into the Canyon, and only a single path, difficult and dangerous in places, follows the upper half of the river. The middle section of the run is completely pathless.

Rafting
The canyon is too tight and difficult for rafts so commercial trips are mainly restricted to two man inflatable canoes (les 'hot-dogs') with a guide . It's a long hard day's expedition which involves some portaging and you need to be fit and mentally prepared. It is also relatively expensive - over 100 euros per person and it can only be run when there is sufficient water. But, this is a unique expedition, immensely satisfying, and well worth the cost which compares favourably with the daily rate to raft the Grand Canyon of the Colorado.

For those with previous experience it is also possible to make a descent using hydro-speeds ('nage en eau vive'). In low water conditions, the alternative is a guided walking/swimming expedition through the Canyon - about 80 euros per person. It is feasible (although not encouraged) for a competent small group to do this on their own with the help of a detailed map and guide book.

Access and Logistics

A trip down the Grand Canyon is a mini-expedition so requires careful planning and preparation. This is a **long trip** - local experts who know the canyon intimately have raced through in 4 hours, but typically most groups will take over 8 hours to do it safely - there's a great deal of scouting, scrambling, safety cover and some difficult portages, and besides, this is such a unique and beautiful place that it would be a shame to rush through it. A time analysis of our latest trip showed: actual paddling time 5 hours, inspection, safety cover, and portages 3½ hours, rescue and salvage 1 hour, lunch and photos 1 hour. If you have many swims, then, like many groups before you, you could well end up paddling the last section in the dark!

You need to be well equipped for a full day, self-contained expedition and as well as all normal safety gear, should consider the possibility of a forced bivouac and take head torches, fire lighters, emergency rations, and perhaps a brew kit. Throw bags are essential, and water purifying tablets strongly recommended. Down in the depths of the canyon the sun only penetrates rarely and it is surprisingly cool, even in mid-summer, and we recommend wet suits and dry tops.

Ideally you will have your own reliable shuttle driver. If this shuttle monkey is active, then it is possible (and fun?) for them to hike down from the canyon rim and meet you at L'Estellié, the halfway point - 400m of vertical descent. This provides an added safety factor: if there is a problem you can stash the boats here and hike-out up to your support vehicle.

Whilst it is possible to start at Point Sublime, we suggest that you put in at the Pont de Carajuan - a pleasant 30 minutes fast paddle as opposed to a long carry down a steep path. For the take-out you need to agree clearly with your shuttle driver which side of the lake at Pont du Galetas you are going to finish - we suggest the left is easiest. If you are leaving a vehicle anywhere, be aware that, because of its proximity to Marseilles, this is a bad area for car thefts.

One final idea for the expedition purist - why not make this a relaxed two day trip and bivouac in the untracked wild section of the canyon? (If you do, make sure that you sleep more than 2m above river level in case of sudden flood!)

The Run

This is a legendary run. The first person to explore it (by dinghy!) was a hydrologist, E.A.Martel in 1905. It was tackled between the wars in folding canvas kayaks, but with many long portages and then from the 1950s onwards it was paddled on a fairly regular basis running most of the rapids.

This is not a run for everyone - we can remember one slalom paddler who thought the paddling was mundane, and didn't like having to get out of his boat all the time. He's the exception: everyone else we know has been wildly enthusiastic, including five-times world champion Richard Fox. It is a convoluted run - someone described it as a cross between caving, rock scrambling and kayaking - one of the climaxes of the run is the 'l'Imbut' where a class 4 rapid takes you underground - you then have to paddle in the dark, get out of your kayak and poke it through a hole in the rock and jump down into a pool!

In the depths of the Grand Canyon - below the Styx   *Paul Mackenzie*

The rock is limestone and so there are many undercuts and **siphons** - often quite innocuous looking until you disappear down one - Sue Hornby (of Suzy's Sweat Shop) got sucked down one and fortunately reappeared a few metres downstream, likening it to being flushed down the U bend of a lavatory: she was lucky, many of the siphons are blocked by tree debris.

This is a dangerous run that has had a good number of fatalities and it's often graded as class 5 in guide books for just this reason. It's not a run that is easy to scout from the river: there are many hidden passages, shoots and siphons lurking behind huge boulders and it is reassuring, and time saving, to have someone along who has paddled the river before. We recommend that you limit your team to 3-6 experienced class 4 paddlers, who are familiar with scrambling around on rocks, setting up safety cover, and using ropes.

Water levels in the Grand Canyon are controlled by the barrage upstream at Castellane. Locals used to reckon that the ideal level was about 18 cumecs, but have come around to the view that at the standard release of 10 cumecs, the canyon is still just as feasible and just as much fun. It is still just about runnable, but less fun, at lower water levels - note however that 'navigation est interdit' ('no boating') below 5 cumecs (you can then swim through it then) - more than 25 cumecs is best left to the local experts.

In spring and autumn you stand a reasonable chance of finding adequate water levels on most days. In the main summer months, in recent years, local rafting companies have negotiated **twice weekly water releases** from the dam above Castellane - normally around 10 cumecs, on a Tuesday and a Friday, but sometimes more - check days and times with local rafting companies or the tourist information office in Castellane.

The Verdon paddling weekend in July has now been discontinued but there is normally a huge release of 40 cumecs for the Verdon Rodeo - usually held on the third weekend in September. (A few expert local paddlers who know the river well have kayaked the Canyon at this level - describing it as 'a very committing trip, big , swirly water, huge boils, and powerful stoppers - with mandatory portages at l'Imbut, le Rideau and le Styx.')

Description

Please see the next run description 'Verdon Pre-Canyon' for the 4 km from the Pont de Carajuan to Point Sublime.

The entrance to the Grand Canyon below Point Sublime is suitably dramatic with the vertical rock cliffs of the **'Couloir Samson'** towering straight out of the river for hundreds of metres. The path on the right bank has nowhere to pass, so climbs with some iron ladders and disappears from view into some sinister tunnels in the rock (the remnants of a HEP survey). The paddling is relatively easy, class 3+, with nice technical moves around giant boulders, powerful currents, little shoots, and the occasional undercut. Richard Fox said to us after a run: 'it's a really exceptional river and its nature is summed up by the first shoot'.

After two kilometres the cliffs recede, the river widens and becomes easier with the occasional little play wave - resist the temptation though and save your energy for the challenges ahead. The river stays like this for the next 4 km down to the confluence with the Artuby, easy paddling and the occasional glimpse of the viewpoints on the 'Route des Cretes' some 700m above on the canyon rim.

If you have the time pause for a few minutes to paddle up into the sombre, eerie portals of the **'Canyon de l'Artuby'**. The river now doubles-back on itself, but remains relatively easy for another 3 km. Just after a right-hand bend a giant couloir in high cliffs sweeps up to the canyon rim, with a toy-like hotel perched on the edge. Down at the river level, the water is calm and there are often people bathing and picnicking on the beaches by the riverside in scenes more typical of the Ardeche. This is warning of 'l'Estellié' rapid which is a few hundred metres downstream. When the metal footbridge comes into sight (destroyed by the floods of 1994, but since replaced) then land almost immediately on a small shady beach on the left to inspect.

L'Estellié is a long rapid, class 4+, that extends above and below the footbridge. Take the time to scout it carefully and note how what appear as two of the most obvious break-outs from the river level, on the left both above and below the bridge, both have dangerous siphons in them. These have a record of fatalities and we recommend that you set up safety cover if you intend to run this rapid - see photo of a rescue from the first siphon.

You are now roughly one third of the way through the trip and next to the path up to the canyon rim - time to take stock and check that everyone is happy - from here on the river gets noticeably more serious. There are some ten or so rapids in the next 1.7 km down to the 'Styx' with names such as 'le Cyclope', 'le Niagara' and 'la Guillotine'.

The high performance 'skinny' kayaks popped through
the syphons with ease - their overwieght occupants
however did not have such an easy time....

All of these rapids are technical, class 4, with skilful, confident paddling required, and great fun for the leaders as they dodge from eddy to eddy, and leap ashore occasionally to try and get a glimpse around the next big boulder - don't crowd them! Depending on water level, one or two portages might be advisable, especially at **'la Guillotine'**, about 1 km after 'l'Estellié' where the rapid funnels then siphons under some large rocks in the centre of the river (land and set up safety right).

The **'Styx'** is preceded by relatively calm water and a high cliff with a large couloir/cave can be seen on the right as the river bends around to the left some 200m downstream. It's a good idea for two people to land here, well upstream, to go ahead to signal and assist the others to land just above the 'Styx' (also take throw bags just in case). The 200m down to the 'Styx' are straight-forward, with fast current between rock walls about 2m wide, but there is no big eddy and only room for one boat at a time as you ram your kayak up the bank and scrabble desperately at the rocks to stop it sliding back into the river!

The 'Styx' translates as 'entrance to Hell' - it's a deep gloomy couloir, an undercut cave where the river bends around to the left, with a sheer cave wall rising out of the river on the right. A strong siphon flows under this right wall of the cave - we've seen a high volume C1 disappear here (happily the paddler was rescued with a throw bag but never saw his boat again!). This is dramatic, sombre place and it's a real adrenaline buzz to shoot it, but do set up good safety. The portage is really short and easy, and if you're short of time (you're now about halfway through your trip) you might prefer to give it a miss.

Less than 1km, and a few more rapids, brings you to the **'Chaos de l'Imbut'** where the river goes underground beneath a massive boulder fall. The approach to the l'Imbut is reasonably obvious but a dangerous rapid leads into it, so you should land before, on a boulder beach on the left, to inspect and set up safety cover. The rapid at the entrance to 'l'Imbut' has a fairly obvious siphon under the rock on the left. The choices are to run the rapid (with safety cover), to portage the siphon and to put in immediately below, or to portage the whole of the 'Chaos de l'Imbut'.

The reaction of most paddlers on seeing this rapid disappearing into the bowels of the earth is probably summed up by Suzy: "Pete, I trust you normally, I've followed you down most things, but there's no way I'm I following you into that thing". Fortunately a handsome Frenchman came along, assured Suzy that it would be 'pas de problème' and whilst she wouldn't believe me, of course she believed him!

Just as well, because this next underground section is a unique experience that shouldn't be missed. Once in the portals of the cave, the current slackens and you have time to look around. You realise that in fact, it isn't a real cave, but that the river is gently percolating through a massive boulder choke, and you can see daylight through holes in the roof. After some 100m of bumping along in the dark you come to the end of the passage and have to clamber up to a small hole and then pass the boats up to seal launch or jump into the pool below.

Time to take stock again - there's another 3 hours of paddling and portages ahead of you and if necessary you could stash the boats here and follow the steep and exposed path that climbs some 350m up to the road.

Kayaking through l'imbut (or "Help, what am I doing here"?) *Paul Mackenzie*

The next 3 km are the wildest and perhaps the most beautiful part of the canyon with sheer rock walls on both sides and no way in, or out, except by river. The paddling is easier, class 3+, and there's chance to relax for a while. After these 3 km the cliffs on the left bank retreat from the riverside and make space for a wooded bank which continues for the next kilometre down to Les Cavalets (in case of need there is now a rough path along this left-hand bank).

A huge grey rounded boulder perched on other rocks in the middle of the river looks something like a mushroom and identifies 'le Champignon' rapid - this may require a quick scout, but more importantly gives warning of **'le Rideau'** (the curtain) about 100m below - land just below the mushroom to inspect. 'Le Rideau' is a huge block that appears to bar the river completely. In low water flows there is normally a narrow passage around the left-hand side of the block that you can squeeze through - but many paddlers end up rolling or swimming under the block (to the usual sympathetic kayakers response!). In higher flows, over 18 cumecs, it becomes a sump and should be portaged.

Sheer rock walls guard the approach and mean that once you start your run there is no alternative or escape. Just to make life more interesting, you cannot see the passage from upstream or from the rocks above! The safest way to run 'le Rideau' is for two paddlers to land: one portages and then checks the passage is clear from the pool below, the other stands on the rocks above and directs the others down.

About a kilometre brings you to Les Moulards rapids 1 and 2, then shortly after come **'les Siphons des Cavalets'** - a 2m high chockstone creates a dangerous siphon and mandatory portage at usual levels. The approach is marked by the cliffs on the right retreating from the river and a bush and tree-covered bank above the riverside rocks. Land on the right and climb up through the trees to then descend - this is the most straight-forward portage and takes about 15 minutes of hard work. If you miss this take-out, then you run a small rapid with a sheer rock wall on the left (river bending around to the right) - break out immediately right and commence a scramble of a portage on the rocks above the river. If you miss both these options then you have one last chance, a micro eddy on the left immediately before the siphon with a very dodgy landing and portage - just possible at certain water levels.

There is a second chockstone in calm water some 50m downstream that forms an interesting initiative test. After this 200m of calmer water brings you to 'les Molasses', followed immediately by **'les Assommoirs'** - a tricky rapid bending out of sight to the right. Land left on some boulders to inspect and set up safety. This is almost the last difficult rapid: 500m downstream is **'l'Oublie'** (the forgotten one) which needs care as the river siphons under some rocks on the left, then 100m brings you down to the remains of the old Mayrestre footbridge. A path on the right bank climbs up, 230m of hard ascent, to the road above.

Soon after, the river and valley widen, there are beaches on both sides and the river flattens as it enters the lake. Depending on water levels in the reservoir there are about 4 km of paddling, flat but scenic, to the take-out just past le **Pont de Galétas** where, with luck, your support party is waiting with reviving food, drink, and massage oil (or perhaps they have hired a pedalo and come to meet you with an icebox of cold beer?).

Floods on the Verdon

As I sit in front of a roaring fire, with a bottle of Cotes de Provence at my side to try and lift my spirits, I look gloomily out of my window and am reminded that, apart from the occasional accidental shower, it generally rains twice a year in the South of France. Usually in April or May it seems to rain solidly for a week between the cold blue skies of winter and the warm blue skies of summer - this is called Spring - then with uncanny precision it does the same at the end of October or beginning of November - this is called Autumn. What many people do not realise, is that the average annual rainfall is equivalent or even superior to that of many other regions of France - it's just that we seem to get it all in one go!

This phenomenon is precisely what occurred in the first week of November last year, 1994, and with such intensity that it produced a centennial flood in the valleys of the Verdon and the Var (what this means is that the flood is so big that it is statistically likely only once every hundred years). Before you ask, no, I didn't paddle the Verdon Gorge at this level - apart from the Police and rescue services forbidding all access, the peak level was during an eight hour period overnight. The water table had been generally quite high for a couple of weeks beforehand and all the reservoirs were consequently very near capacity, which was one of the major problems facing Electricite de France when the rain came.

And when the rain came, there was nothing anyone could do to stop it. On the upper Verdon, the road was washed away in six places, two bridges were destroyed, numerous houses wrecked, and the cemetery at Colmars was ripped from the hillside. Arriving at the dams above Castellane, there was nothing the technicians could do but open the flood relief valves. Speaking to the night shift crew as they came off duty, we stood admiring the 40m high jet of water coming out of the base of the dam and they said that I should have seen it earlier. Official figures have been cagily vague but it seems that something in excess of 600 cubic metres per second were released from the dam above Castellane which probably means 1250 cumecs under the bridge at Vinon (a typical summer flow through the Grand Canyon would be 10 cumecs). During the night, with threats of a dam release of 800 cumecs or even more, the lower lying quarters of Castellane were evacuated and the army called in to build a two metre high barricade of rocks upstream of the town.

As you can imagine, this level of water had some spectacular effects when compressed in the confines of the Canyon. At the Degoulinante rapid, the usual starting point for a run of the gorge, the water was up over the road, which it completely eradicated, retaining wall and all. At the Point Sublime the level rose between 8 and 10m and at the Estellie rapid the footbridge was swept away.

All this will obviously have serious consequences for all water sports use of rivers in this area as well as for local residents. Six months on and the roads are not yet rebuilt, although access is possible with weight and height restrictions; the railway is still looking for the estimated 50 Million FF needed to rebuild. And, most important of all, the rivers have suffered from a flood of between 40 and 50 times its normal flow. This is especially so in the limestone of the Verdon where a lot of new syphons have been opened up, some old ones blocked with debris, the Imbut totally choked with trees and both banks scoured clean of anything removable to the height of the flood. It is very impressive to see the mighty power of a river just reminding us that we are maybe not the masters of the universe we like to think we are. It's also a reminder not to be surprised if you come round the corner on the river and there is rapid that wasn't there before!

Robin Knapp

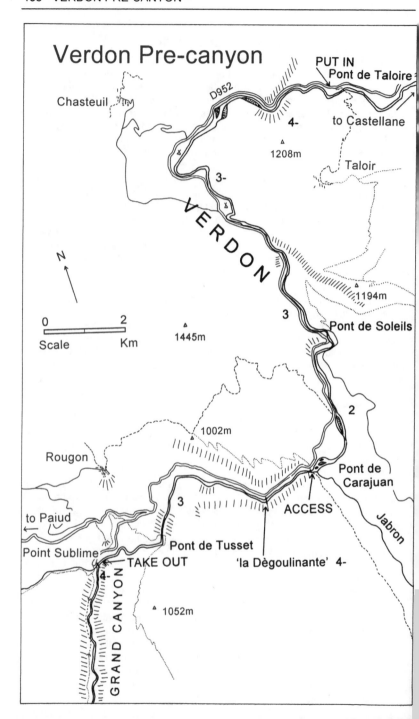

Verdon Pre-canyon

From:	Pont de Taloire	Difficulty:	**3** (4)
To:	Point Sublime	Gradient:	7 m/km
Distance:	13 km	WW Stars:	★★
Time:	2½ hours	Scenery:	❀❀
Best months:	May to Sept,	Flow:	18 cumecs = MW
Bank support:	reasonable	Gauge:	no
Water temp:	warm	Ass. runs:	Grand Canyon,
Water quality:	good		Castellane to Taloire

Summary

A fine paddle that gives much of the flavour of the Grand Canyon without the risk of indigestion! Easy logistics and a good warm-up to a canyon run.

The River

This run includes the first section of the Grand Canyon du Verdon as the river starts to cut a 500m trench through the surrounding limestone. It finishes at the Point Sublime where the main part of the Grand Canyon commences. The nature of the river, with limestone cliffs, huge boulders, clear green water, and pebble beaches is the same as in the Grand Canyon. Water levels are likewise controlled by the dam at Castellane. In the main summer months, local rafting companies have negotiated **twice weekly water releases** from the dam above Castellane - on a Tuesday and a Friday, but sometimes more - check this with local rafting companies or the tourist information office in Castellane. Earlier in the summer and in autumn you stand a reasonable chance of finding adequate water levels on most days.

Rafting

The favourite stretch of the Verdon for rafting and it's a run that we can recommend - friendly, warm, good white water and superb scenery - so if you are in the area then grab the opportunity! This is also a popular stretch for hydro-speeds ('nage en eau vive') if you prefer a more intimate experience.

Access and Logistics

The road is close to the river for most of this run so inspection and shuttles are easy. Take the chance to scout 'la Dégoulinante' on the drive to the start. Put in by driving down a track downstream of the bridge on the right bank - there's parking here in the shade of pine trees, but do not leave valuables in vehicles as this is a bad area for car thefts.

There's a pleasant picnic place and alternative access point at Pont de Carajuan - park in the lay-by and carry your boat over the old bridge to the picnic site. If you're short of time then we recommend starting your trip here.

Take out at the Point Sublime. This entails a 15 minute steep hike, about 75m of ascent, from the river to the parking place, so we suggest that you plan this as an afternoon paddle to arrive in the shade and cool of the early evening.

The Run

This run is normally done as a warm up to the Grand Canyon, or as an easier and less serious alternative. Don't ignore it because it's a bit overshadowed by its neighbour, however this is a fine run in its own right and one that won't disappoint you: the river is a beautiful clear green colour and flows over white rocks, sparkling little rapids wind around big round boulders, a couple of larger falls to get the adrenaline flowing - without being too serious - green wooded banks, orange and white cliffs, and all under the blue skies of Provence.

Like all good runs, it builds variety and interest as you progress down it, saving the best scenery and most entertaining rapids for the last 4 km and with a dramatic climax of a finish in the stupendous 'Couloir de Samson'. If you're short of time then we recommend that you just do this last section.

It normally takes about an hour for the water to flow from the dam down to the Pont de Taloire and then maybe another 3-4 hours to the start of the Grand Canyon. Locals prefer a level of around 18 cumecs, but 10 cumecs gives a fun run with well defined eddies and rocks to dodge, below this it becomes more of a bump and scrape and it may be better to put in at the Pont de Carajuan. Note that 'navigation est interdit' ('no boating') below 5 cumecs.

Description

From the put-in at the **Pont de Taloire** there is just under a kilometre of easy water before the first gorge, the 'Gates of St Jean' with cliffs rising an impressive 500m on either side. There are two obvious rapids here: the second flows against some overhangs on the left and is sometimes a class 4-. The difficulty then eases to class 2 and 3 for the next 4 km as the river passes campsites on the right bank.

The second little gorge provides some more white water interest and takes you down to the Pont de Soleils and another 2 km of easy paddling to the confluence of the Jabron and the **Pont de Carajuan** with a pleasant picnic site on the left bank before the bridge.

Easy water brings you to the big rapid of the run, **'la Dégoulinante'**. This used to be a class 4 with two big shoots and holes following immediately, one after the other, however, the floods of 1994 changed it into an easier shoot. Traditionally amongst kayakers 'la Dégoulinante' was seen as a test piece for a run of the Grand Canyon - if you swam here then you shouldn't be doing the main run!

The river now continues at class 3, with plenty of small rapids, couloirs, boulder shoots, and a couple of 'silly' play waves. All the time the scenery gets more and more impressive - the road climbs away and you're just left with a wild river cutting deeper and deeper, and your own equally deep sense of anticipation as you approach the portals of the 'Couloir de Samson'. First though, is the superb old Roman bridge of **le Pont de Tusset**, beautifully sited just after a little gorge, and highly photogenic.

A couple more bends and the road becomes visible again some 70m up on the right, and then the car park, viewpoint, and also the small stream and valley of 'le Baou' coming in on the right. A huge boulder, **'le Solitaire',** blocks the river here and forms a rapid. You can take out above if you wish, or shoot the rapid - we recommend that you inspect first as the shoots on either side are often blocked by tree trunks. If you have any doubts about your group then it is also probably worth setting up safety cover below, otherwise you may see bodies and boats drifting-off into the portals of the **'Couloir de Samson'** on a 30 km voyage of no return! (Not strictly true, but you'd have some major problems.) Land on the beach just below 'le Solitaire' and take a few minutes to admire your stupendous surroundings as the river disappears from sight into a narrow cleft in the 400m high cliffs.

The main tourist path is just out of sight up through the bushes; it crosses the creek on a footbridge and then winds steeply up to the car park at Point Sublime - a sweaty 10-15 minute walk - we hope you have a shuttle monkey waiting with ice-cold drinks!

Verdon Pre-canyon, 'la Dégoulinante' (12 cumecs?).   *Peter Knowles*

Lesser Classics

Verdon from Castellane

From:	Castellane	Difficulty:	**2** (3)
To:	Pont de Taloire	Gradient:	7 m/km
Distance:	6 km	WW Stars:	★
Time:	1 hour	Scenery:	✤✤
Best months:	June to Sept	Flow:	18 cumecs = MW
Bank support:	reasonable	Gauge:	answerphone

Summary
Relatively easy water and pleasant scenery. A friendly introduction to white water. Put in by the swimming pool and bridge in Castellane. A fun run at high levels.

Upper Verdon from Allos

From:	Allos	Difficulty:	**4**
To:	Colmars	Gradient:	25 m/km
Distance:	7 km	WW Stars:	★
Time:	1 hour	Scenery:	✤✤
Best months:	May & June	Flow:	7 cumecs = MW
Bank support:	reasonable	Gauge:	

Summary
A small fast run easily viewed from the road. Potential hazard from fallen trees. Put in at the 'Base de Loisirs' in Allos (the river has been kayaked from a few km upstream). Take out at the Pont de la Tompine in Colmars.

Upper Verdon from Colmars

From:	Colmars	Difficulty:	**3-**
To:	Pont Clos	Gradient:	14 m/km
Distance:	15 km	WW Stars:	★
Time:	2 hours	Scenery:	✤✤
Best months:	May & June	Flow:	10 cumecs = MW
Bank support:	reasonable	Gauge:	

Summary
A pleasant run with white water rapids interspersed by gravel beds. The first 6km down to Beuvezer used to be a white water race course. Take out at the Pont Clos, 3km downstream of Thorame Haute, where the D52 crosses the river.

Upper Verdon from Pont Clos

From:	Pont Clos	Difficulty:	**3+**
To:	St André	Gradient:	8 m/km
Distance:	18 km	WW Stars:	★★
Time:	2 hours	Scenery:	⊕⊕
Best months:	May & June	Flow:	10 cumecs = MW
Bank support:	good	Gauge:	

Summary

The river narrows and provides some fine white water through the gorges of Font Gaillarde and then spreads out with gravel beds as it approaches St André. If you just want to paddle the most exciting stretch, the first 12 km, then take out at the Pont d'Allons where the D52 goes off to Allons. Otherwise take out at the Pont de Méoulles on the small D955 out of St André towards Méoulles - look out for the ledge underneath the bridge.

Var - Gorges de Daluis

From:	Pont des Roberts	Difficulty:	**3**
To:	Daluis	Gradient:	17 m/km
Distance:	7 km	WW Stars:	★
Time:	1½ hour	Scenery:	✿ ✿
Best months:	May & June	Flow:	10 cumecs = MW
Bank support:	very limited	Gauge:	

Summary

Red sandstone walls drop sheer into the river and make a very picturesque and committing run. It can be dangerous in high water, with no eddies and no escape, so beware of flash floods in stormy weather, but at normal water levels there are no serious problems. Take out at Daluis; below here the valley widens and the river becomes mainly a class 3- conveyor belt running over gravel beds for the next 20 km to Puget-Théniers.

Other rivers

The **Issole** flows into the upper Verdon at St André and can be paddled from Pont de Lambruisse, class 2 and 3. The **Coulomp** is worth a look at if you are driving over to the Var along the N202: 6 km of class 3 (4-) from the Pont de la Done just below the confluence with the Vaire, with a magnificent old bridge, the Pont de la Reine Jeanne, half-way down the run.

The **Jabron** can be paddled from Noyers, 12 km of class 2 and 3, after rain or snow melt. The **Artuby** has 4 km of class 4+ paddling near Châteauvieux in a narrow canyon before it flows into a military area.

The other rivers of the Var watershed can only be paddled in spring or autumn when there is sufficient water. There is some hard technical paddling in fantastic gorges - the **Estéron** probably being the best. Josef Haas and other German guide books have more information.

International river classification of difficulty

Class 1: Easy
Moving water with occasional small rapids. Few or no obstacles.

Class 2: Moderate
Small rapids with regular waves. Some manoeuvring required but easy to navigate.

Class 3: Difficult
Rapids with irregular waves and hazards that need avoiding.   More difficult manoeuvring required but routes are normally obvious. Scouting from the shore is occasionally necessary.

Class 4: Very difficult
Large rapids that require careful manoeuvring. Dangerous hazards. Scouting from the shore is often necessary and rescue is usually difficult. Kayakers should be able to roll. Turbulent water and large irregular waves may flip rafts. In the event of a mishap there is significant risk of loss, damage and/or injury.

Class 5: Extremely difficult
Long and very violent rapids with severe hazards. Continuous, powerful, confused water makes route-finding difficult and scouting from the shore is essential. Precise manoeuvring is critical and for kayakers, rolling ability needs to be 100%. Rescue is difficult or impossible and in the event of a mishap there is a significant hazard to life.

Class 6: Nearly impossible
Difficulties of class 5 carried to the extreme of navigability. Might possibly (but not probably) be run by a team of experts at the right water level, in the right conditions, with all possible safety precautions, but still with considerable hazard to life.

An alternative Alpine grading system

Here's a possible system that complements the international grading system and is particularly useful for Alpine snow-melt rivers, especially if you are visiting for the first time and not used to them.

At the centre of this highly technical system is a regular size jar of peanut butter. The sort that someone in your group sneaks into the supermarche shoping basket when no one really likes it that much and the rest of the group would prefer Nuttela chocolate sauce for those crepes and pancakes! Anyway this jar of peanut butter can sit around the camp site unless its potential is harnessed.

The heart of this scale relates to the consistency of the jar of peanut butter when left in the campsite. Inspection of the jar should take place just before moving off to put on the water. If the contents are quite firm, then the guide book grading should be a fair indication as to the river conditions. If on the other hand you have lazed around the camp all morning it is likely that the jar will be very hot and instead of spreading the butter, you are more likely to pour it. In these circumstances you should add one to the river grading as the sun has melted so much more water into the valley! You could on the other hand write the day off, as its late, and tuck into that cheap wine you bought and enjoy the rest of the weather.

Paul Mackenzie

50 years ago, on the Durance and Verdon

It is now nearly 50 years since the five of us canoed the Durance and Verdon in South East France with Oliver Cock providing road transport and following to make a cine film* of our progress.

Our canoes were of the folding type consisting of a rubberised canvas hull with a canvas deck. Then a framework, or cage, of rods and frames was assembled and slipped into the hull where it was tensioned and held into shape with the addition of a cock-pit coaming. A rubberised spray-deck completed the water-tight arrangements. My Klepper T6, with its distinctive blue deck, had already taken me safely down many Alpine rivers, mainly in Austria. It taught me to take care to choose the correct channel to avoid rocks, to 'read' the river and steer a safe course down rapids without damage to the boat.

The Durance was full with ice-cold glacier water flowing in a milky coloured torrent as we launched our frail craft at L'Argentiere. The Rabious rapid with its bouncy waves provided the highlight of that day's canoeing and we found an excellent camp-site just beyond the tail of them. I saw a wild boar and chased it for some way down stream on the river bank. Fortunately, for me perhaps, it out-distanced me - as I discovered later that they can be very dangerous when confronted!

The next day we continued to Embrun and enjoyed more interesting rapids, some of which I understand are now submerged by a more recent barrage scheme lower down.

We then packed up the canoes and drove up over the mountain pass, the Col d'Allos, to the Upper Verdon at Castellane where a barrage held back the river and created a large lake. Releases were made at set intervals and we heeded the advice to check when the next release was due, before embarking on the river.

We set off from Castellane and on that first stretch we enjoyed a full day of many delightful rapids with a good recovery pool between each - it was such clear water that we were tempted to take a swim in the nude! These rapids led us eventually to the start of the Grand Canyon du Verdon at Point Sublime.

It was possible to inspect the next six miles or so through a series of tunnels and paths drilled and excavated from the rock face on the right bank of the river, which we did. It was a long walk, but well worth while, culminating in a climb up a series of vertical metal ladders. Earlier this century it had been planned to build a dam at the lower end of the gorge. Happily this scheme, which would have drowned the whole canyon, was never completed but the tunnels that have been left do enable the canoeist to reconnoitre much of the gorge before being committed to it .....

Eric Totty

This delightful film is now available as a BCU archive collection video.

French Glossary

Robin and Paul go kayaking

ENGLISH	FRENCH	ENGLISH	FRENCH
Bank (river)	rive	Pop-out	chandelle
Bouyancy	flottabilite	Portage	portage
Bouyancy aid	gilet (de securité)	Pour-over	pleureur*
Bouyancy bag	gonfle	Put-in	embarquement
Breakout	stop	Raft	raft
Bridge	pont	Railway	chemin de fer
Canoe	canoe	Rain	pluie
Capsize	chavirer	Rapid	rapide
Capsize & swim	désaler	Ravine	ravin, canyon
Cliff	falaise	Reverse	marche arrière
Confluence	confluence	Right	droite
Current	courant	River	rivière
Downstream	en aval	Road	route
Drop (1-2m)	seuil	Rock	rocher
Drop (3m+)	chute	Rock or boulder	caillou
Eddy	contre	Roll (verb)	esquimoter
Eddy-line	port-feuille	Rolling wave	rouleau*
Ferry or shuttle	navette	/small stopper	
First aid	premiers secour	Section (of river)	passage
Flow	débit	or gap	
Follow	suivre	Shoot (a rapid)	sauter
Footbridge	passerelle	Spate	crue
Gauge	échelle	Spraydeck	Jupe or Jupette
Gorge	gorge	Stopper	rappel
Gradient	dénivelée	Support stroke	appui
Hole	trou	Swim	nager
Hole [sic]	trou	Syphon	syphon
Karabiner	monsqueton	Take-out	débarquement
Kayak	kayak	Throw line	corde de securité
Left	gauche	Tow back	rappel
Level	niveau	Tree	arbre
Loop	soleil	Tributary	affluent
Metal stake	ferail	Undercut	drossage
Mushroom (sic)	champignon	Un-runnable	infran (chisable)
Navigable	navigable	Upstream	en amont
Paddle	naviguer	Volume	volume
Paddle (noun)	pagaie	Waterfall)	cascade
Path	chemin, sentier.	Weir	barrage
Play-hole	trou à chandelles		

FRENCH	ENGLISH	FRENCH	ENGLISH
Appui	support stroke	Naviguer	paddle
Avant	before	Pagaie	paddle (noun)
Baigner, nager	swim	Pagaille	big mess (almost swearing)
Caillou	rock or boulder	Passage	section (of river) or gap
Cascade	waterfall	Passerelle	footbridge
Champignon	mushroom [sic]	Planiol	flat water (boring)
Chute	drop (3m+?)	Pleureur*	pour-over
Contre	eddy	Port-feuille	eddy-line
Droite	right	Rappel	stopper
Drossage*	water sliding sideways towards or under a cliff found typically on bends.	Rive	bank (of river) = Haha
En amont	upstream	Rocher	rock
En aval	downstream	Rouleau*	rolling wave (small stopper)
Esquimoter	roll (verb)	Sauter	to shoot
Falaise	cliff	Seuil	drop (1-2m)
Gauche	left	Stop	breakout (verb and noun)
Giclé*	literally spurt, or the last stroke	Sous	under or below
Incidence	used with gauche & droite means pointing left or right	Suivere	follow
Infranch-issable	un-runnable	Trou	hole [sic]
Marche arrière	reverse	Vague	wave
Navette	ferry or shuttle	Veine	green tongue

signifies a word with no direct translation

A Guide to river names in this book

Whilst these are not exact phonetic reproductions, they do represent about as close as most English-speaking paddlers will ever come to getting it right. One day everyone will be multi-lingual, but until then, this will have to suffice.

Name of river	Pronunciation	Name of river	Pronunciation
Bonne	bon	Isère	ee-zaire
Dora Baltea	dora bol-tay-er	Romanche	ro-monsh
Dranse	drons	Sesia	say-zee-a
Durance	dur-rons	Séveraise	say-ver-raise
Guil	geel (hard g)	Ubaye	Uh-by
Guisane	gee-zann (hard g)	Verdon	vair-don

Common expressions used by ordinary folk in their day-to-day lives:

ENGLISH	FRENCH	ENGLISH	FRENCH
Hi	Salut	Pinch	piquer*
Bye	Ciao	Gang or boys	les gars
Mate (male)	copain	Stupid or stupid git	con ***
Mate (female)	copinne	Arsing around	deconner ***
Cute	chouette	Face	guelle**
Thing	truc	Shut your face	ta guelle! ***
What's his name	machin	Unwound	decontracté
A sort of	un espèce de	Relaxed	relaxe
Bloke	mec	[Sic]	cool
Geezer	type *	[Sic]	stressé
Company	boite	Awful (tricky one)	pas terrible
Joke	blague	Shitty, awkward	merdique **
Grub	bouffe*	Naff	nul*
Eat	bouffer*	Oh fuck	oh putain!**
Car	bagnole		(lit. Whore)
Purloin	squatter*		

*   *star ratings indicate inadvisability of use in polite society, though it must be
remembered that the French do swear considerably more than the British*

**Now try this little extract
and see how you get on;**

"Oh, salut les gars. J'ai fait la navette jusqu'a la passerelle en amont de l'infran et putain! Il y a un passage bien merdique dans la gorge. J'ai parlé au mec de la boite de rafting qui m'a dit qu'il faut faire un stop dans la contre derrière un grande caillou près de la falaise, puis passer la chute avec incidence gauche pour rester a gauche parçe qu'a droite il y a un espèce de syphon. Si je tombe dans le rappel je sais que je ne pourrai pas esquimoter et j'ai pas envie de nager la-dedans"

"Sans blague? Decontracte toi! Reste cool! Je l'ai fait l'année dernière avec machin de Sisteron et c'est chouette, tu saute le truc avec un bon giclé droite et c'est tout. Allez! Viens bouffer avant qu'on cherche la bagnole"

*Good luck and Bon voyage,
Robin Knapp.*

Books and Maps

(All prices are approximate)

Books

Michelin Green Guide to the French Alps 2001, 14 euros.
Probably the best general English language guidebook to this area with excellent up-to-date information in full colour, maps, town plans and photographs.

Alpes - Dauphiné. Le Canotier éditions. 1999. 20 euros.
Written by local experts - 'les Caskaboulons', this guidebook gives accurate details on almost all the paddleable rivers - 97 runs - in the region of Briancon, Grenoble and Embrun. Great value and well worth buying if you are spending time in the area. It has an innovative international format, relying on good maps, diagrams, so you don't need to be able to read French. At first sight this deviant format puts many paddlers off, but the more you use it - the more you will like it and appreciate its humour. Especially recommended if you are here early season and wanting to run some of the smaller and more extreme runs that are not covered in White Water South Alps.

Gems of Whitewater of the High Alps. Josef Haas, translated from German by Fred Wondre. Rosgarten Verlag, 1989. 30 euros.
A large format book with many inspiring colour photographs. It has sketch maps and short descriptions (in English and Italian) for some 46 rivers in the Alps to the south of Grenoble. Descriptions are now out of date and should not be relied on.

Guide-Itineraires 700 Rivieres de France. Daniel Bonnigal. 1991. 23 Euros.
An impressively detailed French language guidebook to almost all the navigable rivers of France. A good reference source for those "what's that river like that we've just driven by?" enquiries. No maps & no illustrations give this a 5 mogadon rating for bedtime reading.

Lacs et Rivieres des Alpes de Haute-Provence, Eric Olive. Édisud, 1994. 11 euros.
A small book in 5 languages and full colour that gives clear information for the tourist paddler on the main rivers and lakes of Haute-Provence. Eric Olive is a local expert, so the information is accurate, and this is an appealing and well-designed book: most of the information, however also appears in White Water South Alps!

Flussführer, Schweiz und benachbartes Ausland. SKV, 1991. 24 euros.
Published by the Swiss Canoe Union, this German language guidebook gives good coverage (but not as detailed as that given by the DKV guides) of most of the rivers in Switzerland and neighbouring areas (including the Sesia, Aosta, and Dranse valleys) that are worth paddling..

Geneva and the Upper Rhone.
In 2003, Canotier is planning to publish a detailed French language guidebook to the Alpine rivers to the South and East of Lac Leman - this will cover both Haute Savoie and Suisse Romande.

Maps

AA map of France 7 euros

We recommend this as an excellent overall map of France that is very clear, easy to use, and shows the difference between toll and non-toll motorways.

Canoe-Kayak Map of France. FFCK and IGN. 1993. Price 6 euros.

Another overall map of France that shows some 490 rivers, colour coded to show their difficulty; information is given in English, French and German; overprinted on a high quality and detailed road map of France at a scale of 1:1,000,000. Recommended. Widely available in France from shops and motorway services stations.

IGN TOP100 maps. 5 euros.

Published by the French Government mapping agency at a scale of 1:100,000. These show all roads, tracks, rivers, streams, contour lines, tourist information, - all in lovely clear detail and are ideal for car touring and cycling. They are widely available in France but only available from specialised travel outlets in the UK, e.g. Stanfords. Sheet 54 Grenoble-Gap, covers four centres in this book so is a best buy for many paddlers.

Swiss Canoeing Map. 1999, 15 euros.

An excellent multi-coloured map of Switzerland and surrounding areas at a scale of 1:400,000. Printed on waterproof paper. Shows all the rivers with runs colour coded for difficulty, main roads, towns and campsites.

Websites

The internet is a great source of information. For general information on canoeing, kayaking, and the rivers in France try - www.eauxvives.org. This also has updated river levels.

For maps and books try: www.ign.fr.   www.stanfords.co.uk   www.canotier.com

White Water North Alps - summary of runs

The format and specification of our North Alps guidebook are similar to this book, so if you are enjoying this we hope you will buy it's companion! Available from all good specialist shops or see our webbsite - www.riverspublishing.co.uk

Centre: the Upper Rhine Valley

Name of run	Class	WW Stars	Scenery	Km	Flow cumecs	Notes
Vorderrhein	2+(3)	*	***	21	50	'Grand Canyon'
Upper Hinterrhein	3	**	***	11	6	High Alpine
Landquart	4	**	**	11	16	recommended
Glenner	4(4+)	**	*	8	6	for space aliens
Upper Vorderrhein	4+	**	**	6	15	seldom water
Middle Vorderrhein	3-	*	**	10	20	pleasant run
Upper Landquart	4(5)	**	**	6	6	Access by taxi
Albula	4(5)	**	***	6	20	seldom water

Centre: Engadine

Name of run	Class	WW Stars	Scenery	Km	Flow cumecs	Notes
S-Chanf Gorge	3	*	**	5	18	
Brail Gorge	4+	***	***	5	20	very beautiful
Giarsun Gorge	4	***	**	11	25	superb run
Ardez Gorge	4+(6)	***	**	4	25	1 hard portage
Schuls Gorge	3 (4)	**	**	6	25	
Martina section	3	**	*	9	30	seldom water
Finstermünz Gorge	5+	*	***	9	35	or class 3 (5+)

Centre: Landeck

Name of run	Class	WW Stars	Scenery	Km	Flow cumecs	Notes
Sanna	4	***	**	7	15	Intensive
Landeck Gorge	4	**	*	6	25	Powerful
Rosanna	3+	**	**	10	6	Good training
Trisanna	3(4+)	**	**	18	5	High Alps
Inn Shoot	5	***	*	2	25	'ballsy'
Upper Trisanna	4+	**	**	4	5	
Inn from Tösens	4	*	**	8	30	

Centre: the Lech Valley

Name of run	Class	WW Stars	Scenery	Km	Flow cumecs	Notes
Lech	2 (3-)	**	**	22	12	
Madaubach	3-(3+)	**	**	3	3	Ropes needed
Bschlabsbach	3+	**	**	3	4	Ropes needed
Upper Hornbach	4+	***	**	7	3	abseil start
Lower Hornbach	3 (4)	**	**	5	4	1 portage
Lech gorges	5 (6)	**	***	14	7	an expedition

Centre: Haiming

Name of run	Class	WW Stars	Scenery	Km	Flow cumecs	Notes
Imst Gorge - Inn	3	***	**	12	250	BIG water
Lower Oetz	4 (4+)	**	**	12	60	1 portage
Upper Oetz	4+	***	**	4	30	'stonking' run
Lower Venter Ache	4 (4+)	***	**	6	15	fast and steep
Middle Oetz	5 (6)	***	*	8	30	hard
Lower Pitzbach	3+	**	**	20	8	rarely water
Melach	4+ (6)	***	**	14	6	serious

Centre: Upper Bavaria

Name of run	Class	WW Stars	Scenery	Km	Flow cumecs	Notes
Upper Ammer	3- (3)	**	**	12	8	popular run
Upper Isar	3- (3)	**	***	12	4	Access by taxi
Rissbach	3 (4)	**	**	8	5	
Loisach	3 (4)	***	*	5	8	justly famous
Ammer Cataract	4	**	*	2	15	Spate only
Halbammer	3	**	*	6	6	Spate only
Loisach in Austria	3	**	**	5	6	Seldom water
Middle Isar	2 (3)	*	**	25	15	
Walchen Gorge 1	4 (5)	**	**	1	3	Water critical
Walchen Gorge 2	3 (4)	**	**	3	4	Water critical
Leutascher Ache	3	*	**	4	5	Water critical

Centre: the Kitzbuehel Alps

Name of run	Class	WW Stars	Scenery	Km	Flow cumecs	Notes
Brandenberger Ache						
Kaiser Gorge	5	***	***	1	6	
Pinegg & Wies Gorges	3 (4)	**	**	4	7	
Tiefenbach Gorge	5 (6)	***	**	4	10	
lower Brandenberger	3 (4)	**	**	6	11	popular
Windauer Ache	3+ (4)	**	**	9	6	
Kelchsauer Ache	4 (4+)	**	**	7	10	Full on!
Reither Ache	4	**	*	9	10	
Kössener Ache	2	*	**	8	12	relaxing
Upper Brandenberger	3 (4)	*	**	15	8	Spate only

Centre: Val di Sole

Name of run	Class	WW Stars	Scenery	Km	Flow cumecs	Notes
Upper Noce	4 (4+)	**	**	10	20	National
Lower Noce	4	**	**	15	30	slalom course
Noce Gorge	5	**	**	3	35	Committing
Rabbies	5	***	**	7	7	
Vermigliana	4 (5)	**	**	4	10	

White Water Massif Central - summary of runs

The format and specification of our Massif Central guidebook are similar to this book, but the rivers are easier so this makes a great area for a warm up on your way to the Alps - we especially recommend the Allier and the Ardèche.

Allier

River and run	Class	Km	Stars	Scen.	Fluffy	Busy	Notes
St Etienne >	3 (5)	16	★★★	✿✿✿	-	<10	Technical, fun kayaking, very pretty.
Chapeauroux >	2 (3)	18	★★★	✿✿✿	☺	<50	'Jewel of a run' for canoes, fine gorge
Monistrol >	3-(3+)	10	★★	✿✿	-	<50	Good play boating and rafting run.
Prades >	2+	15	★★	✿✿	☺	<50	Pretty, scenic, friendly, canoe run. .
Langeac >	1-2	17	★★	✿✿	☺☺	<200	Old villages, granite cliffs, green river
Lavoûte Chilhac >	1-2	21	★★	✿✿	☺☺	<50	More of the same.
Brioude to Cournon	1(2)	67	★	✿	☺	<10	Pastoral & ideal canoe-camping.

Ardèche

Chassezac Gorges	1-2(2+)	8	★★	✿✿✿	☺☺	<50	Technical paddling, splendid gorge.
Ardèche les Défilés	1-2	18	★	✿✿	☺	<200	Tamer version of the Gorges below
Ardèche - Pont d'Arc	2 (3-)	6	★★	✿✿✿	☺	>200	Foretaste of the Gorges below
Gorges de l'Ardèche	2 (3)	26	★★★	✿✿✿	☺	>200	A world Classic !

Hérault

Ganges to Aubanel	2 (3-)	13	★★	✿✿	☺☺	<200	small river, diverse scenic run.
Moulin de Bertrand >	2	11	★	✿✿	☺	<50	a wild green canyon.
St Guilhem >	4	5	★★	✿✿	-	<10	convoluted run for deviant kayakers

Orb

Poujol to Tarassac	2+	10	★★★	✿✿	-	<50	Fine rapids and a wild valley.
Tarassc to Roquebrun	2(2+)	15	★★★	✿✿✿	☺	<200	'Gorges de l'Orb' - superb canoeing.

Tarn

le Pont du Tarn >	2-3	18	★★	✿✿	-	<10	*Usually insufficient water in Jul-Aug.*
Montbrun >	1-2	10	★	✿✿	☺☺	<50	Scenic introduction
Sainte Enimie >	1-2	14	★★	✿✿✿	☺☺	<200	Old villages & deep gorges
la Malene to Ps de sc	1	10	★★★	✿✿✿	☺☺	>200	Spectacular and popular run.
les Vignes to le Rozier	1-2(3)	10	★★★	✿✿✿	☺	<200	Wild water and wilder scenery
le Rozier to la Cresse	1-2(2+)	10	★	✿✿	☺	<200	Valley now wider.

Notes

★ **Stars** for paddling are 1-3, a subjective measure of satisfaction at that grade.

❀ **Scenery** - our subjective measure from 1-3.

☺ **Fluffy's** rating 1-2 - an idea of how friendly we think the river is for **children**.

Busy is how many boats you might **expect to meet** on a typical day in high season.

Aveyron

River and run	Class	Km	Stars	Scen.	Fluffy	Busy	Notes
Gorges du Najac	2 (3-)	5	★	❀	☺	<50	Short fun run.
St Antonin to Cazals	1-2	8	★	❀❀	☺	<50	Scenic run with good beaches.

Lot

St Laurent >	3	11	★★★	❀❀	-	<10	*Usually insufficient water in Jul-Aug.*
Pomayrols to St Gn.	2+	5	★★	❀❀	☺	<50	Tight gorge & fun playboating spot.
Barrage >	2-3	11	★★	❀	☺	<10	*Usually insufficient water in Jul-Aug.*
Espalion to Estaing	1-2	14	★	❀	☺	<10	*Usually insufficient water in Jul-Aug.*
Barrage to Hydro plant	3(4+)	3	★★	❀	-	<10	*Usually insufficient water in Jul-Aug.*
Hydro plant >	2-3	5	★★	❀❀	-	<10	*Usually insufficient water in Jul-Aug.*
Entraygues >	2(3-)	10	★★	❀❀	☺	<50	Classic run.
le Port >	1 (2)	11	★★	❀❀	☺☺	<50	Friendly, ideal beginners run.
Grand Vabre >	1	12	★	❀❀	☺	<10	2 weirs
Livinhac to Cahors	1	106	★	❀❀	-	<10	Scenic canoe touring but many weirs

Célé

Boussac to Bouzies	1 (2)	48	★	❀❀	☺☺	<50	Friendly, small, ideal family run.

Dordogne

Argentat to Beaulieu	2(2+)	25	★★	❀❀	☺	<50	Fast wide river, a sporty run.
Beaulieu to Souillac	1 (2)	55	★★	❀❀	☺☺	<200	A Classic canoe touring stretch.
Souillac to Beynac	1	44	★	❀❀	☺☺	>200	Famous villages, popular tourist run
Beynac to Mauzac	1	44	★	❀	☺	<50	Quiet, mellow run.

Vézère

Peyrissac to Uzerche	2	17	★★	❀❀	☺	<10	Delightful, small, unspoilt river.
Vigeois to Estivaux	3	12	★★★	❀❀	-	<10	Granite gorge - a fun kayak run.
Montignac to Limeuil	1	47	★	❀❀	☺	<200	Famous pre-historic caves.

Glossary of river terms

Boulder garden - big rocks tastefully positioned in a rapid to give pleasure to boaters.

Boater / paddler - deviant form of human

Breakout - an 'eddy' that a boat can use to break out of the current and then to stop in.

Camera vulture - avaricious bird with a large black beak that hovers below rapids.

Canoe - an open or Canadian style canoe. Note for American readers: Europeans often use 'canoe' as a generic name for all types of canoes and kayaks.

Chicken shoot - an easier way down a rapid that by-passes the main action.

Continuous - an over-used adjective in this book - denotes a sustained and unremitting stretch of river where the difficulty keeps at the same high level.

Eddy - an area of relatively slack water (or where the current re-circulates upstream) usually behind an obstruction in the river.

Eddy-line - the transition line between the main current and the slower calmer water of the eddy. Best crossed at speed!

Ender / endo / pop-out / loop - where kayakers use the force of a wave to drive their kayak vertically out of the water in a phallic display or kind of cart wheel.

Flip - a capsize of a raft: usually from hitting a hole or wave at the wrong angle/place: may be like an ender and quite spectacular.

Hole - normally formed on the downstream side of a rock or similar underwater obstruction. There is usually a 'stopper' / 'hydraulic jump' on the downstream side of the hole. Individual holes can be playful, tempting, humiliating, or downright dangerous.

High-siding - when a raft is caught broadside in a hole or against a rock the current presses down on the upstream side and tries to flip the raft - rafters need to quickly throw their weight onto the high side of the raft (the downstream side) to prevent this.

Hot Dog - French term for an inflatable canoe, holding one or two persons that can be propelled with single of double paddles.   These are a lot of fun for beginners and also used by experts for some extreme first descents. Americans call these 'duckies'.

Kayak - small boat shaped like a banana, with a hole in the bottom from which the occupant hangs. Can be propelled the wrong way up by experts.

Kayaker - extreme form of deviant paddler (semi-human): uses a double ended paddle. Often called 'river maggots' by rafters because of their habit of infesting holes on a river. Canoeists and paddle rafters reckon that kayakers 'have twice the paddle but half the brains'.

Paddle - length of wood or plastic/metal: people hold one end and dip the other end in water to achieve a dramatic personality change.

Pin - where a boat is held by the current against a rock or other obstruction. May be vertical or horizontal, and underwater. Usually a serious incident and may be life-threatening. Low volume kayaks with sharp ends are particularly susceptible to vertical pins.

Play spot - section of water used by over-grown children for water play with rubber and plastic toys. Those playing should beware the enticements of 'camera vultures'.

Portage - favourite activity of canoeists: not so popular with rafters. Wise boaters portage when in doubt.

Pour-over - the current pours over the top of a rock and then drops vertically, usually into an evil hole. Hard to see from upstream until it's too late, so potentially dangerous.

Put-in - start of excuses and commencement of a river trip.

Raft - inflatable boat used for descending rivers: appeals to those with a rubber fetish. Referred to by kayakers as 'rubber bus', 'cattle wagon', 'river barge', etc.

Roll - short for 'Eskimo roll'.

Self-bailing raft - has an inflatable floor and holes to drain the water out. Recommended for more difficult rivers and high water conditions.

Scout - the act of inspecting a rapid or difficult stretch of river: 'When in doubt: get out and scout'. Exercise for eye muscles and imaginative excuses.

Stopper (British) / Reversal (American) / Hydraulic jump (Engineering) - a breaking wave on the downstream side of a hole that re-circulates like a window blind rolling itself up: bad ones will do this to you!

Surf - kayaks, rafts, canoes, etc. can surf a river wave just like people ride ocean waves.

Take-out - finish point of a river trip - usually followed by a bar and lies.

"They make it look so difficult"

Notes on Contributors

Shaun Baker still sees himself as a local boy - totally at home just scratching around the big Thames weirs where he spent his formative years being "kicked up really badly". His journey through kayaking ultimately led to 4 world records (for waterfalls, gradients and speed on snow) and 9 UK Championship titles in whitewater freestyle. Though, as he says, "There will always be more rivers that need to be run and more hideous recirculations that need to be experienced".

Ian Beecroft started boating about 1952 and soon gained a reputation as the 'oldest young man in Manchester'. In between often sordid bouts of socialising he somehow managed to represent Britain in European slaloms. Subsequently he settled down to some serious sprog making, technical editing, and mountaineering based in Martigny, Switzerland. He still does plenty of Alpine paddling and the odd big trip when his wife will let him. More into having fun than getting infamous, he is founder of the ORDCC (old river dogs canoe club) - motto: 'I'm happy with what I've done'.

Mike Bruce is a keen kayaker and skier who after eleven years of paddling in the Alps finally decided to make his home there in 1990. He is a British and French qualified instructor, fully certified, professional nutter and Alpine bum, who lives in a ski resort and tries to make a living out of arranging white water holidays, guiding and rafting.

Roberto Chilosi writes: ".Please allow me to introduce myself, I'm a man of wealth and taste. I've been around for a long long time, stole many mans soul and fate.". (M.Jagger). I'm 37 years old, tall, handsome, intelligent, modest, kayaker, rafting guide, a lover of ravioli, class five rapids and river trips. I have worked on the Dora Baltea since 1996 and have travelled a great deal - always with my kayak - but I still haven't found what I'm looking for....

Ian Fairclough is a veteran of Southampton University Canoe Club. Despite looking terrible in a shorty wetsuit, he is passionate about Alpine paddling, and even proposed to Dawn whilst they were running the mighty l'Ange Guardien gorge.

Fiona Firth describes herself as a 'purely recreational paddler' and explains that the pleasure she derives from canoeing trips comes as much from the accompanying red wine, good company, pain au chocolate, and games of baby foot as from testing rocks for bounce.

Alan Fox is known to many as 'Foxy' for his cartoon work. He is a man of many talents; a film maker, engineer, author, expedition organiser and lecturer. He is married with two daughters. His books include 'Run River Run' a river guide to British Rivers and 'The Blind Probe' a collection of cartoons inspired by river adventure. He is currently working on his next book.

Steve Fullard is a chemistry graduate who puts his degree to good use in the summer months and can be found surfing the Rabioux Wave or drinking a beer in a hammock on the banks of the Gyronde in France. The rest of the year he spends in Pokhara, Nepal and if you can drag him away from the pool table in the Moon Dance Bar, then he may well join you to act as a kayak guide and translator on a Himalayan Expedition.

Matt Funnell describes himself as a lazy boater who would surf all the time if it was possible. He finds most of his vices, in which canoeing is only a small one, were fine tuned at Uni under the ever helpful influence of Muz and Tim.

Heather Gunn spent her formative years in the Thames Valley so, inevitably got mixed up with weir paddling and the playboating and Rodeo scene. A career as a photographer dragged her out of her playboat and she now runs the publication 'Playboater UK'. She is worried that she is still under the influence of playboaters, but is waiting to be invited on a river expedition somewhere nice and friendly to stretch her playboating horizons.

Mark Herriott was rescued by his parents at the age of 18 months from an Atlantic breaker and according to them has remained obsessed with water and has a death wish. He started white water paddling when he was 14 and remembers his Dad, stripped to his Y-fronts wading into the floods at Skelwith Force to recover his broached boat. Still obsessed with water, rafting drove him to more far-flung places like Canada, Mongolia and the Wye. He got together with Sara after a romantic interlude on Roy Bridge, but the obsession continues!

Colin Hill held four Guinness Book of Records - one was for doing 3700 rolls in a kayak! Too many rolls probably sent him over edge as he spent 9 years running rivers full time - in some of the wildest places in the World - Vietnam, Papua New Guinea, Mozambique, Sikkim, to name but a few. Achieving a few first descents along the way, such as the Ugandan White Nile. His favourite place was working as a raft guide in Austria, where he kept fit with pre-breakfast paddles in his river racer down the Finster Monster. Now with two kids (Indus & Zac) & Kiwi wife, he finally has a base in the Lake District from which to travel from!

Robin Knapp comes from a long line of Polish individualists. He progressed from building his first kayak at the age of 14 to doing a two-man unsupported descent of the Inn, journeying with plastic kayaks from their home and back using public transport (buses, trains and ferries). He now lives in France, some twenty minutes from the Grand Canyon du Verdon, where he can usually be found in the village bar talking mountain bike trails.

Paul Mackenzie has many world descents to his name, the most memorable however was his first descent of the Hoggs Mill river in the outskirts of London. This solo epic narrowly ended in tragedy in a stopper beneath a bridge. Paul had to lasso a sewage outfall pipe with his throw bag to extricate himself - much to the amazement of passing shoppers. Perhaps he should stick paddling in the Alps and marketing?

Caragh Mathew started paddling at the age of 12 with the guides. Has had some great days out paddling with Hinckley Canoe Club at various locations in England and Europe. She also enjoys photography and Skiing.

Mark Nichols first started canoeing at the age of eleven and claims to be still 26, his face however, is reminiscent of the many knarly rivers he has explored and suggests otherwise. Mark is something of a expedition photographer and his photos (and his face) are well known to readers of canoeing magazines.

Laurent Nicolet spent his early chidlhood playing with rubber toys in the bath. He tehn progressed to plastic, colder water and more distant climes, leading paddling expeditions to Canada, Alaska, and Arabia. He was one of the founders of AN Rafting and now runs River Equipment services in Thonon les Bains, where he has regressed to rubber toys - producing high performance 'hot dogs'.

Conor O'Neill learnt to paddle with the scouts, and spent the next 25 years learning to paddle white water, injuring himself too much, then easing off to paddle just the easy rivers. He will happily offer advice on the harder stuff, but this should be treated with the respect it deserves. He enjoys paddling in the sun in France, but is normally limited to rivers within a day-trip distance of Bristol. He can't really get to grips with these newfangled playboat type things.

Mark Pedley's initial kayaking adventures concentrated on the swimming possibilities on UK rivers but his ambitions soon expanded to breast stroke on alpine and Himalayan rivers. During a recent six year sojourn in California, Mark has been able to research in detail the re-circulation possibilities of west coast pourovers. and if anyone's heading over to the west coast, he says to make sure to run the New River in the Trinity Alps in northern California - it's a little gem. His coldest swim was when he fell through the sea ice in Antartica - whilst pretending to do research but actually perfecting his penguin mating calls.

Iain Penketh decided after his first trip with Southampton University Canoe Club that 36 swims in a single weekend was excessive. Since then, he has enjoyed probing rivers in Europe, Nepal and Canada, and has been constantly amused by the antics of those who dare to follow his line.

Gianluca Ricci. We first bumped into Gianluca in a bar next to the Kawerau river in New Zealand, then a year or two later in a dusty wine cellar in Corsica, a year later in Rum Doudle's bar in Kathmandu (where he was training for a second descent of the Humla Karnali); and then last year we were drinking home made beer in a mud hut in the Simien mountains of Ethiopia when an Italian truck rolls up, and who should it be? Of course, we've also met him in a few bars in Alps: in the summer he works in the Aosta valley where he is one of Italy's premier raft guides and kayak instructors. He's also famous for his mother's ravioli - one of the best of its kind!

Julie Rowan has kayaked/ rafted/ shuttle-bunnied some of Europes finest whitewater. When not getting up early to fetch the best pain au chocolat or the elusive pain au raisin, she can be found mountain biking high passes or losing wedding rings in the Rio Noguerra Pallaresa.

Francesco Salvato is one of Italy's top expedition kayakers. He has his own kayak school, Free Flow, that works on different rivers of the Alps - like the Soca, Durance and Sesia. He also works as a technical consultant and is a kayak journalist and photographer who loves to explore new rivers in remote corners of the world.

Marcus Schmid is a leading member of the Alpiner Kayak Club and was raised and nurtured on the rivers in the Alps. A visit to the 1985 Mike Jones Rally broadened his horizons and he starred in several filmed expeditions. In 1990 he was nearly converted to a true Brit on the 'Taming of the Lion' expedition: forced to drink cup after cup of English tea, only the thought of real Bavarian beer kept him alive.

Pat Thoyts has paddled extensively for the past seven years all over the Bristol docks. In between moments he's also managed to get around the Alps and tick off some wine. He is well known for waving people down "inconsequential" drops and for providing subtly incomplete river information ('Pat's Guide') to unsuspecting enquirers.

Tony Tickle's name is synonymous with slalom photography and his photos are used worldwide in publications from Olympic programmes to quality guidebooks. He first started paddling in 1967, reached the dizzy heights of Div. 2, and claims several first descents of local rivers, none of which you will have heard of! He still paddles today with his kids, who are probably the best turned out paddlers on the water. As time pass on he can now be found travelling the world creating bonsai trees and lecturing at international conferences. Visit: www.tickle.co.uk and see what he does for a living!

Eric Totty started canoeing prior to the Second World War and after demob. in 1945 he became a white water river addict and spent all his holidays on Alpine rivers. He was a member of the British Team at the 1952 International Slalom at Lippstadt and was in Div. 1 until the age of 50 when he devoted his energies more to expeditions, including Finnish Lapland, Northern Ontario, and a crossing of the Baltic Sea. More recently, he has done several sea kayaking trips off the coast of Greenland and was dubbed the 'Ancient Mariner' by his friends after an encounter with an albatross on his 80th birthday!

Jeannie Tracey is an enthusiastic touring kayak paddler, especially in a double behind Jerry. Her ideal trips are hot days with clear water and plenty of stops to nibble chocolate and sip wine. She's not too keen on rough water because it gets her sketch books wet. When not paddling she teaches five year olds how to use chairs and not to drink paint.

Jerry Tracey spent a great deal of time in the Alps in his younger days: much of it is now a blur, but he does remember some great river runs, as well as a few epic! He is now making a come-back in Division 2 slalom. When not on the water he teaches French to Geordies..

Charlie Wood has completed no first descents, been on no major expeditions and won no honours in any competition. His singular achievement is to have been awarded a Swimmer of the Year trophy with both Monklands Canoe Club and, more recently, Edinburgh Kayak Club. He can still be found on the banks of Scottish rivers in a leaky dry suit wondering where the nearest tea room might be.

Harry Wood is 'the Digimeister' of Imperial College Canoe Club because of his excessive digital photography habit. He is at his happiest on an Alpine campsite, drinking his way through the club's beer supply while trying to focus on the stars... lying back and relaxing... He adopts a similar posture on Alpine whitewater. It is his effortless paddling style, and his ability to run rapids while sleeping, that make him a kayaking legend in the eyes of his fellow canoe club members

Stuart Woodward still gets a huge thrill when its time once more to travel south for another French Alpine summer. He runs his Kayak School (Canoe Control) from a lovely private campsite set in pine woods on the banks of the Gyronde. He says he always feels lucky to be in this beautiful area from spring to the start of autumn - to get up in the morning and just go boating, put on almost where and when you want, no access problems, no permits, and no tickets to book! Stuart also likes expedition paddling (he was on the second descent of the mighty Thule Bheri river in far west Nepal, from the flanks of 8000m Daulaghiri to the plains of India) and he returns most years to the Himalayas to lead adventure and aid expeditions. But trips like these he says, make you appreciate the different attractions of paddling in France - its great when there's a bar close to the take out!

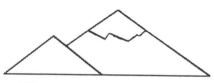

SUPPLIERS DIRECTORY

get out **more**!

Canoeing & **Multi-Activity**
Instructors

PGL is the UK's largest employer and trainer of canoeists – every year over 150 of our canoe instructors teach paddling skills and lead river trips in the **UK** and **France**.

Ardèche, Southern Alps, Wales, Scotland...with 25 centres situated in some of Europe's most stunning locations PGL has something to offer to paddlers of all standards. Our season operates from February to November, providing an excellent gateway to a career in the outdoors or the opportunity to spend a few months sharing your love of sport with others.

Each season several hundred star tests are awarded, 200+ coaching awards are gained and more than 35 employees complete Assessor training and WCA/BCU Raft Guide Assessments.

So, if you are vibrant and energetic, love the outdoors and get on well with kids, we'll help you achieve the skills and qualifications you need. For a highly rewarding position, excellent training opportunities, accommodation, meals and the chance for rapid career progression – *get out and get in touch now!*

We also offer the chance for experienced white water paddlers to train as Raft Guides in the **Southern Alps**.

PGL is Britain's leading provider of adventure holidays and courses for children. For over 100,000 children each year, a PGL holiday means the adventure of a lifetime. For more information about PGL – employment, trips for children and families – visit www.pgl.co.uk

KAYAK
RIVER VEST

GUL

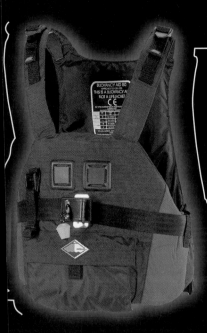

- 30mm Corex foam in the back and 40mm Corex foam in the front body for preferred buoyancy posture
- Main outer panels constructed in high durability 420D rip stop nylon
- Lining panels and side gussets constructed in 210D Oxford nylon for comfort, durability and adjustment
- Rescue harness system fitted centrally for easy access - (ambidextrous)
- File compression points for optimal comfort/fit in shoulders and waist
- Cowtail park fitted to right side as worn
- Large cargo pocket with drain eyelets
- Lash tab points for knife or securing accessories
- High visibility design, back centre panel/harness area is easily identifiable

Sizes: S/M and L/XL
Code: GK 0002

Gul International Ltd

Callywith | Bodmin | Cornwall | England | PL31 2RQ | Tel: +44 (0) 1208 262400 | Fax: +44 (0) 1208 262474
email: gul@gul.com | www.gul.com

Other Great Guidebooks

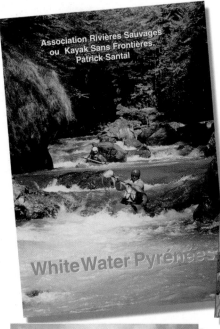

Association Rivières Sauvages ou Kayak Sans Frontières. Patrick Santal

White Water Pyrénées

White Water Nepal

Peter Knowles

White Water Europe

Book One
North Alps

Peter Knowles   Pete Bandtock

White Water
Massif Central

Peter Knowles

Fluffy's guide to the friendly rivers of Southern France

www.riverspublishing.co.uk